BIRDS, BEES &
BUTTERFLIES

BIRDS, BEES & BUTTERFLIES

Bringing Nature Into Your Yard & Garden

Nancy J. Hajeski

NATIONAL GEOGRAPHIC

WASHINGTON, D.C.

Contents

∾ PART THREE ∾
BUTTERFLIES & MOTHS
in the Garden

Introduction

Welcoming Wildlife

LANDSCAPES THAT NURTURE BIRDS, BEES & BUTTERFLIES

(left) How do you create a yard that is comfortable for humans and welcoming to wildlife? Create a balance between attractive groomed landscaping that is a pleasure to behold and a wilder, less groomed area that acts as a haven for birds, insects, and other animals.

(right) Before logging wiped out much of its habitat, the red-cockaded woodpecker *(Leuconotopicus borealis)* was plentiful in the old-growth pine forests of the East and Southeast. Efforts to restore its numbers include drilling nesting cavities into trees and inserting man-made nests.

Your yard is probably already a mini oasis, the place you go to relax, play with the kids or your dog, and socialize with family and friends. Your garden, likewise, has doubtless achieved some level of tranquility and beauty. But what if you could increase the ambiance of these pleasant spaces with the addition of native fauna—the wildlife that surrounds many homes but only occasionally comes to call? With a just a few landscaping alterations—planting native food and host plants, allowing some lawn areas to fill in, and offering water resources, shelter, and nesting sites—birds, bees, and butterflies will all become frequent visitors.

WILDLIFE CHALLENGES

These changes will not only draw new animal guests to your yardscape, they can also benefit many species that are in peril. Various threats to birds, bees, and butterflies have been making headlines lately: songbirds face increasing loss of habitat and poisoning by toxic chemicals; bee colonies are suffering nationwide collapse from a mysterious agent; and some butterflies, most notably the beautiful, migratory monarch, experience diminishing food resources and habitats, and destruction of larval plant hosts. Yet on a local scale, concerned homeowners can—and do— make a real difference.

Embattled Birds

During the 1960s and '70s, the danger to bird populations from the agricultural insecticide DDT became increasingly evident. DDT was eventually banned, but other toxic pesticides still take a heavy toll on songbirds—more than seven million a year die from lawn chemicals alone. Other threats include loss of food resources, nesting sites, and local and migratory habitats.

Beleaguered Bees

Without the pollination provided by bees, roughly one third of crop plants would fail worldwide, and there would not be enough food to support the planet. Industrial crops would also suffer, as well as flowers, some woods, and sources of fiber, spices, fragrance, and animal feed. In the United States alone, bees pollinate an estimated $15 billion worth of crops yearly. Bees also produce valuable commercial products, such as honey, pollen, royal jelly, and propolis.

Imagine the blow to agriculture in 2006, when entire colonies of honeybees began to die without explanation. These events were first attributed by beekeepers to bad husbandry by other beekeepers. The critics were quickly silenced when their hives, too, began to fail. Large commercial apiarists that seasonally truck their hives across the country were soon going bankrupt as millions of bees went out to forage and simply never returned to their hives—a syndrome known as colony collapse disorder. Current thinking is that neonicotinoids, synthetic pesticides applied to crop seeds, are slowly destroying the nervous systems of bees. These pesticides are still in wide use in the United States, but many countries have banned them pending further study.

A beekeeper examines a hive frame to assess the health of the colony. Small-scale apiaries and individual beekeepers have been more successful than the large commercial apiarists at avoiding the catastrophic effects of colony collapse disorder and other potential menaces to honeybee populations. Raising bees yourself is one way to help keep them from vanishing, but it's not an effort for everyone. Instead, you can do your part by supporting your local beekeepers and purchasing their honey and other related products.

The Karner blue (*Lycaeides melissa samuelis)* is one of three members of the blue family of butterflies to appear on threatened or endangered species lists. Classified as endangered in the United States in 1992, it was listed as locally extinct in Canada in 2000. Efforts to boost populations focus mainly on replanting large areas of blue lupine—this butterfly's host species—that have been lost to development. These efforts are meeting with modest success. It is now found mainly in the Great Lakes states, in small areas of New Jersey, the Capital District region of New York, and in southern New Hampshire, where it is the state butterfly.

Besieged Butterflies

Butterflies and moths are important indicator species of healthy and stable ecosystems, model organisms to study when there are concerns over the impact of habitat destruction. These same insect pollinators are placed at risk when homeowners blanket their lawns and gardens with toxic chemicals. Additional threats include the loss of native food resources and breeding habitats—possibly due to climate change. Threats to monarch populations have been widely reported, but increasing numbers of other butterflies and moths will also suffer losses unless humans work toward nurturing and protecting them.

THE GOOD STEWARD

There are numerous landscape changes homeowners can make to help preserve threatened wildlife. This does not necessarily mean increased effort, but rather *a redirection of effort,* a letting go of the need for neatness and a willingness to bow before the whims of nature. Focus on planting native species; don't deadhead perennials in the fall; rake piles of fallen leaves under shrubs; and conserve water by letting part of your lawn go wild. Determine not to use toxic chemicals on your lawn or plants, and instead seek out safe alternatives, such as ladybugs or nematodes. And finally, speak out as an activist, encouraging others in your community to become conscientious custodians of our planet and its wildlife.

. . . .

This book is intended to furnish a starting-off point for making your outdoor spaces welcoming havens for wildlife, especially birds and insects that might be endangered. For more information, investigate the many websites devoted to bird conservation, beekeeping, and nurturing Lepidoptera. And remember, your revamped yard or garden is not just meant as a refuge for wild creatures; you will equally benefit from relaxing there and viewing your new visitors up close. Keep in mind this sage advice from the Zen masters: "You should sit in nature for 20 minutes every day. Unless you are busy. Then you should sit there for an hour."

How to Use This Book

This book is presented in three parts—Birds of the Yard & Garden; Bees & Other Beneficial Wildlife; and Butterflies & Moths in the Garden —covering the attractive and engaging animal visitors that many homeowners desire to bring onto their property.

Each part is divided into two chapters. The first chapter covers habitat, including information on history, anatomy, biology, life cycle, reproduction, and appropriate landscaping and garden options, along with a sample garden plan and a list of ten plants that are guaranteed to make your yard the most popular dining spot in town.

The second opens with an introduction that explains the various classifications of animals

that will be covered, followed by individual species spreads that feature an informative overview, a favorite plants list, a stat box, feeding tips, and photos. Some spreads contain a box that provides a handy tip or an interesting fact or showcases a similar species.

Throughout the book you will find Focus On features, which offer a more in-depth treatment of specific topics. The bluebird comeback, the monarch butterfly migrations, and creating a moon garden for moths are just some examples.

The book's appendix includes a growing guide for a selected list of the plants mentioned on the species pages, a glossary, and an index.

1 common name

2 key illustration

3 favorite plants

4 Latin name

5 explanatory text

6 feeding suggestions

7 statistical information

8 photo captions

9 supplemental box covering tips, facts, or similar species

Bumblebees

genus *Bombus*

They feed on nectar, lapping it up with their long tongue, or proboscis, which folds under the head during flight. There are more than 250 species worldwide, with roughly 50 found in North America.

These are social insects, like honeybees, that form small colonies of perhaps 50 to 400 bees with one queen. It is she who searches in spring for a nesting site beneath the ground or in a tangled clump of grass, flying in a zigzag close above the lawn. Once the queen is settled, she lays her eggs; newly hatched workers begin gathering nectar and pollen to feed her and also start tending the nest. Unlike the neat precision of honeybee hives, bumblebee nests are haphazard, often having dead bees or grubs near the entrance. Clearly, these bees live as casually as they fly. Workers also make honey, but it is not edible by humans.

In summer, the queen produces a new generation of workers and, finally, in late summer, new queens and drones. After mating, only the fertilized queens survive— they will hibernate underground during the winter and emerge the following spring to begin the process anew.

BRINGING THE BUMBLEBEES
Bumblebees sample the bounty of each passing season—in early spring feeding on apple, pear, plum, and cherry blossoms,

California poppies, bluebells, and pussy willow, followed in late spring by foxgloves, geraniums, honeysuckle, roses, salvia, and wisteria. They will sample from herbs like chives, oregano, and mint and fruit such as raspberries, strawberries, and blueberries. Summer favorites include viper's bugloss, sunflowers, delphinium, snapdragons, lavender, hollyhocks, cosmos, and cornflowers. In early fall, they feed on pumpkins, melons, and zucchini. Due to their varied tastes, they are able to pollinate flowers, herbs, vegetables, shrubs, fruit trees, and agricultural crops.

These busy pollinators will become garden regulars if you provide them with nest boxes. Typically 15 to 25 inches in diameter, the boxes feature one entry hole and two or three for ventilation, which require a net covering to keep out ants. It helps if your garden is set up for long-term or staggered blooming times—bumblebees require nectar from March to September.

Basics

SIZE
Worker, 0.25 inch to 1 inch; queen, 0.75 inch to 1.25 inch

LONGEVITY
One season or less; fertilized queens overwinter and lay eggs in spring.

DISTRIBUTION
Temperate to tropical zones worldwide, except Africa or Australia; introduced to New Zealand, spread to Tasmania

(opposite page) While sipping nectar, a common eastern bumblebee *(Bombus impatiens)* can dust itself in the flower's pollen. This species ranges through eastern North America, along with the western desert areas, California, and Oregon.

(top) An American bumblebee *(Bombus pennsylvanicus)* drinks nectar from oregano blossoms. This species is one of the bumblebees most often encountered in eastern North America.

Favorite plants

- foxglove
- comfrey
- viper's bugloss
- rosemary
- clover
- wood geranium
- cornflower
- rhododendron

Bumblebees are among the most familiar garden pollinators. Doddering along from blossom to blossom with their fuzzy bodies, legs packed with pollen and wings buzzing softly, they seem both personable and comical. By nature, they are placid creatures and rarely confrontational, even going out of their way to avoid human contact. If threatened, however, they will sting.

Native to most temperate or semitropical zones, these bees prefer cool, open, flower-rich grasslands with one long adverse season—usually winter. They have large, rounded bodies that are covered with soft hair—long, branched setae— called pile. Their coloration is aposematic: contrasting color bands that warn animals an insect may sting. Most bumblebees are black with buff, yellow, or orange markings.

similar species: *stingless bees*

The Meliponini—tiny, stingless bees—are a sister tribe to the Bombini and are found in the tropics. Pre-Columbian peoples cultivated them for their honey, but their output is low by modern standards. Still, these bees are vital pollinators of tropical plants, especially of the vanilla orchid, source of the vanilla bean. The vine blooms just one day a year and has a hidden source of pollen that only these bees know how to access.

A stingless bee. These bees are "stingless" because their stingers are simply too small to deploy.

178 • BEES & OTHER POLLINATORS

BUMBLEBEES • 179

~ PART ONE ~

BIRDS *of the*
YARD & GARDEN

Creating a Habitat for Birds

· ·

(opposite page) Plant a variety of flowers and greenery and provide shelter and food to create a welcome environment for birds.

Bird Basics

Birds are warm-blooded, feathered animals that lay eggs to reproduce and have the ability to fly. There are approximately 8,500 species of birds on earth, totaling more than 600 billion individuals. They are found on every continent and at nearly every altitude, deep within dense tropical rain forests and far out to sea. They consume seeds,

Small birds may consume their entire body weight in food daily in order to maintain their necessary high metabolic rate. With the highest rate of all birds—and all animals other than insects—the hummingbird has a heart rate that can beat as fast as 1,260 beats per minute,

buds, fruit, sap, and flowers, as well as insects, arthropods, mollusks, fish, amphibians, reptiles, mammals, and other birds and their eggs. They range in size from the tiny bee hummingbird, barely two inches long, to the imposing ostrich, seven feet tall and 260 pounds.

A BRIEF HISTORY

During the Triassic Period, 200 million years ago, insects were the only creatures that could fly. Fifty millions years later, during the Jurassic era, a large flying reptile with a membrane between its elongated fingers evolved. It was called

pterodactylus. A more refined flier, archaeopteryx, from the Greek for "ancient feather," appeared in the late Jurassic. It became the link between certain dinosaur contemporaries—they shared jaws with sharp teeth, three fingers with claws, long bony tails, a retractable "killing" hind claw, and feathers—and today's modern birds.

THE MIRACLE OF FLIGHT

Several combined factors allow birds to fly: bone structure, metabolism, wing structure, and feather design. To achieve lift, an object needs to be light, and so the interiors of birds' bones are strutted and full of open spaces. Birds also need a quick burst of energy and enough thrust to defy gravity. This is provided by a high metabolism fueled by a calorie-rich diet and strong, flexible wings.

ADAPTING TO WINGS

After their front legs evolved into wings, birds learned to use their "hind" feet, their bills, and their tongues to manipulate objects and food resources. These skills help with weaving natural materials into complex nests; "caching" food under tree bark; opening hard-shelled nuts; and capturing prey while on the wing.

MIGRATION

Flight has given birds more than the ability to hunt or escape predators—it allows them to expand their territories as the seasons progress, following ripening fruit and crops or hatching insects, as well as avoiding harsh weather. Many species migrate thousands of miles from their breeding grounds. Other species remain year-round in one spot, adapting their food requirements to the resources that are available, switching from insects to seeds and dried fruit, for instance.

THE MYSTERIES OF NAVIGATION

The actual mechanics of bird navigation during migration are still being studied There is some evidence that birds use variations in the earth's magnetic field to maintain their routes. Other researchers believe that those that fly at night navigate by the stars or that birds "inherit" a visual terrain map with signposts of the correct routes to follow to reach winter locations and to return to their breeding grounds. Whatever methods birds use to navigate, the fact remains that banded first-year birds that have never before visited their hereditary wintering spots and who get separated from their flock during migration still manage to rejoin them at journey's end. That's a tough one to explain.

(left) A sparrow preening. Birds repair "flight damage" by preening their feathers to remove dust, dirt, and parasites and to also relock the barbules and properly align each feather.

(middle and right) Bills are used as tools and have evolved in different ways to meet the needs of different species—woodpeckers drilling holes in trees or finches using their nutcracker beaks to hull seeds, for example.

A Bird's Life Cycle

THE AVIAN YEAR FROM EGG TO ADULT

tip

What should you do if you find a baby bird in your yard? If it is a feathered fledgling that can hop, place it in a nearby bush, where its parents can watch over it and feed it. If the baby is naked or downy and helpless, attempt to return it to its nest. (It is not true that the parents will abandon a chick if you touch it.) If that fails, place it in a cloth-lined shoebox and locate a wildlife center or rehabber in your area by checking online. Don't try to hand-raise a chick; the needs of baby birds are too complicated for untrained individuals.

Throughout the calendar year, birds are compelled by nature to repeat age-old seasonal patterns: courtship and mating in spring, followed by nesting and the raising of their young. Summer brings the training of fledglings and perhaps the production of a second brood. Late summer's bounty allows birds to fatten up, either for the coming winter months, when food will likely be scarce, or to prepare for long, winged migrations to warmer climates.

EGG INTO CHICK

Birds lay eggs because their need for mobility in flight prohibits them from retaining their young inside their bodies. Females begin forming eggs after mating and, because of their size, lay the eggs as soon as they form. Mother birds incubate their eggs, and when a chick is ready to hatch, it uses an egg tooth, a small projection at the end of the bill, to chip away at the shell. This tooth will drop off the chick a few days later. Chicks are born naked or with patches of down. Yet, amazingly, many are feathered and ready to fly in two weeks.

One or both of the parents feed the hatchlings, who may be helped by members of earlier broods that act as "babysitters." Some species raise two or more broods in a single season.

THE URGE TO MIGRATE

Many birds that breed in temperate North America, especially insectivores, migrate to the southern United States, Central America, or even South America

as autumn ushers in colder weather. Some birds travel thousands of miles to the tropics, while other species travel only a few states away. Often, mountain birds simply move to sheltered, low-altitude meadows once winter arrives. Shorter days, lower temperatures, loss of food resources, or a genetic imperative—or a combination of these factors—may trigger migration.

BREEDING SEASON

When winter's icy blast lets up, migrant birds return to their breeding territories. Some species are monogamous and remain with the same mate for life. Other males mate for only one season, and each spring begin the task of courting a desirable female anew. Extreme posturing, seductive singing, and impressive aerial displays—even fights between males—are all forms of wooing. Once the female accepts a male, the pair might engage in bill stroking, neck twining, mutual feeding, and other intimacies.

When it comes to nesting, most male birds limit their input to locating a good site, leaving the female to construct the nest. Other males, such as bushtits, help with the work. Male European starlings are known to carry bits of odd materials to the nest, which the picky female then tosses out. Once the nest is completed, the female lays her eggs and incubates them until they hatch . . . and the whole remarkable cycle begins again.

1 **egg**
Each species of bird has its own way of nesting and raising its young, but all birds begin life as an egg.

2 **hatchling**
A baby bird that has just hatched is called a hatchling.

3 **nestling**
While it is growing in the nest and being fed by one or both of its parents, the baby bird is called a nestling.

4 **fledgling**
When it is ready to leave the nest, it is called a fledgling. As its flight feathers continue to grow, its wing muscles will get stronger. Some fledglings remain close to their parents: large, awkward youngsters with unkempt juvenile plumage can often be seen posturing pitifully to be fed by an exasperated parent.

5 **juvenile to adult**
As the juvenile bird continues to mature, it often stays with adults to learn important skills, such as singing, foraging for food, roosting in trees, and recognizing dangers. When it has finished growing, an adult bird will begin the cycle anew—attracting a mate, building a nest, and raising its young.

A Bird Garden

SELECTING & ARRANGING PLANTS TO ATTRACT BIRDS

tip

Once you invite songbirds into your garden, they shouldn't have to share the space with predatory felines. Keep your cat indoors to prolong its life and to stop it from menacing the birds you want to observe. If a neighbor's cat prowls your garden, there are several deterrents: motion-activated sprinklers; ultrasonic high-frequency alarms; plants like rue or *Coleus canina* (called Scaredy Cat) with odors cats dislike; scattered lemon or orange peels, cayenne pepper, pipe tobacco, coffee grounds; or commercial repellents.

There are many ways to bring birds onto your property—providing shelter, bird feeders, a water source, and nesting sites all work well. But foremost among them, arguably, is a thriving garden. Both ornamental flower gardens and utilitarian kitchen gardens containing vegetables, herbs, and fruit not only attract birds that prey upon insect pests, they also draw birds that consume plant matter, including insectivores that feed off seed heads in winter.

EMBELLISHING YOUR GARDEN

It's possible, with a minimum adjustment and minor expense, to augment your garden—and your landscape—to attract a variety of bird species and also create a haven for beneficial insects and wildlife. Just a few simple ideas can get you started.

Including native grasses, shrubs, vines, and trees in your landscape plan offers birds foods they recognize, plants they grew up eating. Make sure to take into account the watering requirements and preferred levels of sunlight of the plants.

Grow seed-bearing perennial flowers, such as coneflowers, black-eyed Susans, and bee balm, in lush clumps, and stop deadheading them by midsummer. This allows a good crop of seed heads to form, which will support birds through winter. Make sure to choose flowers that will do well in your climate or growing zone.

Create dense layers of flowers in varying heights. This will furnish birds with cover as they feed. Choosing flowers that go to seed at staggered intervals will ensure an ongoing supply of food.

1 trumpet honeysuckle
(Lonicera sempervirens)
This plant has it all: nectar for hummingbirds and berries and fruit for songbirds. It also offers shelter for many birds.

2 sunflower
(Helianthus anuus)
The large cheerful yellow flowers produce the fruit known as sunflower seeds—a favorite food of a score of birds.

3 purple coneflower
(Echinacea purpurea)
Their spiny heads yield a multitude of seeds that keeps birds well fed into the fall.

4 American elder
(Sambucus canadensis)
In summer, the foaming white flowers brighten the garden, and, in fall, drooping clumps of berries are a source of nutrients for many birds.

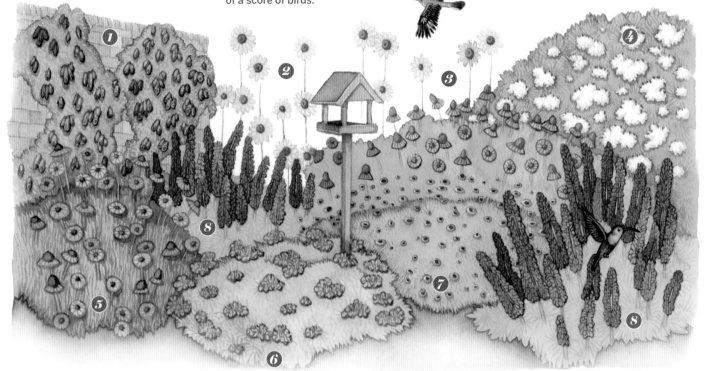

5 black-eyed Susan
(Rudbeckia hirta)
This North American native is rich in seeds that are loved by goldfinches, sparrows, chickadees, cardinals, and nuthatches.

6 wild bee balm
(Monarda fistulosa)
Its tubular flowers are hummingbird magnets, and its leaves exude a delightfully spicy scent that also attracts bees and butterflies.

7 golden tickseed
(Coreopsis tinctoria)
The small flowers bloom in a profusion and produce fall and winter seeds for birds.

8 cardinal flower
(Lobelia cardinalis)
Brilliant red, nectar-filled, and pollen-rich blossoms draw hummers and bees.

Include ornamental birdhouses and birdbaths in your yard or garden, for aesthetic as well as practical purposes.

You can also let one edge of your garden go a bit wild by placing dead stalks, branches, and trimmings there to furnish birds with shelter from storms and year-round cover. Dried garden debris also supplies nesting materials.

A SONGBIRD BORDER

Create a songbird border, or windbreak, along one side of your property. Clump similar species of native trees and shrubs, placing the tallest in back and the shortest in front to establish a small, contained ecosystem that will benefit birds all year long. Include a few thorny species for nesting, such as hawthorn or raspberry, as well as berry-producing shrubs like dogwood, serviceberry, and viburnum that offer fruit throughout the fall and winter. Make sure to use several evergreens—holly, spruce, or juniper—to provide cover. Ask at your garden center or contact your local cooperative extension for guidance on which plants are native to your region.

A bird-friendly plan
Following a template can help you when you are making over a section of garden or yard. Here is a plan for a bird-friendly garden plot. Use it as a starting-off point, and combine it with your own ideas. The plants shown here should come back each year and spread moderately of their own accord. All are illustrated in bloom, but not every species shown will flower at the same time—in a real garden this will create a shifting landscape of shapes and colors for you and multiple food options for your feathered friends.

Repurposing Your Yard

FROM MANICURED LAWN TO WILDLIFE HAVEN

(left) Replant your lawn with drought-tolerant and low-maintenance mints or lavenders. Some birds use the leaves of aromatic plants to line their nests, which helps kill bacteria. The nectar of lavender will also attract hummingbirds, along with scores of bees and butterflies.

(right) One landscaping trick to help your new "veldt belt" complement the remaining green lawn is to give it a swooping, curved perimeter.

You may be like many homeowners who are not interested in gardening, the ones who are fine with a landscape that consists mostly of manicured green grass, perhaps dotted with a few evergreen shrubs and an urn of seasonal flowers. At the same time, you'd like to bring wildlife, like birds, bees, and butterflies, onto your property for your family to enjoy. So how do you create a proper habitat with a minimum of effort?

The first step is to consider giving up some of that lush lawn. In the United States, an area eight times the size of New Jersey is devoted to lawns. Just imagine the enormous amount of water and the mowing and maintenance time this expanse requires. Lawns are an inefficient use of resources—on average a 25-by-40-foot lawn drinks up 10,000 gallons of water in one summer.

Clearly, it makes sense to transition to a less-formal landscape, one that will require less time and fewer resources to maintain *and* invite birds into your space.

The good news is that the less you do to groom your yard, the more birds will like it. Most pairs looking to nest are drawn to real estate in which native plants and grasses grow in unregulated profusion—that is their idea of "location, location, location." This doesn't mean your yard needs to be messy, only that certain areas will be designated as free-growing meadows.

LETTING GO OF THE GREEN

It is not an all-or-nothing proposition: consider reducing the area of your lawn by as little as 25 or 30 percent and replacing it with meadow plants and tall grasses that need no watering and get cut only once a year. You can also simply stop mowing a portion of your lawn, which will sprout up with a mix of grasses and wildflowers. Birds will feed on seeds there and maybe even build a nest. Allow the remainder of your lawn to reach three or five inches before mowing it.

Take the "healthy yard pledge" to stop using water-wasting sprinklers and toxic weed killers and pesticides. Half of American households use lawn chemicals—70 million pounds worth—that end up killing seven million birds a year. Remember "food chain" math: insects ingest chemicals, birds eat hundreds of insects, chemical effects multiply inside birds. These harmful chemicals also find their way into groundwater, and from there they spread to wells, streams, rivers, and oceans.

ROUGHING IT

If you arrange a deadfall, or brush pile, in a corner of your yard, it will shelter birds from bad weather. Every time a rain- or windstorm takes down tree branches, collect them and layer them with the larger limbs on the bottom. Add trimmed boughs from your shrubs and even old Christmas trees. Before long, your brush pile will be supporting a few garter snakes and a toad or two—great for controlling destructive insects. You will soon notice different species of birds flitting in and out of the tangled branches.

Also try raking fallen leaves underneath your shrubs to create mulch. This will attract ground-feeding birds like sparrows, towhees, and thrashers that will feast on the pill bugs, insects, earthworms, and spiders that will soon abound in the decomposing leaves.

tip

As a good steward of the planet, you might consider mixing up a batch of this safe herbicide to replace toxic ones. Just take 1 gallon white or apple cider vinegar, and mix in 2 cups Epsom salts and ¼ cup Dawn dish liquid. Pour the mix into a sprayer bottle, and spray it on weeds first thing in the morning, after the dew has evaporated.

Consider giving up a portion of your high-maintenance lawn and planting the area with low-maintenance native species that offer birds both food and shelter.

Xeriscaping

USING WATERWISE & BIRD-FRIENDLY NATIVE PLANTS

Water scarcity has been in the news recently, raising the public's awareness of the increased need for water conservation. Unfortunately, the traditional suburban grass lawn we have come to cherish is a great waster of water resources. Yet, there is an alternative to that wide expanse of grassy green that has been gaining popularity: a landscape method known as xeriscaping. This process involves reducing lawn area and landscaping with native species that have lower water requirements and that are more drought-tolerant than non-native, water-thirsty plants.

Although the trend began in dry desert areas, xeriscaping has been catching on in nearly every geographic region of the country. It not only uses up to two-thirds less water than grass lawns, it also lowers maintenance time and the expense of fertilizers, insecticides, and weed controls, and it reduces the amount of lawn waste that ends up in landfills. Xeriscaping also encourages native wildlife, like birds, to visit your yard for the plants they would naturally choose to dine on or nest in.

The method is not without drawbacks, however; the "spare" aesthetic of many xeriscapes does not match some people's idea of backyard beauty: areas for playing sports or games might now be limited, and xeriscapes often contain spiky cactus and agaves that can be threats to children and pets. And, like any garden makeover, creating a xeriscape initially costs money. But the savings in water and upkeep time will soon make up for the expense—and possibly for any other negative aspects.

THE SEVEN STEPS TO XERISCAPING:

1 Plan out your yard by determining how you intend to use the space—for instance, play, picnic, and pet areas—and what kind of aesthetic look you want to achieve. "Statement" rocks and stone or brick edging can increase appeal.

2 Create a functional turf area in a flat, easy-to-water location, and be sure to choose turf with low water requirements. You can also replace grass with ground covers or ecoturf.

3 Choose plants suitable to your climate. Your garden shop should be able to help you find local species or check out plant suppliers online.

4 Condition your soil with compost and organic matter until it is sponge-like and crumbly. This ensures that your plants receive the correct levels of physical support, air, water, nutrients, and beneficial organisms.

5 Mulch your planting areas up to three inches in depth to prevent evaporation, weed growth, and erosion, and to keep the soil cool.

6 Water wisely by grouping plants according to their water usage, and hand water them whenever possible.

7 Maintain your landscape regularly; chances are you can do without chemical pesticides, weed killers, or fertilizer.

(top left) Xeriscaping in the Northwest can use grasses like fescue or oat grass, and plants like yucca, juniper, and cedar, along with a host of others, to create a lush but eco-friendly look.

(top right) In the central states, turn a corner of your backyard into a bird haven by letting prairie flowers grow in natural profusion.

(bottom left) Xeriscaping a luxury home in the Arizona desert meant letting native cacti, shrubs, and trees, which provide food and shelter for birds, grow wild.

(bottom right) In both the Northeast and Southeast, replace a grass front yard with masses of hardy natives like black-eyed Susans and coneflowers.

Feeding Stations

FITTING THE FEEDER TO THE BIRD

(left) Three house finches at a platform feeder. These open feeders allow multiple birds to feed at one time.

(middle) Two male northern cardinals, a blue jay, and a black-capped chickadee share a meal at a hopper feeder. These covered feeders protect the bird food from the elements in the winter months,

(right) Three American goldfinches rest on the staggered perches of a tube feeder. You can fill them with any seed mix, but they are great for dispensing nyjer and other thistle seeds that finches thrive on.

The best way to observe wild birds around your garden and backyard is by offering them a varied range of dining options. In addition to creating gardens and landscapes that allow birds to eat "from their own larder," you can also supply them with commercial food sources, which is especially critical during the lean colder months. Make sure to position these feeding stations near windows, patio doors, and outdoor decks for easy viewing.

Birds habitually feed in the same way, and different species use different methods: some feed on the ground; others feed sideways, hanging from branches, or head-on, clinging to tree trunks; while others hover over their source of food.

By supplying a variety of bird feeders that cater to these different requirements, you can attract a wider spectrum of species to your yard. Feeders needn't be expensive, but they should be sturdy and easy to clean. Experts suggest that you disinfect them frequently by mixing a quarter cup bleach or white vinegar into one gallon of water.

PLATFORM FEEDERS

These open-sided, open-top feeders, also called tray feeders, allow larger birds to feed. They also allow small birds to keep an eye out for predators. They attract jays, sparrows, grosbeaks, purple finches, house finches, doves, starlings, and more.

HOPPER FEEDERS

These substantial, covered feeders typically have clear sides so that the homeowner can monitor the level of seeds. The food falls to a tray area at the bottom and offers perches big enough for larger birds. Hoppers attract doves, jays, woodpeckers, nuthatches, cardinals, chickadees, and finches.

TUBE FEEDERS

These cylindrical feeders dispense birdseed from multiple ports. Small perches keep large birds from landing. Some examples have small ports that are ideal for dispensing tiny seeds, like thistle. Soft sock feeders are similarly effective for small seeds. They attract finches, chickadees, nuthatches, and grosbeaks.

SUET FEEDERS

These cagelike feeders hold cakes of commercial suet that is often blended with seeds, berries, and/or nuts. They are made for birds that feed vertically by clinging to tree bark as they hunt for insects and larvae. They can also hold nesting materials in spring. They attract woodpeckers, nuthatches, titmice, chickadees, jays, wrens, and more.

NECTAR FEEDERS

These plastic or glass feeders are engineered for hummingbirds, which hover over the tiny open ports to sip a nectar-like solution with their tongues. The solution is made from a simple recipe of one part sugar to four parts water. Some versions have blossom-like extensions to increase their appeal. It is important to clean nectar feeders every week during hot weather with a quarter cup bleach to one gallon of water. They attract orioles and hummingbirds.

GROUND FEEDERS

These feeders sit close to the ground and offer a flat, low-sided surface for the dispersal of seeds, nuts, and insects like mealworms. They attract robins, cardinals, sparrows, mourning doves, juncos, and grackles.

fact

Birds will happily feed on leftovers such as toast, bagels, cake, stale cheese, baked potato skins, spaghetti, and bacon rinds. Many also enjoy sliced fruit, raisins, nuts, coconut meat, and homemade balls or logs made of peanut butter or suet mixed with seeds.

(left) A northern flicker will find a suet feeder hard to resist. It allows it to feed in its natural clinging position and provides it with the high-energy food that is so important during the nesting season, migration, and long, cold winters.

(middle) A group of ruby-throated hummingbirds—called a charm—flock to a nectar-filled feeder.

(right) Inquisitive mourning doves take a break from feeding at a ground feeder. Open like a platform feeder, these allow more than one bird to eat. You can also place them on the railing of a deck to create a relaxing bird-watching area.

Enabling Birds to Nest

PROVIDING PLANTS & MATERIALS THAT PROMOTE NESTING

It might begin as an oversight. A hanging patio planter gets left out over the winter and before you can take it down in spring, there are sparrows or finches nesting in it. So begins the delightful odyssey of watching birds raise their young . . . virtually under your nose. You can likewise intentionally encourage birds to breed on your property by

A mated pair of cedar waxwings work together to bring a length of twine to their nesting site. Providing birds with natural nest-building materials may encourage them to build a home in your backyard.

offering natural, protected nesting sites in dense, leafy trees and shrubs. Here are some nest-friendly landscape options.

DECIDUOUS TREES
It is likely that at least one species of bird-attracting deciduous tree will grow in your area.

• *Mulberry (Morus* spp.) These medium-sized trees provide summer berries and nesting sites, attracting waxwings, cardinals, and robins. Fallen fruit can be messy, so plant mulberries away from walks and driveways.

• *Serviceberry (Amelanchier* spp.) Another medium-sized species, these summer-fruiting trees bring cardinals, robins, thrushes, waxwings, vireos, tanagers, and grosbeaks to dine and nest.

• *Flowering dogwood (Cornus florida)* This popular landscaping tree furnishes fall fruit and nesting sites to robins, bluebirds, cardinals, tanagers, and others.

• *Crabapple (Malus* spp.) These mid-sized garden favorites offer plentiful fall fruits that persist through the winter. They also furnish seeds, buds, flowers, and fruit, plus nest sites, for robins, bluebirds, catbirds, cardinals, waxwings, and finches.

EVERGREENS

These trees supply year-round beauty, while also offering birds food and shelter. There are many choices, and one is sure to be right for your yard.

• *Eastern red cedar (Juniperus virginia)* Tall and cone-shaped, this evergreen offers pale blue fall and winter fruit and nesting spots for waxwings and others.

• *Spruce (Picea* spp.*)* These tall evergreens' seed-bearing cones provide for seedeaters in winter and harbor insects for migrating warblers in spring. Spruce trees also offer cover for nests.

SHRUBS

Many shrub species give backyard birds places to nest and food to eat. Try northern bayberry *(Myrica pensylvanica),* red-osier dogwood *(Cornus sericea),* or gray dogwood *(C. racemosa),* which all provide nesting sites and ample fruit. The latter may even lure wild turkeys and grouse.

VINES

Vines can be pretty and useful, providing both food and nesting sites, including grape *(Vitis* spp.) and Virginia creeper *(Parthenocissus quinquefolia).*

NESTING MATERIALS

Breeding pairs will be more likely to choose your yard if you supply them with a variety of nesting materials. These include short strips of natural-fiber cloth, twine, batting, or yarn; pet fur; short hanks of horsehair; snakeskin; evergreen needles, straw, twigs, or other yard debris; and the coir fiber from hanging baskets. Do not offer synthetic fibers or dryer lint, which may contain chemicals. To distribute the materials, scatter them on the ground, dangle from branches, or place in a suet feeder.

tip

Birdhouses and nesting boxes are engineered for species that nest in tree cavities. Position these boxes up a pole or on a tree trunk, or hang from a sturdy branch. To guarantee tenants, install them outside in early spring, before courtship season begins. When selecting boxes, look for substantial, insulating walls of untreated wood, holes that allow ventilation and drainage, and an extended, sloped roof to keep out rain.

(top) Chipping sparrow eggs. Many trees can supply birds with a place to incubate and raise their young.

(bottom) Mourning doves build their loose, unlined, and rather flimsy nests out of pine needles, twigs, and grass stems and usually place them amid dense foliage or on a tree branch, such as an evergreen.

(right) A yellow warbler sits incubating her eggs. Dense springtime shrubs in out-of-the-way corners of your property can provide cover for nesting songbirds.

Water Features

BIRDBATHS TO BUBBLERS TO PONDS

A ceramic jar or urn bubbler fountain set in a single tray is a great way to add the sound of splashing water—which attracts birds—to a small-space garden.

In addition to food and shelter, wild creatures require a source of clean water, so almost any type of water offering will bring birds to your property. Sometimes just setting up a sprinkler in the yard can help to refresh birds, but many homeowners are now exploring more elaborate options like birdbaths, fountains, and even ponds. Not that it's all for the birds—what is more relaxing to humans than the soothing trickle of a fountain or a serene view of standing water in the yardscape?

BIRDBATHS

Birdbaths are among the simplest types of water features, providing birds a rim to perch on as they drink and a shallow bowl to aid in their bathing rituals. Inexpensive plastic models are available, as well as attractive masonry or cement versions with separate pedestals and bowls. Resin birdbaths, typically in shades of stone or antique bronze, offer a middle ground price-wise, with some models featuring small fountains.

FOUNTAINS

The sound of moving water provided by a fountain not only restores the human spirit, it entices birds to drop in and linger. Fountains can range in size from battery-operated tabletop models to ornate tiered affairs that cost thousands. Many gardeners opt for a bubbler, which is an attractively glazed ceramic urn set in a bed of gravel or river stones that spouts water and uses a basic recycling pump. Half-barrels also make

(left) A gray catbird splashes into a birdbath. Installing a birdbath may be one of the easiest ways to attract visitors to your yard or garden. Just about all birds—from the bigger songbirds to tiny hummers— enjoy a bath and a drink.

(right) Even a small seating area will feel lush surrounded by a rich variety of flowering plants and shrubs intersected by a simple small stream. A basic feeder pipe supplies the sound of a waterfall.

(bottom) A shallow pond rimmed with a variety of bird-pleasing plants adds beauty to a yard. Plenty of trees and shrubs and limited lawn space make this yard a bird haven.

charming country-style fountains, and they also allow you to create a small bog or water garden. Look for versions that come packaged in kits that include a pump and hosing.

PONDS

Ponds are the ultimate water features, whether they are small and self-contained or expanded into artificial streambeds that meander through the property and offer overlooks and waterfalls. Preformed pond liners and all the necessary equipment to outfit and maintain them can be purchased at most home and garden centers and are not difficult projects for do-it-yourselfers. Simulated streams and waterfalls, on the other hand, will likely require the services of an experienced contractor.

Unexpected Visitors

WHO'S CHECKING OUT YOUR LANDSCAPE?

Once your garden makeover is underway, you may discover many birds, besides songbirds, investigating your enhanced landscape. If it's not the flitting and feeding around your seed-headed perennials that attracts them, it might be the serene lure of your water feature. So don't be shocked if you look out your window one morning and see

(top) A red-winged blackbird perches on a great blue heron *(Ardea herodias).* Homes adjacent to wetlands may get a visit from waders like herons and egrets.

(bottom) A belted kingfisher *(Megaceryle alcyon)* might leave its woodland perch to fish in your backyard pond.

a great blue heron standing statue still in your pond, witness the hatching of mallard ducklings in a patch of native grasses, or marvel at the sight of a peregrine falcon in your tallest tree.

WADING BIRDS

Wading birds, like egrets and herons, enjoy backyard ponds and will while away an afternoon in a shaded water feature. If you keep koi, carp, or goldfish, however, your visiting wader may eat them. Kingfishers—top-heavy, deep blue woodland birds with a cackling call—will also hunt in your pond if it contains fish.

DUCKS

Some wild ducks, such as mallards, make the most of ponds—they will even cavort in a large mud puddle—so be prepared for web-footed guests if you create any water feature large enough for paddling, especially one with plenty of plant cover. Ducks will also nest in yards close to water; if you do find a nest, avoid the area until the ducklings hatch. Mother duck will soon have them off and swimming.

Elegant wood ducks sometimes breed in yards close to wetlands if provided with a nesting box on a tree. It's amazing to watch as the fluff-ball fledglings leave

the nest and plummet to the ground, and lie there stunned . . . only to bounce back to life and head for water.

GEESE

Canada geese (*Branta canadensis*) are large gray and black migratory waterfowl that typically breed in Canada and winter across the South. In recent decades, some birds have established large, year-round colonies in suburban areas of the United States. Unfortunately, their noise, aggression, and droppings have made them nuisances at golf courses, school campuses, and public parks. If you're pleased that they are visiting your yard, offer a nesting box, and they may breed there. If you'd rather not encourage them, place plastic mesh on the lawn—they have trouble walking on it.

HAWKS

Hawks, falcons, and other raptors are always a thrilling sight, but they are not ideal garden guests, having an unfortunate tendency to snack on their smaller fellows. If you hear your resident chickadees give a shrill warning *s-e-e-e,* it's likely that there is a hawk nearby. Still, if you provide enough bushy ground cover around the feeders or in the garden, your birds should be safe until the raptor departs.

If you really don't like the idea of "death from the skies" lurking near your feeding stations, take all feeders inside for several days, encouraging the hawk to move on by removing its dining options. You can also purchase feeders with wire surrounds that let small birds in, but keep raptors out.

(top) A mallard hen *(Anas platyrhynchos)* with her brood of ducklings. A backyard pond may lure these ducks to nest nearby. High, unmowed grasses growing near the edge will help protect the nest and its inhabitants from predators.

(bottom) A family of Canada geese nibble on the grass in a suburban park. These birds are now ubiquitous sights wherever there are open lawns near a source of fresh water.

(right) An American kestrel *(Falco sparverius).* This small falcon is a thing of beauty, but may be a danger to your songbird visitors.

PLANTS TO ATTRACT SONGBIRDS

Ideally, the best plants for attracting songbirds furnish edible seeds or fruit and possibly nest-building materials. It's best to opt for hardy perennials native to your region, which should thrive in most gardens. Seed-producing annuals, such as sunflowers, are also avian favorites.

1 SUNFLOWER (*Helianthus* spp.)
The king of seed flowers. Plant this easy-to-grow annual in full sun near windows where you can watch songbirds fuel up for migration.

2 CONEFLOWER (*Echinacea* spp.)
This hardy perennial boasts long-lasting blooms on tall stalks. The bristly seeds are a favorite of birds and butterflies.

3 CORNFLOWER (*Centaurea cyanus*)
The seeds, nectar, pollen, sap, and foliage of cornflowers (also known as bachelor's buttons) nourish, birds, bees, and butterflies.

4 BLACK-EYED SUSAN (*Rudbeckia hirta*)
Long blooming and easy to grow, these perennials blend well with other seed-bearers like coneflowers and asters.

5 DAISY (*Bellis perennis*)
Garden favorites, cheerful daisies form nutritious seeds that are vital winter fare for finches, sparrows, cardinals, and towhees.

6 ASTER (*Symphyotrichum* spp.)
These fall bloomers—in purple, pink, blue, or white—are perfect for those who desire a garden of staggered seed-bearing plants.

7 MARIGOLD (*Tagetes* spp.)
Many birds eat the dried seeds of these pungent annuals, but some, including grackles and crows, tear apart the orange blooms.

8 VIRGINIA CREEPER (*Parthenocissus quinqefolia*)
The fruit of this vine is an important food source for winter birds, such as mockingbirds, nuthatches, woodpeckers, and blue jays.

9 ELDERBERRY (*Sambucus canadensis*)
This versatile shrub sustains many bird species, including brown thrashers and red-eyed vireos, with it dark blue fruit.

10 STAGHORN SUMAC (*Rhus typhina*)
This shrub furnishes autumn and winter fruit to robins, thrushes, catbirds, cardinals, chickadees, and starlings.

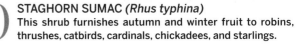

PLANTS TO ATTRACT HUMMINGBIRDS

In addition to using nectar feeders to attract hummingbirds, try growing nectar-rich, brightly colored flowers in your garden. Hummingbirds have no sense of smell, so it is not a heady fragrance that attracts them to a particular flower, but rather the bright hue of its blossoms.

1 TRUMPET VINE (*Campsis radicans*)
Often called hummingbird vine, this aggressive climber of the Northeast is ideal for disguising a messy wall or old fence.

2 CARDINAL FLOWER (*Lobelia cardinalis*)
This striking red perennial summer bloomer depends on the ruby-throated hummingbird for pollination.

3 TRUMPET HONEYSUCKLE (*Lonicera sempervirens*)
The flowers draw hummers, butterflies, and finches. Thrushes will eat the fruit, and orioles eat the flowers for their nectar.

4 COLUMBINE (*Aguilegia* spp.)
These delicate, multi-hued, old-fashioned perennials provide hummingbirds with an early-spring feast.

5 NICOTIANA *(Nicotiana spp.)*
The sweet scent of this all-season blooming annual will permeate your window boxes, and its color will draw hummingbirds to feed.

6 PENSTEMON *(Penstemon spp.)*
Hummingbirds love penstemon's tubular flowers, which come in red, pink, purple, or white. They also attract bees and butterflies.

7 ORIENTAL POPPY *(Papaver orientale)*
Spectacular, papery scarlet red blossoms are sure to grab the attention of passing hummers in late spring or early summer.

8 CORAL BELLS *(Heuchera sanguinea)*
Low clusters of variegated leaves and spikes of petite coral, red, or pink flowers make this a great early-season hummingbird plant.

9 PETUNIA *(Petunia spp.)*
With blooms of nearly every color, they provide hungry hummers with plentiful nectar. Hang them in baskets for easy viewing.

10 HOLLYHOCK *(Alcea spp.)*
Hummers love this towering plant with its oversized papery blooms. It also furnishes food for other birds and butterflies.

CHAPTER TWO
Backyard Birds

· ·

(opposite page) Familiar to many backyard bird-watchers, the blue jay is known for its perky crest and stunning tricolor plumage.

Know Your Backyard Birds

THE BIRDS MOST LIKELY TO VISIT YOUR YARD AND GARDEN

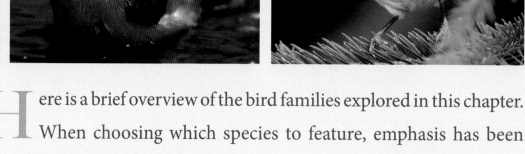

(left) A pair of house finches visit a backyard feeder. Members of the Fringillidae, or finch family, they display the typical sturdy bills of finches, which are adapted for eating seeds.

(middle) A scarlet tanager takes a break from his bath. Until recently, tanagers were classified in their own family, the Thraupidae, but are now listed as members of the Cardinalidae.

(right) A golden-crowned kinglet perches on a pine. The kinglets, or Regulidae, are small, chubby birds.

Here is a brief overview of the bird families explored in this chapter. When choosing which species to feature, emphasis has been placed on widespread geographic location, attractive or beneficial attributes, and, naturally, tolerance for humans and their habitations.

NEW WORLD SPARROWS

New World sparrows—or Emberizidae—are small songbirds. North American species are gray or brown, seed-eating birds with distinct wing and head patterns.

FINCHES

The colorful, small- to medium-sized songbirds of the family Fringillidae possess the strong conical bills of seedeaters and range through many habitats worldwide.

CARDINALS

Members of the Cardinalidae are medium-sized songbirds with large, powerful bills perfect for opening seed and nut hulls. This family includes grosbeaks, tanagers, and buntings.

TITS & BUSHTITS

The tit family, or Paridae, includes "snowbirds" like chickadees and titmice that overwinter in the North and feed on nuts and seeds. The bushtit family, or Aegithalidae, are drab, long-tailed birds with only one New World representative, which lives in the woodlands of the West.

WAXWINGS
These slender, delicately hued songbirds, family Bombycillidae, feast on berries and often nest near shallow creeks, where they enjoy bathing.

THRUSHES
The worldwide thrush family, or Turdidae, comprises small- to medium-sized plump birds known for their beautiful songs.

KINGLETS
These tiny, migratory birds of the underbrush—family Regulidae—feed on insects and are best adapted to conifer forests in temperate regions.

WOOD WARBLERS
The family Parulidae are colorful migrants known for their trilling songs—and confusing fall plumage.

WRENS
These small, brownish perching birds, of the family Troglodytidae, are found in shrubby woodlands and near human habitation.

SWALLOWS
The Hirundinidae, including swallows and martins, are agile, graceful fliers that have adapted to eating insects on the wing.

DOVES & PIGEONS
These large, sleek seed-and-grain eaters—family Columbidae—are prolific and adaptable. They are found throughout North America.

NUTHATCHES & CREEPERS
The large-headed members of families Sittidae and Certhiidae are avian acrobats that explore tree trunks in all directions for insects and spiders.

TYRANT FLYCATCHERS
Tyrannidae—tyrant flycatchers of the New World—are the largest bird family, boasting more

than 400 species. Typically gray or brown, some of these birds have colorful markings. They hunt for flying insects on the wing.

MOCKINGBIRDS & THRASHERS
These alert, leggy songbirds of the New World family Mimidae are known for replicating the calls of other birds. The group includes mockingbirds, thrashers, and catbirds.

BLACKBIRDS, ORIOLES & STARLINGS
The family Icteridae includes blackbirds, orioles, grackles, and other birds that feed on insects and seeds; some are migratory. Starlings, which often flock with blackbirds, are an introduced species—from the Old World family Sturnidae—that has proliferated in North America.

CROWS, MAGPIES & JAYS
The Corvidae family of the New World features large, sleek, and highly intelligent birds that have little fear of humans. Most will consume anything edible, including carrion, reptiles, and nestlings.

WOODPECKERS
These distinctive, colorful woodland dwellers of the Picidae family, which contains about 200 species, explore tree trunks for insects with their powerful chisel-like bills.

HUMMINGBIRDS
These tiny, agile nectar feeders of the New World family Trochilidae are beloved for their iridescent plumage and scrappy personalities.

(left) A Baltimore oriole. These birds, which are members of the Icteridae, love both the color and taste of oranges.

(right) Two northern flickers hold a log-side conference. These colorful birds are members of the Picidae, or woodpecker family.

(bottom) A tree swallow (family Hirundinidae) perches outside a nest box.

fact

The habit of investigating deep crevices in rock walls gives the wren family its name, Troglodytidae, from the Latin words for "cave dweller."

Chipping Sparrow

Spizella passerina

Favorite plants

- sunflower
- cherry
- chives
- marjoram
- fountain grass

Chipping sparrows, of the family Emberizidae, are a familiar sight in many backyards across the United States, the bold trill of their song often heralding their appearance.

These sparrows are small, slender birds with long tails. Their plumage is a frosty gray below and a streaked brown above and features both a black eye line and a white brow line. During courtship, the male displays a rusty crown, and his bill turns from brown to black.

They prefer woodlands, farmlands, grassy meadows, parks, and urban and suburban areas, consuming the seeds of grasses and herbs, as well as insects. Chipping sparrows forage on the ground in loose flocks and will pick through groomed lawns or rough ground but are especially keen on dining below feeders. They can be

tempted with a variety of seeds and crumbs scattered in a wide area. In 1929, ornithologist Edward Forbush called the chipping sparrow "the little brown-capped pensioner of the dooryard and lawn, that comes about farmhouse doors to glean crumbs shaken from the tablecloth by thrifty housewives." They will also peck at mineral salt blocks.

Although originally native to pine forests, chipping sparrows of the eastern United States have adapted to suburban life, and many seem unafraid of humans.

These birds are partially migratory—during the colder months, populations of mid- and high-latitude birds will journey to the southern United States or Mexico. If they do migrate, they typically fly at night. During the spring and fall months, their distinctive, undulating calls of *se-e-e-en* can be heard after dark.

Chipping sparrows prefer to perch in low bushes and shrubs, but when they sing it is often from the outer limbs of piney treetops. Females build their delicate nests—which are nearly translucent—of grasses, weeds, and rootlets in conifers, shrubs, or tangled vines. These birds sometimes improvise and will nest in hanging strands of chili peppers, inside rotary lawnmowers, or in hanging baskets. Males attend sitting females, which lay two to seven pale blue, streaked or spotted eggs. The chicks fledge after 10 or 12 days.

FEEDING CHIPPING SPARROWS

These small birds are a mainstay of suburban neighborhoods and consume a variety of commercial foods, including cracked corn, hulled sunflower seeds, millet, milo, and nyjer. They are not fussy eaters and will congregate at a platform, ground, tube, or hopper feeder . . . or simply scavenge the birdseed that has fallen to the ground below any hanging feeder. Also try planting a variety of grasses or grains to tempt them.

Basics

LENGTH
5 to 5.79 inches

WINGSPAN
7 to 9 inches

WEIGHT
0.39 to 0.55 ounce

LONGEVITY
Record in the wild is 11 years, 10 months.

VOCALIZATION
Note is a dry *chip;* call in flight is an undulating *seen;* courting males produce a loud, trilling *chi-chi-chi.*

DISTRIBUTION
Summer from coast to coast, and in the West up to Alaska and Canada. Some populations winter in the Deep South.

(opposite page) A chipping sparrow in its summer breeding plumage. In winter, its colors will be subdued.

(top) A chipping sparrow dining at a tube feeder. These sprightly birds are frequent backyard guests.

similar species: *house sparrow*

This ruddy, chunky import *(Passer domesticus)* is an Old World sparrow of the family Passeridae. It was introduced to New York City in 1852 and soon became one of the most abundant birds in the United States. It has likewise spread, after introduction or due to natural dispersal, throughout many other regions of the globe, making it the mostly widely distributed wild bird. Even though it vies with native birds for food and nesting resources, like most introduced species, the house sparrow is an entertaining addition to the feeder station.

A house sparrow drinking at a birdbath. You are very likely to see this non-native at your feeder.

Song Sparrow

Melospiza melodia

Favorite plants

- buckwheat
- ragweed
- clover
- sunflower
- wheat
- wild cherry
- wild berries

As its common name suggests, this delightful sparrow can be recognized by its distinctive, clattering song, which rises from the low, exposed branches of small trees.

The typical song sparrow is a slightly bulky, medium-sized bird with a red-brown and slate gray head. Its plumage is a streaky russet brown above and white below. Even though these birds can show a number of regional differences, most have a dark spot in the center of the breast. Some coastal sparrows have noticeably darker plumage, and scientists believe that this coloration may be a defense against feather mites and other parasites that live in moist, humid regions. Dark feathers contain more of a pigment called melanin, which makes them tougher and harder to degrade.

Pishing for Birds

Song sparrows sing all through the year and are known to respond to "pishing," which is an imitation of the scold or alarm call of tits or chickadees. When other songbirds hear this call, they will often respond by investigating the threat and then "mobbing" the invader. (This same call might also signal an invitation to join a mixed-species feeding flock.) Researchers use pishing during bird diversity surveys, and birders use it to attract unusual species.

Song sparrows will dine on insects in spring and summer and on seeds in autumn and winter, searching through dense underbrush or low branches. They are ground foragers that will sometimes scratch at the soil.

Their flight pattern is short and fluttery and features a signature downward pump of the tail. When roosting, they often hold their tails cocked upward.

Their loud, clanking songs are complex, containing, on average, four to six phrases that may alter in tempo or quality. The songs of these widespread birds also vary depending on geographic location.

Although song sparrows will flock and migrate in groups, they are solitary and territorial during courtship and nesting season. Males court by singing, and studies show that females are not only attracted to the music, but also value the male's ability to improvise, in other words, they judge how many "learned components" —phrases copied from the adult bird that taught him—the male utilizes in his songs.

The female builds the nest, which is an open cup of leaves, grass, and bark situated in low branches or shrubbery or on the ground. The clutch of one to six eggs is incubated for 12 to 14 days; both parents attend the young. Although the fledglings leave the nest in 10 or 12 days, most remain nearby for feeding and flight training for another three weeks. When resources are plentiful, song sparrows might lay a second or even a third clutch of eggs. As many as seven clutches are not unknown, and four have been raised successfully in one season.

ENCOURAGING SONG SPARROWS

These birds are not flashy, but they make up for their drab appearance with their pleasing songs. Bring them into your yard with offerings of black-oil or hulled sunflower seeds, cracked corn, millet, milo, nyjer, peanut hearts, and safflower. They find it easiest to dine on platform or ground feeders. You might also plant a variety of berries and add cherry or mulberry trees to your landscape.

Basics

LENGTH
4.7 to 6.7 inches

WINGSPAN
7.1 to 9.4 inches

WEIGHT
0.4 to 1.9 ounce

LONGEVITY
11.3 years in the wild

VOCALIZATION
Alarm is a sharp *chip;* females chatter harshly during nest building; the clattering song ends with a buzz or trill.

DISTRIBUTION
Year-round across the northern United States; some birds summer in Canada, some winter across the Southwest to the Deep South.

(opposite page) A song sparrow performing a tune from its varied repertoire. This species is known for the variety and intricacy of its songs, which combine a complex series of repeated notes, quick isolated notes, and melodious trills.

(left) A song sparrow in flight flits through low vegetation to find a perch.

(middle) While foraging in the snow, this bird strikes a typical sparrow pose: head alert and tail cocked upward.

(left) Before taking a drink, a curious song sparrow investigates the fishy decoration in a birdbath.

Spotted Towhee

Pipilo maculatus

Favorite plants

- thistle
- raspberry
- sumac
- buckwheat
- oat
- wheat
- cherry
- oak acorns

A widespread bird of the American West, the spotted towhee—as its name suggests—is spotted on its back and wings. Scientists believe these white spots help the birds blend in with sun-dappled foliage. In addition to its black back and wings, the male has warm rusty red sides and a white belly. The long black tail shows white near the tip. The head is black, the bill is pointed and thick, and the eyes are a piercing red-orange. Females are similar, but brown where the males are black.

The spotted towhee is found year-round from the Pacific Northwest down to the Baja and Mexico. Some populations that breed in the northern interior are migrants and may winter on the Great Plains and in Texas. Vagrants have been found as far to the east as the Atlantic coast.

These birds inhabit arid chaparral, manzanita thickets on mountainsides, scrubs oaks, overgrown fields, forest edges, and pinyon-juniper woods with dense ground cover. They enjoy scratching through leaf litter in heavy thickets—a noise that often gives away their presence. Insects such as beetles, caterpillars, moths, bees, wasps, crickets, and grasshoppers, and arthropods like spiders, sowbugs, and millipedes make up their diet, augmented with seeds, berries, and small fruit, especially in winter.

Courting males chase females to show interest and defend their nesting territories by singing. Researchers have discovered that early in the breeding season, male spotted towhees are so determined to find mates that they spend from 70 to 90 percent of the morning singing. Once they find their "soul mates," however, they are soon busy performing domestic duties and sing only 5 percent of the time. The female builds the nest—an open cup of grass, twigs, and strips of bark—and locates it on the ground, under a protective shrub, or in a low bush. She lays three to five creamy white eggs that hatch in 14 days. Both sexes tend the nestlings, which are ready to leave the nest in 10 or 11 days—but which often stay

with the parents beyond that. Some spotted towhees may produce two or, rarely, three broods a year.

ENTICING TOWHEES

These birds will come to ground or platform feeders that offer black-oil and hulled sunflower seeds, corn, millet, milo, and peanut hearts. Towhees also enjoy scratching through rough cover for insects and would welcome a cluster of dense shrubs or a small deadfall of tangled branches in your yard.

Basics

LENGTH
6.7 to 8.3 inches

WINGSPAN
11 inches

WEIGHT
1.2 to 1.7 ounces

LONGEVITY
Record is 10 years, 8 months.

VOCALIZATION
Song is a long, buzzing *chewee;* call is a catlike *meeww* with a *chip.*

DISTRIBUTION
Year-round in the West; some northern populations may migrate to the Plains states and Texas.

(opposite page) The color-blocked plumage of the spotted towhee is enhanced by its white spots and intense red eyes.

(top) A juvenile spotted towhee perches on an apple tree branch. Although its eyes are still brown, it has begun to show the spotted wings of its species.

related species: *eastern towhee*

The unspotted eastern towhee *(Pipilo erythrophthalmus),* which was formerly known as the rufous-sided towhee, was once believed to be conspecific with the spotted. The male has a rich black head, chest, back, wings, and tail and rusty orange sides. The bill is dark, stout, and conical, and the eyes are bright red. Their differing plumage is not the only distinction between the two: the spotted towhee's calls and songs are more varied and harsher than those of its eastern cousin. Still, where their ranges overlap along a narrow stretch of the Great Plains, these two species can interbreed.

Like the female spotted towhees, female eastern towhees are brown where the males are black.

Dark-eyed Junco

Junco hyemalis

Favorite plants

- chickweed
- buckwheat
- lamb's quarters
- sorrel

The dapper dark-eyed junco is a familiar sight at winter feeders alongside other "snowbirds," such as tufted titmice and black-capped chickadees—the bird's specific name, *hyemalis,* actually means "of the winter." A member of the Emberizidae family, the junco is one of several species of dark gray sparrows—although their color patterns vary widely across the continent.

The junco's body is plump, and the head, back, and breast are usually gray, while the back is gray or brown, the belly white, and the bill pink. The white outer tail feathers are visible during the bird's vigorous flight. (Studies indicate that females show a definite preference for the males with wider bands of white.)

These seedeaters prefer to forage close to the ground, moving along with a hopping motion as they peck through the leaf litter or lawn thatch, but they sometimes take flight to catch an insect in a tree. This is especially true during breeding season, when they require extra energy and will consume insects such as beetles, butterflies, moths, caterpillars, wasps, and flies.

Juncos breed in the western states, the Appalachians, and throughout Canada, including the Arctic regions. The rest of the year they range across the United States from coast to coast, flocking in conifer and mixed-wood forests, open woodlands, fields, parks, weedy verges, and backyards. They are one of the most abundant forest birds on the continent: the total North American population was recently estimated to be 630 million.

During breeding season, courting males display by hopping up and down, offering nesting materials, flicking their wings, and fanning out their tails. Females construct the cup-shaped nest, using their bills to weave together fine grasses and pine needles and then shaping the sides around their bodies. It is then lined with grasses,

ferns, hair, and fine bits of moss. The nest is situated in a ground hollow or supported by twigs and rootlets and is usually obscured by vegetation. The females lay three to six gray or bluish white eggs that incubate for 12 days. Nestlings are ready to fledge in 10 to 13 days.

BRINGING JUNCOS TO THE YARD

These attractive cold-weather visitors will feed with chickadees in your yard. Make sure you provide these snowbirds with a good mix of millet, black-oil and hulled sunflower seeds, cracked corn, milo, nyjer, oats, peanut hearts, and safflower. You might also tempt them with live mealworms. These birds prefer to dine at ground, hopper, and platform feeders.

A Bird by Any Color

There are 15 described races of juncos—six forms that are easily recognizable in the field and five that used to be considered separate species until the 1980s. Among the many subtypes are the slate-colored, found in Alaska and east of the Rockies; the gray-headed, found in the southern Rockies; and the Oregon junco found in the northern Rockies and farther west. Less common are the white-winged, which breeds in the mountains of Wyoming, Montana, and South Dakota, and the pink-sided, which breeds in Montana and Wyoming.

Basics

LENGTH
5.5 to 6.7 inches

WINGSPAN
7.1 to 9.8 inches

WEIGHT
0.63 to 1.06 ounces

LONGEVITY
3 to 11 years; record is 11 years, 4 months.

VOCALIZATION
Song is a loose trill, similar to a chipping sparrow's; call is a *smack* note. It also utters a high, twinkly *chip* while foraging.

DISTRIBUTION
Summers and breeds in Canada—as far north as the Arctic, Western states, Appalachians; balance of year across the country

(opposite page) West of the Great Plains, dark-eyed juncos come in a wide variety of plumage, often showing reddish brown on the back or sides or both. This subtype is known as the Oregon junco.

(top) A gray-headed dark-eyed junco sports a gray hood, gray underparts, and a reddish brown back.

(bottom) A slate-colored dark-eyed junco forages in the winter snow. Coloration varies widely across the country, but in the East, these birds are always gray and white, with males tending to display darker markings than females.

American Goldfinch

Spinus tristis

Favorite plants

- thistle
- aster
- milkweed
- dandelion
- alder
- birch
- western red cedar
- mullein

These showy and active members of the finch family, Fringillidae, are perennial favorites at feeding stations, entertaining viewers with their acrobatic stunts. American goldfinches are especially fond of nyjer seeds and will also flock to mature thistle, aster, or milkweed in the garden.

They are one of the most recognizable songbirds in the country and have been chosen as the state birds of New Jersey, Iowa, and Washington. Although the coloration of both sexes is similar—a yellow head and body with black-and-white wings—the breeding male far surpasses the female in flashiness, his vivid, almost neon-yellow body contrasting with his striped wings and forehead patch.

These birds have the typical finch bill—short, strong, conical—which is ideal for tackling plant seeds, tree buds, and berries, as well as for dispatching insects. The wings are long, and the short tail is notched. The flight pattern is distinctive: the undulating up-and-down motion of a roller coaster, accompanied by calls of *po-ta-to-chip* or *per-twee-twee-twee.*

Goldfinches seek out the overgrown fields and floodplains where their favorite bristly weeds grow, as well as roadsides, orchards, and suburban backyards. Some populations remain year-round across the temperate regions of the United States; others summer and breed across southern Canada and winter in the southern states and parts of Mexico.

Although males may sing their hearts out in the spring—these birds continue to learn new song patterns throughout their lives—goldfinches actually breed late in the season, after their weedy dietary staples have gone to seed. Males begin courtship in July with aerial pursuit, and then both sexes search together for a nesting site, usually high up in a sapling or shrub situated out in the open. The pair may join to collect materials like plants and rootlets, but only the female builds the cuplike nest, lashing it to branches with spider silk and lining it with pappus, the fluffy material gleaned from the seed heads they love to consume. She lays a clutch of two to seven bluish, sometimes brown-dotted, eggs that incubate for 12 to 14 days. The nestlings are ready to strike out on their own after two weeks or so.

GOING FOR THE GOLD

These beautiful, lively birds are easily lured to suburban yards; the trick is a nonstop supply of nyjer seed in a tube or sock feeder. They will also eat hulled and black-oil sunflower seeds from any type of songbird feeder. Letting your thistles, asters, milkweed, and dandelions go to seed will also bring a quantity of hungry goldfinches to your property from midsummer through to fall.

Basics

LENGTH
4.3 to 5.5 inches

WINGSPAN
7.5 to 8.7 inches

WEIGHT
0.39 to 0.71 ounce

LONGEVITY
Record is 10 years.

VOCALIZATION
The canary-like song is a sustained and clear series of twitters and warbles; call is *po-ta-to-chip.*

DISTRIBUTION
Year-round in temperate North America; some breed in Canada and summer in the South.

(opposite page) A male American goldfinch in its brilliant breeding plumage takes a break from nibbling on the seed heads of purple coneflowers. In winter, it will be a far drabber bird, with unstreaked brown plumage, blackish brown wings, and two pale wing bars.

(left) An agile female gathers the silken threads of a thistle plant, which she will use to craft a nest. Adult females are dull yellow beneath and olive above.

(right) A juvenile looks secure nestled in a leaf. Unlike other songbirds, which promptly investigate avian warning calls and mob invading predators to chase them away, goldfinches do not respond to these community alarms.

House Finch

Haemorhous mexicanus

Favorite plants

- strawberry
- blackberry
- fig
- knotweed
- thistle
- mulberry
- stone fruit
- wild mustard seed

This gregarious feeder bird was not originally indigenous to the East Coast, but rather belonged to the deserts, grasslands, and chaparral of the American West. In 1940, a few birds were released on Long Island, New York, after they failed to sell to the public as caged "Hollywood finches." This adaptable species had soon established itself throughout the Atlantic and Great Lakes states as well as southern Canada. Sometime before 1870, house finches were introduced to Oahu, and by 1901 they were abundant on all the major Hawaiian islands.

This is a small-bodied finch, with a long, somewhat flat head and heavy, oversized bill. The females are grayish brown with thick, blurry stripes. Males display a rosy red head and chest—and a red rump visible in flight—with dark stripes on the

similar species: *purple finch*

Roger Tory Peterson of field guide fame described the purple finch (*Haemorhous purpureus*) as "a sparrow dipped in raspberry sauce." This finch's saturated coloring makes it hard to miss when it is dining at bird feeders or perched in evergreen trees. It breeds in southern Canada and during the winter ranges from the East Coast to the Central Plains and is also found in pockets in the Far West. Some populations remain year-round near the Great Lakes, New England, and the Pacific coast.

The cool pinkish cast of this chunky finch differentiates it from the warmer-toned house finch.

sides and belly. The coloration of males can vary greatly, but not because of regional differences but rather due to variations in their diet during the molt. Birds cannot make red or yellow colors, so they rely on pigmented food. Females seem to show a preference for brighter males.

The birds' tails are long in comparison to their stubby wings. Most finches have a distinct tail notch, but the notch on a house finch's tail is barely noticeable. These birds do, however, show the typically bouncy finch flight pattern.

House finches feed on the ground or clinging to weed stalks, dining on seeds, buds, and fruits. They are found near forest edges, farms, city parks, urban centers, and backyards, where males can be heard singing a short-noted warble throughout most of the year.

These versatile birds build their nests in coniferous or deciduous trees as well as on cactus plants and rock ledges, in building vents, on street lamps, and in hanging planters. They sometimes take over abandoned nests.

Courting males may feed females, who first gently peck at their bills while fluttering their wings. Females lay two to six white or pale blue eggs in a cup-shaped nest made of fine stems, leaves, string, wool, and feathers. These birds are unusual in that they feed their offspring only plant matter, unlike most other birds that, even if vegetarian themselves, feed their growing chicks animal and insect matter for increased protein. Nestlings are ready to fledge in 12 to 19 days.

ATTRACTING HOUSE FINCHES

Hopper, tube, or platform feeders full of black-oil and hulled sunflower seeds, nyjer, and safflower seeds can bring noisy groups of these birds to your yard. Provide a choice of several nesting spots, including hanging planters and ledges placed in porch eaves to draw a courting couple.

Basics

LENGTH
5.5 to 5.5 inches

WINGSPAN
7.9 to 9.8 inches

WEIGHT
0.6 to 1 ounce

LONGEVITY
Record is 11 years, 7 months.

VOCALIZATION
Male song is a long, jumbled warbling ending with an upward or downward slur; the female song similar, but shorter.

DISTRIBUTION
Year-round through most of temperate North America except the Central Plains

(*opposite page*) A male house finch perched on a blossoming peach tree. House finches are some of the most common feeder birds throughout the continental United States.

(*bottom*) A female house finch lacks the red tones of her male counterpart.

Pine Siskin

Spinus pinus

Favorite plants

- larch
- hemlock
- spruce
- alder
- maple
- dandelion
- chickweed
- sunflower

This small, brownish finch is an erratic wanderer, following cone crops across the continent. Some populations live year-round in eastern Canada and throughout the Rockies; others summer and breed in western Canada up as far north as Alaska and winter from the Plains states east to the Atlantic coast and south to Mexico, as well as in California and the Pacific Northwest.

Pine siskins are known for feeding in large flocks in coniferous or mixed woodlands with open canopies and will also hunt for seeds in scrubland, weedy fields, overgrown thickets, cemeteries, parks, and backyards. In particular, they will seek out gardens with thistle or nyjer bird feeders. They are also attracted to mineral deposits, including ashpits, fresh cement, and road salt.

Turn Up the Heat

To keep warm on cold winter nights, pine siskins are capable of increasing their metabolism by as much as 40 percent more than other songbirds of similar size. This enables incubating mother birds to keep their eggs warm when temperatures drop. Pine siskins can also store seeds equaling 10 percent of their body mass in their crop—providing enough food energy to sustain them through five hours of subzero evening temperatures.

The sexes have a similar streaky brown coloring with yellow edges on their long wings and relatively short tails. Males tend to be a showier yellow, which become more noticeable during courting displays. The bill of both sexes is slender, dark, and sharply pointed, and the tail shows the typical finch notch.

Agile fliers, pine siskins flutter around feeding stations or explode from the trees in sudden flight. It is not uncommon to spot these acrobatic birds hanging upside down from branches as they excavate cone seeds. Even when flocks keep to the shelter of high treetops, their incessant, wheezy twitters give them away.

During courtship, males fly in circles around females, spreading their wings and tails and singing. Although pine siskins form monogamous pairs, it is the female that builds the saucer-shaped nest. She constructs it on a well-concealed horizontal branch—sometimes so loosely that it is vulnerable to gusts of wind— usually midway up a tall conifer. Favored materials are twigs, grasses, weed stems, bark, rootlets, and lichens, occasionally supplied by the male. It is not uncommon for siskins to nest in flocks, each a few trees away from the others. The female stays put on her clutch of three to five eggs, dependent on the male to feed her during incubation. Chicks are born with dark gray down on their heads and backs and are ready to fledge in 14 to 17 days.

PLEASING THE PINE SISKIN

Like most other finches, pine siskins are fond of black-oil and hulled sunflower seeds, as well as millet and nyjer. They will feed at ground feeders and at tube, platform, and hopper feeders, and they will scavenge below larger finches that are messy eaters. They sometimes eat suet from cage feeders. Dandelion seeds also offer them a nutritious food source.

Basics

LENGTH
4.3 to 5.5 inches

WINGSPAN
7.1 to 8.7 inches

WEIGHT
0.4 to 0.6 ounce

LONGEVITY
No available data

VOCALIZATION
Call is a rising *bzzzzt;* the song sounds like a hoarse goldfinch.

DISTRIBUTION
Year-round along the Canadian border and the Rocky Mountains, may breed in northern Canada; sporadic migration in winter to continental United States and Mexico

(opposite page) Clinging to the branch tips of pines and other conifers is a typical pose for a pine siskin. The yellow edging on the wings is especially noticeable on the male birds.

(bottom) Gregarious pine siskins travel in flocks and often descend en masse onto bird feeders. You can expect to see them year-round, even in winter.

Evening Grosbeak

Coccothraustes vespertinus

Favorite plants

- maple
- box elder
- ash
- cherry
- apple
- tulip tree
- juniper berry
- crabapple

A large, husky finch, the evening grosbeak breeds in the pine or aspen forests of the North and the mountains of the West. These are barrel-chested birds, with short necks and tails and, as the name suggests, heavy, conical bills. Grosbeaks are pros at cracking large, thick-hulled seeds, much more so than pine siskins. As a result, these smaller birds often follow them and glean their leavings.

Males have an ivory-colored bill, and the body is bright yellow with a darker, shaded head and a slashing yellow eyebrow stripe. The wings are black with a large white patch. Females are a pale gray with a golden sheen on the neck and flanks and black-and-white wings; the bill is a greenish yellow.

During the late 19th and early 20th centuries, this bird began extending its

consumers of caterpillars, aphids, and the destructive spruce budworm. They will also ingest maple sap by breaking twigs off maple trees.

They are irruptive, or irregular, migrants. Some years certain populations migrate south to the central and southern states, where they become feeder favorites. Other years they spend the cold months in dense forests, often at higher elevations. There are at least three distinct regional populations of evening grosbeaks in North America, and although they do not differ in plumage, each has a distinct call.

Courting males perform a curious dance—swiveling their bodies while they raise their head and tail and allow their wings to droop and vibrate. Males may attentively feed females during breeding season, but the females construct the nests by themselves, usually on horizontal branches or in the fork of a tree.

breeding range eastward, possibly due to the increased planting of box elders, a favorite food, and the presence of backyard feeders. Sadly, these birds are now becoming increasingly uncommon, especially in the eastern United States.

Evening grosbeaks are highly social, flocking together in large numbers to feed, especially in winter when they forage for seeds, berries, and buds in deciduous groves. During the summer, they seek insect larvae in treetops and are great

TEMPTING EVENING GROSBEAKS

Although grosbeaks are intermittent winter visitors, you can make sure any nearby birds will visit your yard by offering sunflower seeds on platform feeders and also by including maple trees and box elders—two evening grosbeak favorites that supply seeds, buds, and berries—in your landscaping plans.

Basics

LENGTH
6.3 to 8.7 inches

WINGSPAN
12 to 14 inches

WEIGHT
1.4 to 3.04 ounces

LONGEVITY
Record is 16 years, 3 months.

VOCALIZATION
Call is a ringing *cleer;* the song an uneven, musical warble.

DISTRIBUTION
Across northern North America, with some migration to the lower states in winter

(opposite page) A male evening grosbeak is an impressive sight, with its massive bill and distinctive markings on its mostly yellow body.

(top) A female evening grosbeak may not be as bright as the male, but her bill is no less striking.

similar species: *rose-breasted grosbeak*

A colorful songbird, the rose-breasted grosbeak *(Pheucticus ludovicianus)* is marginally smaller than the evening grosbeak. A denizen of eastern forests, it can also be found at backyard bird feeders feasting on sunflower seeds or searching the grass for insects. The male is black above, white below, and has a festive patch of red on the upper chest. Females and juveniles are streaked brown and white. Although it is finch-like in appearance, this bird is a member of the cardinal family.

Along with its red breast, the male rose-breasted grosbeak flashes pink-red under his wings.

Northern Cardinal

Cardinalis cardinalis

Favorite plants

- sunflower
- dogwood
- grape
- buckwheat
- tulip tree
- staghorn sumac
- berries
- grasses

With its vibrant coloring and melodic song, the northern cardinal of the central, southern, and eastern states is one of America's most recognizable birds. It is also a frequent feeder at backyard stations, especially during the chillier months.

The male cardinal is crested, and his body is a riveting shade of scarlet, showing slightly dusky wings and a black mask around the conical, deep coral bill. (Cardinals take their name from the high-ranking Roman Catholic cardinals who wear bright red robes and caps.) The female is also crested with a coral bill, but her body is a rich buff, with warm red showing on the crest, wings, and tail.

Cardinals do not molt into dull fall plumage like most other songbirds, so they furnish a welcome note of brightness to a snowy yard or gray winter landscape. Their stunning looks have inspired Illinois, Indiana, Kentucky, North Carolina, Ohio, Virginia, and West Virginia to name this species the official state bird.

If their striking colors were not enough of a clue to their identity, their trilling, familiar calls of *birdy-birdy* and *what-cheer-cheer-cheer,* often rising from the treetops, make northern cardinals easy to identify, even for novice birders.

These birds are found in dense shrubs at forest edges, overgrown fields, hedgerows, marshy thickets, mesquite, new-growth woodlands, and backyards and ornamental landscaping. They feed primarily on seeds, grain, and fruit, sometimes augmented with beetles, cicadas, grasshoppers, and snails. The increase of towns and suburbs across eastern North America has helped the cardinal expand its range northward.

Cardinals are monogamous and will remain together in their established territory throughout the year. Both sexes can be fiercely protective of nesting sites—to the point of attacking their own images in window glass. During courtship, males bring tasty tidbits to females and feed them beak-to-beak. The females build cup-shaped nests wedged into dense shrubs, low trees, or tangles of vines by weaving together twigs they have crushed with their powerful bills. They lay two to five off-white eggs, which hatch in 11 to 13 days. The chicks are ready to fledge in another two weeks.

CALLING ALL CARDINALS

These charismatic birds need little urging to come into your yard to dine in winter; some individuals even wait by kitchen windows for homeowners to fill empty feeders. You can keep your cardinal guests happy with a supply of black-oil and hulled sunflower seeds, cracked corn, millet, milo, peanut hearts, and safflower. Needless to say, cardinals will help themselves from most types of feeders—ground, hopper, platform, and large tube.

Basics

LENGTH
7.9 to 9.3 inches

WINGSPAN
9.8 to 12.2 inches

WEIGHT
1.19 to 2.29 ounces

LONGEVITY
Record in the wild is 15 years, 9 months; 28 years in captivity.

VOCALIZATION
Warning call is a sharp metallic *chip.* Repeated chipping allows couples to find each other. Song is *birdy-birdy-birdy* or *what-cheer-cheer.*

DISTRIBUTION
Eastern and central United States from Maine to Texas; Mexico; and southeastern Canada

(opposite page) Cardinals are all-season visitors. A male brightens a gray winter landscape with a swash of brilliant scarlet plumage.

(left) A female perches in a branch of an apple tree.

(top) Northern cardinals mate for life. To encourage a nesting pair, leave some undergrowth in your yard so that they can build a nest hidden by foliage.

(bottom) A female feeds a chick. Unlike most other songbirds, female cardinals sing, primarily while sitting on the nest. These songs, which can be more complex than the male's, may possibly relay information about when to bring food.

Unwanted Visitors

DETERRING DESTRUCTIVE WILDLIFE

Hanging a feeder in your yard may tempt visitors other than birds. Squirrels find the food inside irresistible and prove themselves able gymnasts in the quest for treats.

It's no surprise that after you've improved your garden soil, you find weeds springing up everywhere. In a similar vein, creating a pleasant habitat for wildlife—with food, water, and shelter—is bound to attract some unwelcome guests. Large animals, such as deer, can destroy landscaping and gardens (and carry ticks that cause Lyme disease), while smaller mammals like rabbits or skunks can dig up plants and damage wooden structures. As a good steward of the planet, you don't want to use toxic chemicals or harmful traps to dissuade these invaders—and building an eight-foot deer-proof fence is impractical—so it's a relief to know that there are plenty of safe ways to say "Keep Out!"

Your first step is to identify the pest you're dealing with so that you can devise an appropriate control strategy. Check with your local cooperative extension or state wildlife agency, which can offer you helpful tips to determine what type of animal caused the damage.

DEER & RABBITS

Many country and suburban homeowners enjoy the sight of a deer or two grazing on the lawn or a glimpse of wild rabbits romping across the grass. What they don't enjoy is waking up to find the tulips beheaded and the hostas decimated. Alas, deer and rabbits will happily make canapés of your blooming flowers and tender young vegetables.

Fortunately, there are a number of nontoxic products that use scent to drive nibblers from the yard. The spray initially smells bad to humans, but long past the time your nose can detect it, the scent will remain repulsive to deer and rabbits. Bars of strongly scented soap (like Irish Spring) scattered throughout the garden will also keep pests away. Sprinkling bloodmeal (a by-product of meat packing) on the ground deters deer and rabbits, and it is good for the soil. Predator urine is also quite effective: coyote urine will repel deer, while fox urine works on small mammals like rabbits, squirrels, and skunks.

SQUIRRELS

No animal is more determined than a squirrel intent on robbing your bird feeder. These inventive animals can climb almost anything and can leap great distances, even straight upward. If possible, set up feeders with ten feet of air around them. If that is not doable, try using baffles—cylindrical or dome-shaped guards that keep squirrels from reaching the goodies. There is some evidence that if you feed squirrels away from the bird feeder—they love peanuts, sunflower seeds, and cracked corn—they will establish territory there and leave the feeder alone. Two other tricks are switching to the safflower

Bears Be Gone

If you live in the country, and problem bears pay repeat visits to your yard, it is likely that they are attracted by bagged kitchen trash or quantities of birdseed lying about. Make sure to keep all refuse cans and birdseed storage containers tightly lidded. If the bears are making a beeline for your bird feeders, leave the feeders empty for at least two weeks—or until the bears find better foraging spots.

seeds they dislike and buying some pepper additive: squirrels avoid it, but birds don't mind the heat.

SLUGS & SNAILS

Deter these slimy garden gourmands by placing coffee grounds around your plants, which will also keep cats away. Copper mesh or circles of copper sheeting placed around your plants is also an effective shield against slugs and snails. If you would prefer to trap them, place the rind of an orange or grapefruit on the ground overnight. Come morning, dispose of all the slugs that flocked there. Shallow saucers of beer set level with the ground will likewise attract and then drown slugs.

No animal is more determined than a squirrel intent on robbing your bird feeder.

(left) Rabbits may look cute, but their natural urge to dig and chew can wreak havoc in your backyard garden.

(right) Gardens planned to attract birds will also attract other wildlife. Once a country denizen, deer have become increasingly common in suburban areas.

Indigo Bunting

Passerina cyanea

Favorite plants

- thistle
- dandelion
- goldenrod
- mullein
- blueberry
- blackberry
- serviceberry
- elderberry

The male of this avian species—nicknamed the "blue canary"—with its brilliant cobalt plumage and black-edged wings is surely one of our most beautiful native birds.

These sparrow-sized, stocky songbirds have short conical bills, and short, rounded tails. The male is blue only during breeding season; in fall its plumage is brown, with hints of blue on the wings and tail. The female is a warm brown above, with a streaked beige breast; outer feathers may show a tinge of blue.

These members of the cardinal family enjoy small seeds, grains, berries, and buds, and they also feed on insects such as caterpillars—including the noxiously hairy brown-tail moth larvae, grasshoppers, aphids, cicadas and beetles, and spiders.

Indigo buntings summer throughout the eastern United States from Maine to Florida, and as far west as California in the South and into the Midwest in the North. They seek out weedy and brushy areas, hedgerows, power line cuts, overgrown fields, and suburban lawns. They can be found along the edges of rural roads, singing endlessly from telephone lines or from treetops. Their song, with its bouncy paired notes, soon becomes easy to recognize. Oddly, chicks learn this song not from their fathers but from male buntings nesting nearby. These "neighborhood" songs can be quite different from the songs of other buntings only a few hundred yards away. The local songs can persist through many generations, changing only gradually.

These birds winter in Central America and the Caribbean Islands, traveling as many as 1,200 miles, migrating at night and using the stars for navigation. They tend to migrate due south from wherever they spend the summer. Indigo buntings form great flocks at this time and can be seen feeding en masse in farm fields or on suburban lawns.

During breeding season, males may grapple with each other in the air while singing loudly and then fall to the ground with their claws locked, still singing. One

male may take several mates. Females weave the cuplike nests out of leaves and grasses and wrap them with spider web. The nests are located in a dense shrub or low tree, a yard off the ground. The eggs incubate for two weeks or so, and the chicks are ready to leave the nest in another two weeks. Females generally tend to the chicks, though males may feed fledglings if females attempt a second brood.

BRINGING BUNTINGS TO FEEDERS
Feeding stations stocked with small seeds, particularly with thistle or nyjer, will draw indigo buntings to your yard. They also eat insects, so a treat of live mealworms may also be welcome.

Basics

LENGTH
4.7 to 5.1 inches

WINGSPAN
7.5 to 8.7 inches

WEIGHT
0.4 to 0.6 ounce

LONGEVITY
Record in the wild is 8 years, 3 months.

VOCALIZATION
Song is an excited warble with each note or phrase sung twice; alarm is *chip*.

DISTRIBUTION
Summers in eastern United States, west to California in South, west to central states in North

(opposite page) A male indigo bunting. Its feathers actually contain no blue pigment: the color comes from microscopic structures in the feathers that reflect and refract blue light. This is true of all blue birds.

(top) A female indigo bunting. When perching, they are known for swishing their tails from side to side.

similar species: *painted bunting*

The flamboyant male painted bunting *(Passerina ciris)*, dabbed as he is with primary school colors of red, blue, green, and yellow, seems to have stepped out of a storybook. Painted buntings breed in the coastal Southeast and the southern central states. Even though they inhabit dense woodland edges and hedgerows, they are frequent feeder visitors. Sadly, these protected songbirds are sometimes illegally caught and sold as cage birds in Mexico and the Caribbean, stressing the current breeding populations.

A colorful male painted bunting. Even the female is a bright lime green with a pale eye ring.

Western Tanager

Piranga ludoviciana

Favorite plants

- mulberry
- elderberry
- hawthorn
- wild cherry
- blackberry
- serviceberry

The brightly colored plumage of this small, stocky songbird, the western cousin of the scarlet tanager, has been compared to a flame—fiery red at the cap, shading to red-orange on the head and then bright yellow on the body. The wings are black with yellow wing bars. The females of the species are a muddy yellow with a gray back and wings.

Unlike most red birds that derive their coloration from plant pigments called carotenoids, the male western tanager's cap color comes from a pigment called rhodoxanthin. Because they cannot manufacture this pigment themselves, it is believed the birds ingest it in their primary diet of insects.

Western tanagers prey on wasps, bees, ants, beetles, grasshoppers, termites, and cicadas, and they are known for searching methodically through the foliage for insects—a feeding method called gleaning. They will also dart out to catch insects on the wing, a behavior called sallying. In addition to insects, they will eat berries and some fruit, including mulberries, elderberries, and cultivated cherries. (A hundred years ago, they were considered a menace to commercial fruit crops and many birds were poisoned or shot.) They have a curious habit of feeding at flowers, possibly to both catch insects and sip nectar.

These birds breed throughout the American West and well up into Canada and have the northernmost range of any tanager. They migrate south in winter to the pine and oak woodlands of Mexico and Central America. Their preferred habitat is open conifer or mixed forests and mountains. Although they are not easily spotted among their pine bough roosts, they can be located by their loud, fluting songs or their rattling calls. During

migration, they often flock with other tanagers or black-headed grosbeaks.

A courting male may chase a female through the trees—and sometimes tumble past her in the air to show off his flashy plumage. Once nesting occurs, the male sings to defend his territory. The female is believed to build the nest, a shallow cup made of twigs, grasses, and rootlets that is lined with fine rootlets and animal fur. She typically places it in a fir or pine tree, sometimes in an oak, on a fork that is at least 15 feet from the ground. She then lays three to five blue or blue-green blotched eggs and incubates them for 13 days. Once the babies hatch, both parents tend them; the young are usually ready to leave the nest in two weeks.

WOOING WESTERN TANAGERS
Although they are not typically seedeaters, these birds will sometimes approach ground or platform feeders stocked with dried fruit and sliced oranges or other fresh fruit. They will also favor yards with a trickling birdbath or a pond.

Basics

LENGTH
6.3 to 7.5 inches

WINGSPAN
11.5 inches

WEIGHT
0.8 to 1.3 ounces

LONGEVITY
Record is 6 years, 11 months for a banded wild bird.

VOCALIZATION
Song is fluty, with a pause between phrases; call is a rolling *pit-r-ick.*

DISTRIBUTION
Breeds throughout the western states and up to northern Canada; winters in Mexico and Central America

(opposite page) Looking like a goldfinch that stuck his head in a bottle of red ink, the male western tanager is a colorful sight.

(top) A duller yellow than the male and with no red markings, the female can remain inconspicuous as she perches in a tree.

(bottom) A male comes in for a landing in a backyard birdbath. Water features can attract western tanagers.

Scarlet Tanager

Piranga olivacea

Favorite plants

- mulberry
- blackberry
- huckleberry
- serviceberry
- black chokeberry
- elderberry
- staghorn sumac

Although the male scarlet tanager displays vivid coloring during the breeding season—a stunning flame red body with ebony wings and tail—this flashy bird prefers to remain obscured by the foliage of tall shade trees. Even if one does venture out of hiding to snatch a beetle on the wing or to hover with rapid wingbeats over a garden in search of caterpillars, it will quickly dart back to the safety of its leafy haven in a feeding method known as sallying.

These medium-sized, stocky members of the cardinal family have a relatively large head, but a short, broad tail. The female is yellowish green with a bright yellow face and throat. After the fall molt, the male turns a similar shade of green with black wings and tail. The rounded, bulging bill is adapted to catching insects

similar species: *summer tanager*

The chunky, tomato-colored male of this eye-catching species is the only completely red bird in North America. Females are a warm mustard yellow that lets them blend in with foliage. Summer tanagers (*Piranga rubra*) breed in the South and Southwest, migrating to Central America and the northern reaches of South America in the fall. In spring and summer, listen for them singing in the canopies of tall forest trees or observe them sallying out to catch flying insects, especially bees and wasps, which they strike against a branch in order to kill them and remove their stingers.

Erecting a birdbath may help persuade the summer tanager to stop for a visit to your yard or garden. A dazzling flash of scarlet will alert you to this insect-loving bird's presence.

and eating seeds. The male's is a silver-gray color, the female's olive-gray.

These birds breed in the deciduous and deciduous-coniferous forests of the temperate eastern states as far west as Kansas and prefer to nest and perch in towering trees like oak, maple, and beech. In the fall, they migrate great distances to the rain forests of western South America, crossing the Gulf of Mexico and typically traveling at night. Their preferred summer diet consists of caterpillars, beetles, moths, wasps, bees, aphids, spiders, and worms, as well as wild fruit and berries. Their winter diet in South America is poorly understood.

Unfortunately, scarlet tanagers are suffering from loss of habitat in both their seasonal ranges due to forest fragmentation—they require large, unbroken blocks of woodland in order to breed and keep populations stable.

Courting males will display on the branches below perching females—drooping their wings and spreading their tails to show off their contrasting plumage. Pairs remain monogamous for one season, typically nesting on the horizontal limbs of deciduous trees high above the ground. The female prepares a shallow, saucer-shaped nest made of twigs, grasses, stalks, and bark strips for two to five pale blue-green eggs. Both parents feed the young, although females handle the brunt of the work and will attend the fledglings for several weeks after they have left the nest.

TEMPTING SCARLET TANAGERS

These birds will often flock with other songbirds during the late summer and fall migrations, when they visit suburban yards. You can coax them to linger by offering a variety of berry bushes.

Basics

LENGTH
6.3 to 7.5 inches

WINGSPAN
9.8 to 11.8 inches

WEIGHT
0.83 to 1.34 ounces

LONGEVITY
Record is 12 years.

VOCALIZATION
Call note is a nasal *chip-bang* or *chip-burr;* the song is a repetitive, raspy, warble similar to a robin's.

DISTRIBUTION
Summers in temperate eastern United States; winters in South America

(opposite page) The thick, rounded bills of scarlet tanagers are adapted for grabbing berries, as well as insects and seeds.

(bottom) Scarlet tanagers are elusive birds, and the female is especially hard to spot. Her yellowish green body and dark wings will camouflage her when she perches amid a backdrop of leafy tree branches.

Blue Grosbeak

Passerina caerulea

Favorite plants

- bristlegrass
- panicgrass
- wheat
- oat
- rice
- corn
- alfalfa

A member of the Cardinalidae, the stocky, medium-sized blue grosbeak shares its family with northern cardinals, "tropical" or New World buntings, and the "cardinal-grosbeaks" or New World grosbeaks. The vividly blue male shows a black mask, warm red wing bars, and a silver bill, while the female is cinnamon colored, with rusty wing bars and a gray bill. As well as the powerful bill typical of cardinals, the male vocalizes with the same rich, sweet song of its brilliant red cousin.

These sociable birds forage in large flocks except during the breeding season, consuming a mix of insects and seeds. Their summer diet may include a range of insects—grasshoppers, beetles, caterpillars, cicadas, and praying mantids—as well as spiders and snails.

They are capable of hovering over plants to pluck up insects or will make short sorties from their tree roosts to snatch them in flight. Seeds of weeds, grass, and waste grain may make up a majority of their diet during some seasons.

These colorful birds can be found year-round in Mexico and Central America, but many populations migrate north, covering long distances to breed in the South, Mid-Atlantic, Midwest, and Southwest.

Despite their eye-catching plumage, blue grosbeaks are retiring, preferring to remain hidden in the foliage of small trees or shrubs. Still, their distinctive song, or their loud clinking note, allows birders to locate them. They are most often found in old fields with returning woodland growth, cedar and southern pine forests, and in bushy scrub along streambeds in arid regions. Spring and summer sightings are not uncommon at seed feeders in shrubby yards.

During nesting season, which can last into late summer in some regions, males sing to defend their territory. The female prepares a cup-shaped nest of twigs, weeds, bark strips, and rootlets that might be augmented with odd bits like snakeskin, string, paper, or rags. She places it low in a shrub, small tree, or tangle of vines. (There are some reports

of these birds also nesting in bluebird boxes.) The female lays three to five pale blue or whitish eggs, and then takes responsibility for feeding the nestlings, which are ready to fly after nine or ten days. The male is more likely to tend to their offspring at this point, especially if the female has started a second brood.

PIQUING BLUE GROSBEAKS

Although they are reputedly shy birds, these grosbeaks have been known to seek seeds and grains at backyard feeders. A tempting offering of meal worms might also lure these insectivores to dine.

Basics

LENGTH
5.9 to 6.3 inches

WINGSPAN
11 inches

WEIGHT
0.9 to 1.1 ounces

LONGEVITY
6 years in the wild

VOCALIZATION
Song is a husky, sweet warble, often jumbled; the note is a sharp metallic *klink*.

DISTRIBUTION
Summers and breeds in the southern, central, and southwestern states

(opposite page) Blue grosbeaks can now be found as far north as New Jersey in the East and North Dakota in the central states. Scientists believe that these birds have expanded their range in the past 200 years or so due to the clearing of the forests.

(top) A water feature can lure blue grosbeaks, such as this female that has stopped by a park fountain for a drink and a bath.

similar species: *lazuli bunting*

Named for the deep blue gemstone, the lazuli bunting *(Passerina amoena)* is as lovely as its cousin. With a smaller and lighter body than the blue grosbeak, the breeding male has a bright blue head and a buff-colored breast edged in orange. Its dark wings are also edged in lapis lazuli blue and feature two broad white wing bars; the tail is black with thin blue edging. Lazuli buntings are common in shrubby areas throughout the West, where their sweet warbling song is a welcome sign of spring.

Genetic evidence indicates that the blue grosbeak's closest relative is the lazuli bunting.

Black-capped Chickadee

Poecile atricapillus

Favorite plants

- sunflower
- ragweed
- hemlock
- birch
- pine
- walnut
- aspen
- elm

An attractive, acrobatic, and inquisitive visitor, the black-capped chickadee makes its presence known with a distinctive call of *chicka-dee-dee-dee* or a descending two-note song. This year-round feeder favorite, often called a "snowbird," along with tufted titmice and dark-eyed juncos, has an oversized head, a small body, a long narrow tail, and a short bill. Males and females share the same coloring: crisp black cap and bib with white cheeks, gray back, and buff underbody.

During warm weather, these members of the Paridae, or tit family, consume insects, caterpillars, spiders, and other animal matter, along with a sprinkling of plant seeds, and in winter they switch to roughly 50 percent seeds, berries, and suet and 50 percent frozen animal matter.

They are known for stashing, or caching, seeds and bits of fat in bark crevices for later consumption and can remember thousands of hiding places.

Recent research on the biology of black-capped chickadees yielded a startling discovery: every fall, chickadees lose thousands of neurons in their brains. Their brains then produce new neurons, allowing the birds to adapt to changes in the flock and the environment.

Many other species of birds—like warblers, woodpeckers, nuthatches, kinglets, creepers, and vireos—flock with chickadees, possibly because these alert sentinels have such an effective alarm system. Chickadee flocks are made up of nesting pairs and lone birds. Some loners "float" between flocks during winter, receiving a different rank or status in each flock. In severely cold weather, these birds have been known to excavate hollows in rotting wood and entomb themselves to keep warm.

They are found across temperate North America, including much of Canada, and although they are nonmigratory, some large groups stage "fall invasions," moving from the northeastern states or Canada to the southern boundaries of their range. They breed in the shrubby edges of forest clearings, in cattail marshes, wooded lots, and parks. Males and females will pair up in the fall and overwinter with the flock, before departing to breed in late winter. Both sexes will defend their chosen territory.

Females prefer to nest in birch or alder trees, where the pair will excavate a hole. They may also co-opt a nesting box, especially one filled with sawdust or shavings. Females lay from 1 to 13 white, brown-dotted eggs, which incubate for two weeks. Males feed sitting females and initially feed the offspring, but are soon joined by the female in this task. The chicks are typically ready to fledge 16 days after hatching.

CHICKADEE DELIGHTS

Although these birds will select their favorite treats from feeders, they typically light on a branch to consume them. They especially enjoy suet, sunflowers, nyjer, safflower, and peanuts and peanut hearts. Or try an offering of live mealworms during the winter. They will dine from any type of songbird feeder and suet cages.

Basics

LENGTH
4.7 to 5.9 inches

WINGSPAN
6.3 to 8.3 inches

WEIGHT
0.32 to 0.49 ounces

LONGEVITY
Record in the wild is 12 years, 5 months.

VOCALIZATION
Whistled song of *fee-dee* with second note lower. Complex language conveys information and alarms—added *dees* to a call of *chickadee-dee-dee* denotes danger.

DISTRIBUTION
Most temperate regions of the United States and well into Canada, extending to Alaska

(opposite page) A black-capped chickadee. This charming bird is the official state bird of both Maine and Massachusetts.

(top) Chickadees are perfectly comfortable around humans, so consider placing their favorite seeds and foods in a suction-cup window feeder where you can enjoy the view.

(bottom) These cavity-nesters will move into abandoned bluebird boxes and happily use nesting boxes erected especially for them. You can install a guard to deter house sparrows and other larger birds from taking over.

Tufted Titmouse

Baeolophus bicolor

Favorite plants

- staghorn sumac
- beechnut
- cherry
- oak

This small, perky songbird is the namesake of the Paridae, or tit family, often called the titmice family. Its soft blue-gray back and crest, rusty or buff wash of color on the flanks, and large luminous eyes make it an attractive and appealing backyard visitor.

Its stout bill is ideal for whacking the tough nuts and seeds it forages in winter. Although both sexes have a pointed topknot, it is not always visible—it is more likely to stand upright when the birds are excited or challenging interlopers at a feeder. Yet, they do not view all other birds as a threat; it is common to see titmice flocking with their chickadee cousins at feeding stations, especially in winter.

These birds eat insects, caterpillars and moth pupae, spiders, and snails during the warm months and switch to

Cheeky Thieves

In addition to plant fibers, tufted titmice use hair to create a soft lining in their nesting cavities. Rather than waiting to find odd bits of animal hair, some bold titmice have been observed pulling hair from small mammals and pets—and even human heads. Naturalists studying abandoned nests have identified the hair of raccoons, opossums, squirrels, rabbits, mice, woodchucks, horses, cows, dogs, and humans.

fruits and berries in winter, often clinging precariously to thin branches to snatch a meal. They also hoard food during the late summer and fall and cache it for cold-weather consumption

Tufted titmice are found across the eastern and central United States, ranging south from the Great Lakes to Texas, and they remain in their territories throughout the year. Populations have recently been expanding northward, possibly due to the availability of food at home feeders.

These birds inhabit woodlands with groves of tall, deciduous shade trees, but they will breed in mixed forests and can also be found in orchards, city parks with large trees, and suburban yards and gardens. They are so fearless around humans, they appear to be almost tame.

Titmice couples pair up over the winter and will remain together all year. The male courts the female by feeding her, a ritual that continues as she incubates her eggs. Once the chicks hatch, he will help feed them as well.

These birds build cup-shaped nests in existing tree cavities or abandoned woodpecker holes, especially those of pileated woodpeckers and northern flickers, lining the space with leaves, bark, moss, and hair. They will also investigate human-supplied nesting boxes. The female incubates her creamy white eggs for up to 14 days and cares for the nestlings until they are ready to fledge at 16 days. Young birds from the previous year's brood may serve as "helpers," tending the current crop of offspring.

TITMOUSE TREATS

Tufted titmice enjoy many of the same foods as chickadees—black-oil and hulled sunflower seeds, nyjer, safflower, peanuts, bread, and suet. They also appreciate live mealworms during the colder months. They prefer hanging feeders and will happily cling to a suet cage.

Basics

LENGTH
5.5 to 6.3 inches

WINGSPAN
7.9 to 10.2 inches

WEIGHT
0.6 to 0.9 ounce

LONGEVITY
Average is 3 to 4 years; record is 13 years.

VOCALIZATION
Song is a whistled *peter-peter* consisting of 4 to 8 notes; interflock call is *tseep;* alarm is a harsh *jay-jay-jay*.

DISTRIBUTION
Eastern and central United States, from Canadian border south to eastern Texas

(opposite page) A jaunty tufted titmouse showing the distinctive crest that it is named for. This species is also known as the crested titmouse, crested tomtit, tufted tit, tufted chickadee, and pete bird.

(left) The impressive wings and tail of this diminutive bird are visible as it comes in for a landing.

(right) Friendly little titmice will pick their favorite seeds right out of an offering hand. These birds are very relaxed around humans and are frequent guests at backyard feeders.

Bushtit

Psaltriparus minimus

Favorite plants

- sunflower
- native shrubs
- small trees

This tiny bird of western woodlands and southwestern scrublands is usually referred to simply as the bushtit. It is the lone member of the family Aegithalidae—bushtits or long-tailed tits—found in the New World, and the only member of the genus *Psaltriparus*.

The bushtit is notable for its rounded head, compact, fluffy taupe and gray body, and brownish cap. Its tail is long, and its black bill is tiny and slightly curved. Males have dark eyes, and females are born with dark eyes that eventually turn pale. Inland birds of the Southwest display a dark mask. These birds, called the black-eared bushtit, were once thought to be a separate species (*P. melanotis*).

With their subdued gray-brown coloring, these birds are so well camouflaged that a passerby might not suspect the presence of dozens in a thicket . . . except that their incessant soft twittering gives them away as they flit about after insects. In summer bushtits feed on leafhoppers, treehoppers, caterpillars, aphids, and spiders, and will hang upside down to search the underside of leaves for tiny scale insects. In colder weather, they supplement their diet with seeds and fruit.

Bushtits are not migratory, remaining in their territory all year long, although some mountain populations seek lower altitudes during brisk weather. These adaptable birds can be found in coastal lowlands and inland at altitudes of up to 11,000 feet. They prefer shrubby, open terrain, chaparral, oak forests, pinyon-juniper woods, streamside groves, and suburbs.

A Most Unusual Nest

Bushtits make their remarkable sock-like nests from plant materials and stretchy spider webs and line them with feathers, fur, and downy plant floss. The nest, which descends a foot or more from its anchor branches, is camouflaged with foliage from nearby plants as well as the host tree. It can take a month to construct. An entrance hole near the top leads to the bowl of the nest. During breeding season, this hanging sac is home to the nesting pair, their chicks, and any helper adults. The nest is frequently used to host a second brood.

These social birds flock and forage with other small songbirds such as chickadees, warblers, and kinglets, especially in winter, when they are most likely to visit feeders. During the spring breeding season, couples leave the flock to pair off. The male and female then build a distinctive hanging "sock" nest that is made of moss, spider webs, and grasses suspended by twigs. These birds become very sensitive at this time and can be easily rattled. If disturbed early in the nesting process, the pair might abandon the nest, and males may even seek a different mate.

Females lay up to ten white eggs and incubate them for 13 days. Once the chicks hatch, some breeding pairs are lucky enough to have a helper bird, which in this species is, surprisingly, an adult male.

A BOUNTY FOR BUSHTITS
These small birds seek out feeders stocked with black-oil and hulled sunflower seeds, breadcrumbs, peanuts, and peanut hearts. They will also eat from suet blocks and will be pleased by offerings of live mealworms during cold weather, when their normal insect prey is unavailable. These birds enjoy bathing, so make sure you offer some kind of shallow water source.

Basics

LENGTH
2.8 to 3.1 inches

WINGSPAN
6 inches

WEIGHT
0.18 to 0.21 ounce

LONGEVITY
Average is 7 years; record in the wild is 9 years.

VOCALIZATION
Calls are continuous soft chips and high twitters of *tsit-tsit-tsit* while browsing in vegetation. Alarm is a trill.

DISTRIBUTION
Year-round on the Pacific coast, most of the Southwest and into Mexico

(opposite page) Two male bushtits take a rare rest. You can often spot these little birds in the low branches of trees located in woodlands and suburban yards and parkland, usually quietly chittering to one another.

(top) A female bushtit. Acrobatic bushtits move almost constantly, often hanging upside down on tree branches or bird feeders to grab their food.

Cedar Waxwing

Bombycilla cedrorum

Favorite plants

- eastern red cedar
- dogwood
- serviceberry
- juniper
- hawthorn
- winterberry
- crabapple

This sleek, crested, medium-sized member of the Bombycilladae, or waxwing family, is one of nature's most delicately hued birds. The silky body is a shaded taupe fading to blue-gray on the back, with touches of lemon yellow on the belly and scarlet wing tips, reminiscent of old-fashioned sealing wax. The cinnamon-colored head features a crisp black mask tipped with white.

Waxwings may be obscured by foliage while feeding, so look for a slender silhouette flitting among fruit tree branches, with a slightly ragged crest and a notched tail edged in bright yellow.

These birds feed on cedar cones, fruit, and insects, and prefer a habitat of open woodlands that offers a selection of berries and a water supply—they will readily bathe in shallow streams.

similar species: *Bohemian waxwing*

Bohemian waxwings *(Bombycilla garrulus)* are bulkier and grayer overall than cedar waxwings and have a rufous undertail, although they do display the same taupe-to-gray shading as their cousins, as well as the black face markings and pointed crests. They are indigenous to the northwestern and north-central regions of this country, and are occasionally seen as far east as New England. Bohemians consume wild fruit and insects and prefer to breed in remote coniferous forests near water.

Bohemians and cedars, which share a love of berries and fruit, are the only two waxwing species in North America, although Bohemians are also found in the northern forests of Eurasia.

They are sociable birds that crave the companionship of the flock; grooming one another is a favorite pastime. In flight, they resemble flycatchers, darting and hovering as they pluck whole berries from bushes on the wing or hunt for insects above rivers and lakes. They will also congregate in cemeteries and on golf courses.

Waxwings tend to be erratic migrants. Some populations remain year-round across the northern temperate states, and they seem to lose any fear of humans during the colder months, as they search for food in parks, yards, and gardens. Other groups spend spring and summer breeding in Canada, and, as the weather cools, they depart for the "sun belt" states and Mexico and Central America.

Cedar waxwings typically delay breeding until well into summer. They defend only a narrow territory, so small colonies where they nest close together are not uncommon. Courtship involves perching side-by-side and posturing, touching bills, and passing food. Males may do a hopping dance for females, who hop back if they are interested. The nest, a loosely constructed cup of plant fibers and twigs lined with soft moss, grass, and hair, is built by both sexes and situated on a horizontal tree limb or a fork. Nestlings hatch after 13 days and are tended by both parents. Most waxwing couples produce two broods a year.

WINNING OVER WAXWINGS

Although they are not known as habitual feeder birds, waxwings will come to your yard to investigate offerings of sliced fruit placed on a platform feeder. You can almost guarantee waxwing visitors in summer if your landscape includes berry bushes and fruiting trees.

Basics

LENGTH
6 to 7 inches

WINGSPAN
8.7 to 11.8 inches

WEIGHT
1.1 ounces

LONGEVITY
Record is 8 years.

VOCALIZATION
Song is a high, thin *tseeee,* often trilled.

DISTRIBUTION
Year-round in northern United States, some breed in southern Canada and winter in the temperate central states and the South.

(opposite) Cedar waxwings specialize in eating fruit—sometimes eating nothing else for several months. Gorging on overripe berries that have started to ferment and produce alcohol can make them intoxicated, however, and even kill them.

(bottom) This is a stunning bird, with a black mask, elegant crest, and warmly shaded plumage.

American Robin

Turdus migratorius

Favorite plants

- chokecherry
- hawthorn
- dogwood fruit
- sumac fruit
- juniper berry
- holly

The American robin is certainly the most familiar of the thrushes and, possibly the most recognized backyard bird in the United States. It is also one of the most abundant species in the country, with populations estimated at more than 300 million birds.

This alert, migratory songbird is known as a harbinger of warmer weather in the northern states because it is one of the first returnees to appear in spring—though it may have left a secluded wintering flock only 100 miles away.

Birding snobs don't give these abundant birds their due—robins are surprisingly attractive! They have the plump thrush body, as well as the large eyes, strong legs, and the slender beak typical of that family. And, unlike woodland thrushes, which display russet coats and spotted chests,

American robins were named after the robin of Europe (*Erithacus rubecula*), which also has a rusty red breast and throat, but the two species are not closely related.

the robin's plumage is a deep brown-black above with a chestnut, trending to red, breast and whitish eye arcs.

The proverbial "early birds," robins can be heard singing at dawn or seen hopping upright across suburban lawns seeking earthworms, grubs, or caterpillars—keep this in mind when using toxic insecticides. They will also feed on berries and fruit.

Robins coexist peacefully with humans, often nesting on porch ledges, in barn or garage eaves, or on exterior windowsills. And even though they are a common sight in cities and suburbs, they inhabit woodlands and mountains across North America and coniferous forests in the Southwest. Some populations summer and breed in Canada and then migrate to the United States, sometimes as far south as Mexico, where they form large flocks at night; others never leave the States.

Robins lay their eggs relatively early, in April, allowing them to raise two or three broods a year—males will attend fledglings while the female incubates a new clutch. The female builds her nest from the inside out, creating a cup shape of coarse grass and twigs with the pressure of her wing "wrist." She might also include papers, feathers, and yard debris in the nest, then stabilize it with a base of mud. Females produce three to seven pale, blue-green eggs—of that particular shade so familiar to both bird-watchers and schoolchildren—that take two weeks to hatch. Both parents are known to be aggressive defenders of their chicks. They also have the ability to detect invasive cowbird eggs and eject them from the nest.

RALLYING ROBINS

A healthy lawn replete with earthworms is guaranteed to attract robins. They will also eat sliced fruit, hulled sunflower seeds, peanut hearts, and mealworms from a ground or platform feeder, and suet from a hanging cage feeder.

Basics

LENGTH
9.1 to 11.0 inches

WINGSPAN
12 to 16 inches

WEIGHT
2.5 to 3.3 ounces

LONGEVITY
Record in the wild is 14 years.

VOCALIZATION
Song is a rich, rolling repetition of *cheer-up, cheerily;* call is a whinny.

DISTRIBUTION
Summers across the United States and Canada; some seek southern states or Mexico during winter.

(opposite page) A "robin red-breast" hops among early spring blooms. This familiar species is the state bird of Connecticut, Michigan, and Wisconsin.

(top) Acclimated to human presence, an American robin feeds her young in a nest built on a windowsill.

(bottom) A robin with an earthworm. These birds employ a number of their senses while hunting invertebrates: auditory, olfactory, and possibly even vibrotactile (the perception of vibration through touch)—but the main way they locate prey is visually.

Eastern Bluebird

Sialia sialis

Favorite plants

- mistletoe
- sumac
- blueberry
- black cherry
- holly
- dogwood fruit
- honeysuckle
- juniper berry

This small thrush's habit of perching out in the open on telephone wires or fence posts makes it popular with birders. The male bluebird's plumage is a bright cerulean blue above and a warm chestnut brown on the throat and breast, with a white belly. Females are drabber— gray-blue above, faded orange below, while juveniles are darker above and have spotted breasts. Adults have an upright posture, rounded heads with short, straight bills, and plump bodies.

Eastern bluebirds prefer open woodland with patchy vegetation, farmland, roadsides, and orchards and are also found in cut-over or burned-out fields. Suburban gardens that offer wide lawns and ideal nesting sites—cavities in freestanding trees—might tempt them. They are found across eastern North

Basics

LENGTH
6.3 to 8.3 inches

WINGSPAN
9.8 to 12.6 inches

WEIGHT
0.95 to 1.20 ounces

LONGEVITY
6 to 10 years

VOCALIZATION
A male's call is a soft *jeew* or *chir-wi*. Song is *chiti WEEW wewidoo.*

DISTRIBUTION
Year-round in the southern states and Mexico. Some breed across the temperate East and winter in Central America.

America, year round in the American South, migratory in the North, heading off to Texas or Central America in the fall.

Researchers believe these birds were once able to expand their range in the East by following the spread of settlements and agriculture. Yet, as the country's agrarian culture diminished, so too did the bluebirds' prospects. With decreasing habitat and loss of nesting sites to invasive bird species, populations of this charming songbird fell sharply. Fortunately, numbers have gradually been restored through the combined efforts of conservationists and bird lovers (see pages 80–81).

Insects and invertebrates are the mainstays of the bluebird diet, with the addition of small fruit and berries during fall and winter. These birds are agile hunters, often seen hovering over grassy areas or low bushes to pluck up insects.

Bluebirds are highly sociable (unless its breeding season when males become highly territorial) and can form flocks of a hundred or more. In spring, males woo females outside prospective nests with displays of singing and fluttering and offers of nesting materials. Mutual preening may also be part of the courtship ritual. The female constructs a cuplike nest in a former woodpecker hole or other tree cavity several feet off the ground. She lays three to seven light blue eggs that will hatch in roughly 13 to 16 days. Both parents feed the nestlings a diet of almost all insects. The young are ready to fledge after 15 to 20 days. Bluebird pairs typically produce two broods each year.

BRINGING IN BLUEBIRDS
They might visit your yard to check out fruiting bushes and trees—or mealworms on feeders, but bluebirds are even more likely to drop by and settle in if you provide them with a commercial nesting box placed on a pole or solitary tree.

(opposite page) The intense blue of the male inspired Henry David Thoreau to note, "The bluebird carries the sky on his back."

(left) A male eastern bluebird picks choice bits from a mealworm feeder to share among his fledglings.

(right) A female picks insects from a cup feeder nestled in the fork of tree.

similar species: *western bluebird*

The male western bluebird (*Sialia mexicana*) differs from its eastern cousin in showing blue around the throat and a brownish patch on the back. These semi-migratory birds inhabit a number of western and southwestern states, and after suffering habitat loss due to deforestation, they adapted to open terrain, farmland, parkland, and desert. They feed on insects and berries and enjoy taking dips in birdbaths.

Bluebirds are beautiful—and fierce. During breeding season, males engage in ferocious battles, grabbing their rival's legs, each combatant trying to pin the other down and jab it with his bill.

The Bluebird Revival
A SUCCESS STORY

A male eastern bluebird pauses for a photo op as he brings nesting material to a human-supplied box. Scores of volunteers erected these boxes in bluebird habitats to encourage the comeback of this iconic American thrush.

Bluebirds were once plentiful throughout their range—the continental United States and parts of Mexico. Their bright blue and rusty red plumage was a welcome sight as they perched on fence posts scanning the air for insects. But loss of habitat and nesting sites—and the ingestion of pesticide-poisoned invertebrates—began to take a toll. By the 1950s and 1960s, the total population of bluebirds was estimated at one tenth of what it had been in the early 1900s.

These birds lack a powerful bill for excavating nesting cavities, so their preference is for preexisting holes in dead trees—or man-made birdhouses. But as more and more land was cleared for development during the 20th century, many dead trees were felled. Further threatening their territory were starlings and house finches, both introduced species. These birds began to compete with bluebirds, stealing the remaining nesting sites, including birdhouses.

Another Comeback

One of the most celebrated avian comebacks involved raptors, whose population numbers tumbled due to side effects of DDT and other pesticides. As apex predators, eagles, owls, hawks, and falcons were ingesting dangerous amounts of DDT in their diet of fish, birds, and small mammals that ate pesticide-contaminated insects. This eventually weakened the walls of the raptor's eggs, preventing chicks from hatching. In 1972, DDT was banned in the United States, and most raptors populations began to slowly recover. Especially at risk was the peregrine falcon; American falconers, who hunt with raptors, donated some birds to the breeding programs, which used both captive and wild birds.

This popular thrush was not officially considered threatened or endangered, but many birders noticed the dropping numbers. Something had to be done, so volunteers began setting up man-made nesting boxes along "bluebird trails"—in open areas where the birds prefer to raise their young. These boxes were specifically made with openings too small for starlings to enter. Each year, the volunteers would clean out the debris from the previous season, hoping that a new pair would soon move in and start a family.

The efforts of the National Audubon Society, as well as local birding groups,

paid off. Bluebird numbers began to climb, and the jaunty blue thrush was once again seen singing from fence posts.

A PLACE TO CALL HOME

If you decide to locate a nesting box in your yard or garden you won't regret it—bluebirds are voracious consumers of insect pests. Nesting boxes can be ordered online or purchased at garden centers. Situate them away from shrubs and tree lines, facing south, and hanging about five feet off the ground. If you live in the South, boxes should be up by February, by March in cooler climes. Some bluebirds may roost in nesting boxes before the breeding season begins.

Tree swallows will sometimes claim bluebird boxes. If that's a problem, put out two boxes, roughly 20 to 25 feet apart. The territorial swallows will keep other swallows from using the second box, freeing it up for bluebirds. Both these species seem to overlap territories without incident. Swallows have even been known to help bluebird parents raise their chicks and then nest in the box themselves once the offspring have fledged.

> *Bluebird numbers began to climb, and the jaunty blue thrush was once again seen singing from fence posts.*

(left) A bluebird family gathered at their nesting box. These boxes have become a key to maintaining bird population numbers.

(right) A female mountain bluebird is a thing of beauty, spreading her wings with a downward motion to act as a brake as she prepares to enter a birdhouse.

Ruby-crowned Kinglet

Regulus calendula

Favorite plants

- dogwood fruit
- spruce
- fir
- lodgepole pine
- poison oak berry

These tiny, chubby, high-energy birds are found across North America and are members of the kinglet, or Regulidae, family. Ruby-crowned kinglets are big-headed, short-necked birds, with both sexes displaying olive-green plumage with some yellow coloration and two white wing bars and a broken white eye ring. Male ruby-crowns have a jagged, red, pop-up crest that remains hidden unless they become agitated—or are intent on courtship.

They are restless movers, flicking and fluttering their wings as they forage quickly through the low-to-middle levels of foliage. In addition to gleaning, they will also hover to pluck prey from leaves and branches. Their main diet consists of easily obtainable small insects such as beetles, flies, and caterpillars, as well as spiders. They also eat the eggs or larvae of many invertebrates. In winter, they will eat berries and seeds. Kinglets have also been observed picking at oozing sap or visiting flowers, possibly to sip nectar.

With the exception of some year-round populations in the West, they summer and breed in Canada and then migrate to the American South and Central America. They prefer tall, coniferous forests of spruce, fir, and tamarack for nesting, and during the colder months they flock in shrubby fields, deciduous woods, mesquite brush, parks, and suburban yards. A recent bird count indicates that populations of ruby-crowned kinglets are on the rise, possibly because they are breeding farther north in remote, undisturbed areas.

Courting males impress potential mates by singing as they crouch horizontally, flutter their wings, and raise their red crown feathers. They also use their lengthy, powerful songs to warn off other males.

The female builds the nest: a hanging, elastic globe suspended from twigs and composed of moss, lichen, spider webs, cocoon silk, bark strips, and twigs, and lined with feathers, plant floss, and animal hair. Not surprisingly, the nests require frequent maintenance to keep from

disintegrating. They are typically located in spruce trees or other conifers, anywhere from 40 to 90 feet above ground.

In spite of her diminutive size, the female ruby-crowned kinglet is capable of producing large clutches, sometimes up to 12 brown-spotted white eggs at a time, which would weigh as much as she herself. The babies hatch within two weeks and are fed by both parents. The offspring are ready to leave their hanging abode in about 18 days; the breeding pair goes their separate ways once the nest is vacated.

COAXING KINGLETS TO VISIT
These fluttery little birds will come to platform feeders for peanut hearts, hulled sunflower seeds, and mealworms, and they enjoy sampling the fare served at suet feeders. They might also take advantage of a birdbath.

Basics

LENGTH
3.5 to 4.3 inches

WINGSPAN
6.3 to 7.1 inches

WEIGHT
0.2 to 0.4 ounce

LONGEVITY
Record is 4 years, 7 months.

VOCALIZATION
Call is a double-noted *jit* and *jidit;* song a bubbly, musical chattering of surprising volume.

DISTRIBUTION
Summers in Canada, winters coast to coast in United States into Mexico; some year-round populations inhabit the Far West.

(opposite page) A male ruby-crowned kinglet flashes his fiery red crest, which he displays when excited.

(top) A tiny female. Protective parents, these birds will display "broken wing" behavior to lure away predators from nests.

similar species: *golden-crowned kinglet*

The golden-crowned kinglet *(Regulus satrapa)* is an acrobatic songbird only slightly larger than a hummingbird. Its plumage is pale olive gray, with distinctive white wing bars. The crest—lemon-yellow in females, orange in males—is banded in black. These shy birds prefer to remain concealed near the tops of dense fir trees, but their thin, high-pitched calls give them away. They feed mainly on insects, hovering out from secluded boughs to snatch them on the wing or clinging precariously to thin branches to glean. Most breed in Canada and winter throughout North America.

The yellow-and-black "crown" of the golden-crowned kinglet gives this species its royal name.

Black-and-white Warbler

Mniotilta varia

Favorite attractions

- dead trees (for insects)
- tree stumps (for nesting)

Unlike most warblers that display at least some yellow markings, this black-and-white species—of the family Parulidae (New World or wood warblers)—shows only those two colors, arranged in crisp horizontal stripes along the head, back, and wings. Because this distinctive plumage makes them easy to recognize, they are popular with birdwatchers, especially novices.

Birders find warblers a challenge in general. During spring and fall migrations, most warbler species remain at certain locations only a short time, allowing a brief window for birders to spot them. By fall, most have lost their gaudy plumage and gone a muddy olive and yellow, making identification iffy unless the accompanying song can be heard, giving rise to the birding phrase, "confusing fall warblers."

Black-and-white warblers can be found creeping along tree trunks or low branches, probing for insects beneath the bark with their needlelike bills. They feed on moths, butterflies, caterpillars—including gypsy moth larvae—beetles—including bark beetles, click beetles, and wood borers—ants, flies, true bugs, leafhoppers, aphids, and other insects. They also eat spiders and daddy longlegs.

These migratory songbirds breed in most of Canada and in the United States from New England down to the Deep South. Their preference is for mature or second-growth forests, both deciduous and mixed. They will sometimes nest in dry sections of swampy woods or in the trees along rocky hillsides. During migration, they are tolerant of many habitats. They winter in the tropics, from Central America to the northernmost

regions of South America and will roost in coffee plantations, fruit orchards, mangroves, many types of forest, urban settings, and at elevations ranging from sea level to high mountain reaches.

Male black-and-white warblers are one of the earliest returnees in the spring—announcing their arrival with a thin song like a squeaky wheelbarrow. Courting males chase females with a show of singing and fluttering. Females build a cup-shaped nest made of leaves, coarse grasses, bark strips, and rootlets that they line with soft grass or hair. They locate it low down—in a stump or in a depression under dead leaves and lay five creamy, browned-flecked eggs, which hatch in 10 or 12 days. Both parents take responsibility for feeding the young. Although the offspring may leave the nest after 6 to 12 days, they are not yet skilled at flying. Warbler nests are commonly parasitized by brown-headed cowbirds.

BECKONING BLACK & WHITES

These insect-lovers might investigate a platform or ground feeder stocked with mealworms, but these birds are likely already part of your local East Coast landscape. Look for them creeping along the limbs of deciduous trees as they hunt for insects and spiders.

Basics

LENGTH
4.5 to 5.5 inches

WINGSPAN
7.1 to 8.7 inches

WEIGHT
0.3 to 0.5 ounce

LONGEVITY
Record is 11 years.

VOCALIZATION
Song is a high-pitched *wee-see, wee-see, wee-see;* call is a hard *tick* or a soft *fsss.*

DISTRIBUTION
Central and eastern Canada south to the Gulf States; winters in Mexico and as far south as Colombia and Peru.

(opposite page) A black-and-white warbler belts out its song. Its squeaky warbling is one of the first signs of springtime.

(top) This bird was once called the black-and-white creeper for the way it moves along tree trunks. Its genus name, *Mniotilta,* means "moss-plucking," and comes from its habit of doing just that as it probes for insects.

related species: *yellow-rumped warbler*

Yellow-rumped warblers (*Setophaga coronata*) also have some black-and-white striping, and they are show-stoppers during the spring or breeding season when their stripy bodies are splashed with saturated yellow. In fall, these birds cross the continent as they migrate to their winter territories, filling woodland and shrubland with their whistling trills. Their ability—unique among warblers—to digest the waxes found in bayberries and wax-myrtles allows them to winter farther north than other warblers.

These versatile fall foragers may be snatching an insect one minute, hunting for berries the next.

Yellow Warbler

Setophaga petechia

Favorite nesting trees

- dogwood
- hawthorn
- white cedar
- raspberry
- honeysuckle
- willow
- alder
- cottonwood

In a family of colorful gems, the yellow warbler is a bright jewel. It displays a citrine head and body and topaz wings. The male even has narrow ruby streaks down its breast. These small, elegant songbirds, members of the Parulidae—the wood warblers, have evenly proportioned bodies, rounded heads, medium-length tails, and, compared to other warblers, relatively large bills.

They seek out waterways and wetlands, and they prefer thickets and other tangled, second-growth habitats and frequent dwarf birch stands in the tundra, aspen trees in the Rocky Mountains, and the edges of woods, power-line cuts, blueberry bogs, and suburban gardens in the East.

These birds have an extraordinary summer range—from as far north as the Arctic Circle down to Mexico. They breed

Space Invaders

Yellow warblers, like many songbirds, are at risk of brood parasitism. Brown-headed cowbirds (*Molothrus ater*) use the nests of other birds to lay their large speckled eggs, and when the competitive chicks hatch, they vie with the legitimate offspring for food—often successfully. Some female birds, such as tanagers, are wary enough to drive off female cowbirds, but apparently have no means of discriminating once a foreign egg appears in their nest. Yellow warblers, however, simply build another nest over the compromised one. Nests with six tiers have been observed, a testimony to the tenacity of both species.

across most of Canada and the United States, and their migration routes encompass much of the South and the Southwest. They then winter in the Yucatan and the upper regions of South America, where they are found in mangrove forests, scrubland, and marshes. Some populations of this long-distance migrant will journey south nonstop over the Gulf of Mexico, but choose a less arduous overland route heading home in spring.

Yellow warblers are constant foragers, gleaning insects as they probe among tree or shrub foliage or sallying out to capture insects in midflight, a hunting method called hawking. Sometimes they will hover to snatch a bug from the leaves of a plant. Their diet is heavily dependent on caterpillars, including the destructive tent caterpillar, but they also feed on other insects, such as moths and beetles, as well as spiders. They will sometimes consume berries and small, juicy fruit.

Courting males defend their breeding territories with lusty singing and aerial displays; they woo females by pursuing them for three or four days. The female then builds a cup-shaped nest in the fork of a small tree or bush, most often willow, dogwood, hawthorn, raspberry, white cedar, and honeysuckle. It is composed of grass, bark strips, and nettles with an outer layer of spider webs and plant down. The inside is lined with feathers, deer hair, and plant fibers. She lays four to five greenish white speckled eggs that will hatch in 12 days. Both parents tend the offspring, though the female does the majority of the feeding. The baby warblers are ready to fledge after only 9 to 12 days.

WOOING WARBLERS

Yellow warblers are not typically feeder birds, but they are attracted to larger yards with small trees and ponds or other standing water. If the amenities are right, they might even nest there.

Basics

LENGTH
4.7 to 5.1 inches

WINGSPAN
6.3 to 7.9 inches

WEIGHT
0.3 to 0.4 ounce

LONGEVITY
Record is 11 years for a banded wild bird.

VOCALIZATION
Tumbling song sounds like "Sweet, sweet, I'm so sweet"; call is a soft or hard *chip*.

DISTRIBUTION
Breeds across temperate United States and most of Canada; winters in Central America and northern South America

(opposite page) With its feathers the color of bright buttercups, the male yellow warbler is a cheerful sight. Often found nears the tops of moisture-loving trees, such as willows and alders, the sweet, tumbling, whistled songs of warblers fill the woods in the spring and summer.

(bottom) Female yellow warblers build their nests high in trees from 10 to 40 feet off the ground, sometimes stealing nesting materials from nearby nests. To guard against cowbirds that may try to leave eggs in the nest, the female yellow warblers have developed a specific *s-e-e-t* cowbird alarm.

American Redstart

Setophaga ruticilla

Favorite plants

- serviceberry
- barberry
- magnolia

This is another songbird, like the American robin, that has a European counterpart to which it is not closely related. The American redstart is in the wood warbler family, Parulidae, whereas the European version, the common redstart *(Phoenicurus phoenicurus),* is an Old World flycatcher, family Muscicapidae. American redstarts are widespread, migratory warblers of the deep woodlands that are sometimes seen in roadside trees, parks, and gardens.

The male redstart's coloration is distinctive and beautiful—black all over with patches of brilliant red-orange on the breast, wing bars, and tail edges. The female is less showy, with a gray head and belly, olive wings and back, and subdued yellow patches. These birds have a plump chest, a slender middle, a longish,

Basics

LENGTH
4.3 to 5.1 inches

WINGSPAN
6.3 to 7.5 inches

WEIGHT
0.2 to 0.3 ounce

LONGEVITY
5 to 6 years

VOCALIZATION
Song is *chewy-chewy-chewy, chew-chew-chew,* rising or descending at end.

DISTRIBUTION
Breeds across temperate North America; migrates to Florida, Southern California, Central America, and northern South America

(opposite page) A male American redstart singing in early spring. The common name comes from the red markings on the tail—the word *start* is an archaic term meaning "tail."

(left) Warblers are often referred to as the butterflies of the bird world, and redstarts more than earn that title, flitting through trees to glean insects.

(right) A female or juvenile American redstart: both share the same coloration. Some yearling males, still wearing their gray-and-yellow juvenile plumage, will sing furiously in hopes of gaining territory and attracting a mate. Some actually do, but most must wait until the following year, when they achieve their black-and-orange glory.

club-shaped tail, sometimes used to indicate mood, and a bill that is flat and wide. The common name comes from the red markings on the tail—the word *start* is an archaic term for "tail."

Redstarts are almost never still as they flit and hover through the canopy, seeking prey in the foliage, sometimes even flashing the fiery color on their tails to startle hidden insects into flight. They will also flycatch—drooping their wings and leaping high above a field to snatch a treat from the air. They eat beetles, caterpillars, moths, leafhoppers, aphids, midges, and crane flies, as well as spiders and daddy longlegs, and are known to smack caterpillars and moths against a branch prior to consuming them. They also feed on berries and small fruits in late summer.

In spring and summer, they can be found throughout the East, as well as in eastern and northwestern Canada. They seek open deciduous or mixed forests, second-growth woods, river groves, and tree-lined stream banks; in the Northwest they nest in willow and alder thickets. Overall, they prefer large, continuous stretches of habitat. Migration takes them to destinations in Florida, southern California, Mexico, Central America, and the cap of South America. At this time, they will roost in any

wooded areas. They winter in open forests at low and middle elevations, coffee and citrus plantations, mangroves, and isolated trees in urban areas.

Male redstarts challenge rivals with stiffened wingbeats as they complete a sweeping, semicircular flight around their territory. Courtship involves fluffing their plumage, raising their crown feathers, and spreading their wings and tails. Some males mate with and raise broods with two females—establishing the second in a separate territory after the first has started sitting. The female chooses the nesting site, typically an elevated fork in a tree, after the male has shown her several options. She builds the cup-shaped nest using plant fibers and rootlets, adorns the exterior with lichens, birch bark, and feathers, and lines it with feathers. Her clutch of one to five creamy, speckled eggs will hatch in from 10 to 13 days. The chicks are ready to fledge roughly 13 days later.

BRING ON THE BERRIES

If you want to draw these beautiful birds to your yard, your best bet is planting a variety of berry bushes. By late summer, redstarts will be looking for lots of high-energy foods as they prepare for their long migrations to the south.

Carolina Wren

Thryothorus ludovicianus

Favorite plants

- wax-myrtle
- sweetgum
- poison ivy seed

It can be reclusive at times, but you might see this pert, small songbird, with its inquisitive demeanor, in suburban woodpiles, garages, and low bushes. In summer, the male's rolling song of *teakettle-teakettle!* announces his presence throughout the eastern woodlands, although mated pairs may duet in any season, with the female providing a chattering counterpoint.

The Carolina is a relatively large wren, with a round breast and rich plumage—a warm brown above, rusty buff below, with black bars on the tail, a white eyebrow, and a long bill that is slightly decurved. The long tail, frequently cocked sharply upward, becomes the bird's exclamation point as it perches on branches or fence rails.

These members of the wren family, the Troglodytidae, typically forage in pairs as they hunt for prey in shrubby or bushy terrain, under tree bark, and in leaf litter on the forest floor. They feed on many types of insects, including caterpillars and beetles. In fall and winter, they consume berries, small fruit, and, occasionally, seeds and nuts.

These birds occur throughout the eastern United States and have gradually expanded their range northward; they can now be found from Ontario, Canada, to the tip of northeast Mexico. In spite of their "southern" name, Carolina wrens are hardy little birds that can tolerate northern temperatures, although extended cold snaps can impact population numbers.

They seek out dense vegetation that provides cover in deciduous or mixed forests, and can be found in ravines full of hemlock or rhododendron, thickets of tangled vines or shrubs, cypress swamps, and hedgerows. They will also frequent abandoned buildings, overgrown farmlands, and suburban yards where brush piles have been left undisturbed.

Most Carolina wrens mate for life and remain in their breeding territory all year. When nesting, they search for abandoned tree cavities, but will also lay eggs in nesting boxes—or in an overgrown hanging plant or disused planter in a quiet part of the garden. Mated pairs work

together to build their bulky, cup-shaped nests, using a variety of mixed materials, including bark strips, leaves, grasses, hair, feathers, discarded snakeskin, paper, plastic, and string. The female lays a clutch of three to seven white or pinkish eggs with rusty spots that hatch in 12 to 16 days. Even after the offspring have fledged, from 10 to 16 days after hatching, family groups may still feed together.

WRANGLING WRENS

In fall and winter, these birds will eat berries and seeds, and they often visit suet cages or feeders stocked with peanuts. Some Carolina wrens will happily breed in nesting boxes (make sure to put up a predator guard) and, during really cold weather, will also take refuge in boxes that have been lined with dried grasses, especially ones with slotted rather than round openings.

Basics

LENGTH
4.7 to 5.5 inches

WINGSPAN
11.4 inches

WEIGHT
0.6 to 0.8 ounce

LONGEVITY
6 years

VOCALIZATION
Call is *teakettle-teakettle* or *chirpity-chirpity*.

DISTRIBUTION
Year-round from the central United States to the East Coast; Great Lakes region south to the Yucatan

(opposite page) This shy wren is rarely seen but often heard. Although small, this bird lets out its distinctive *teakettle-teakettle* call at amazingly high volume.

(top) Round little Carolina wrens have a long tail that they often cock upward.

related species: *Bewick's wren*

You can distinguish this energetic wren from the Carolina by the white dots that edge its long tail. A bird of the West and Southwest, the Bewick's wren (*Thryomanes bewickii*) is known for the complex vocal stylings of the courting male. Nesting females are dauntless and will scold intruders and may refuse to leave the nest. This bird was named in the 1820s for British engraver Thomas Bewick—a friend of the naturalist and illustrator John James Audubon, who collected the first recognized specimen.

The male Bewick's wren learns its song from males in other territories, not from its own father.

Tree Swallow

Tachycineta bicolor

Favorite plants

• wax-myrtle
• blueberry
• cattail

The swallows are small, graceful, swooping birds that hunt for insects on the wing. Tree swallows are a widespread migratory species known for their impressive aerial displays. These birds are unperturbed by humans and highly sociable with one another—outside breeding season they flock together in groups often numbering in the hundreds of thousands.

The male, with his iridescent blue-green back, crisp white chest and belly, and dark flight feathers, is among the most beautiful birds in the swallow family, Hirundinidae. The female's plumage is similar, but her coloring is more subdued. Both sexes have long wings, slightly notched tails and short, flat bills.

Tree swallows forage while in flight, consuming flies, beetles, winged ants, and others, as well as spiders and small crustaceans like sand fleas. In some regions, they are considered great eradicators of mosquitoes. Unlike other swallows, they will feed on plant matter, including many varieties of berries, especially bayberries. This is critical to their survival: when they return in late winter to stake out nesting sites, before the competition arrives, few insects are about, and berries provide an alternate food source. During egg-laying season, tree swallows may raid compost heaps and eat discarded eggshells to provide themselves with extra calcium.

In summer, these birds range across most temperate regions of the United States and throughout Canada as far north as Alaska. Cool fall weather sends them on their long migrations to Central America and the Caribbean. They also migrate to Florida and Baja California, giving them the northernmost wintering range of any swallow.

During breeding season, these birds prefer open or semi-open areas (the name tree swallow comes from their habit of nesting in tree cavities, not from their chosen terrain, which is often treeless) near any bodies of water that furnish them with insects. They favor agricultural fields, marshes, lakes, riverbanks, beaver ponds, shorelines, and brushy meadows. They bathe by skimming their bodies against the water surface and then veering upward to shake off the droplets.

Male tree swallows woo potential mates by showing them prospective nesting holes. Couples pair up for a year and raise their young in existing tree cavities—typically former woodpecker homes—but they easily adapt to nesting boxes or

birdhouses and will tolerate humans nearby. This quality has made tree swallows ideal subjects for research on nesting habits, and they are now one of the most studied birds in North America.

The female lays four to seven pale pink eggs that hatch within 11 to 20 days. Both parents tend the young, with one feeding the nestlings while the other remains on watch to drive away intruders.

HOUSING TREE SWALLOWS

Tree swallows are not feeder birds, although a few hardy berry bushes might entice them to visit your yard. You can, however, lure them by providing a place to raise a family: they are very willing to set up housekeeping in birdhouses or nesting boxes, even those placed quite close to human habitation. This relaxed attitude has likely evolved because many of the dead trees in which these swallows would normally nest have disappeared as woodlands were developed.

Basics

LENGTH
2.8 to 3.5 inches

WINGSPAN
3.1 to 4.3 inches

WEIGHT
0.071 to 0.212 ounce

LONGEVITY
5 to 7 years

VOCALIZATION
Rapid, squeaky chirps as warning; courting males make a *tik-tik tik-tik* with their wings.

DISTRIBUTION
Eastern North America and the southern Canadian prairies to the Maritime Provinces

(opposite page) A pair of tree swallows survey the landscape from the top of a nesting box before taking off again. These aerial acrobats eat and even drink and bathe while in flight.

(top) Hungry nestlings clamor at the nesting box entrance to receive food from a parent. Both sexes work together to care for their offspring, which can take a long time, up to 25 days, to fledge.

Barn Swallow

Hirundo rustica

Favorite nesting spots

- barns
- open sheds
- carports
- greenhouses
- porch eaves

Like its cousin the tree swallow, the barn swallow is an impressive aerial acrobat, swooping across farm and stable yards—and making a serious dent in the fly population. The male displays glistening, deep blue-purple plumage with a cinnamon belly, rusty forehead and throat, and a distinctive forked—or swallow—tail. The female's plumage is only slightly more subdued.

These birds are the most abundant and most widely distributed swallow on the planet—breeding throughout the Northern Hemisphere and wintering in many regions of the Southern Hemisphere. They breed in every state in the continental United States and migrate, many of them over extremely long distances, to Central America and all of South America. Barn swallows typically travel by day in large flocks, with migration beginning as early as late June in some cases.

Although they are known for nesting in barns and open-sided outbuildings, they have also gradually claimed bridges, wharves, and garages as their domain. Their ancestors originally sought out rock crevices and shallow caves to build their nests, but most modern barn swallows—one exception being a cave-nesting group on the Channel Islands off California—choose human-made structures.

These swallows prefer to hunt over semi-open land near water and usually avoid very dry country and unbroken forest. Often seen near rural outbuildings, agricultural fields, beaches, and ballparks, they forage by skimming with low gliding sweeps over fields and bodies of water. Their diet consists mainly of flying insects, especially bluebottles, houseflies, bees, hoverflies, mayflies, and sometimes moth caterpillars and certain spiders and snails. They only rarely eat berries or seeds.

Courting males express interest in females by pursuing them; once a pair is established, the two may perch side-by-side, touch bills, and preen each other's plumage. It's not uncommon for several pairs to nest near one another, but they do not form large breeding colonies. Both

sexes help build the nest, which is a cup composed of mud and dried grasses and lined with feathers. The female lays four or five brown-spotted white eggs and incubates them for 13 to 17 days with some assistance from her mate. When the babies hatch, both parents feed them, sometimes aided by offspring from a previous brood—and occasionally by unrelated juveniles. The chubby, relatively stubby nestlings are ready to fledge in from 18 to 23 days. Barn swallows typically raise two broods a year.

SHELTERING BARN SWALLOWS

Barn swallows don't frequent feeders, but they will appreciate ground-up eggshells or oyster shells on an open platform feeder, which they may eat to aid the digestion of insect exoskeletons and increase calcium levels.

They tend to build nests where you'd rather not have them, so offer alternatives, such as making unused outbuildings available by leaving doors or windows open. Supplying a small patch of mud will help them when it's nest-building time. Artificial nesting cups that you can attach to elevated surfaces are also available.

A Conservation Catalyst

The impact of the millinery trade on barn swallows, which were killed so that their feathers could adorn ladies' hats, inspired naturalist George Bird Grinnel to write an editorial for *Forest and Stream* in 1886 condemning this waste of bird life. His essay aroused public concern and led to the creation of the first Audubon Society.

(opposite page) Barn swallows showing their distinctive, deeply forked tails. These voracious insectivores can consume hundreds of insects a day, so inviting them to nest can supply you with effective—and free—pest control.

(top) Nestlings in their mud cup high in the rafters appear to be all mouths as they call for food. Barn swallows are entertaining birds, but their nests can create health hazards. Federal laws protect them, however, so be sure to call a specialist in safe, no-kill removal if you feel they are damaging your property. Erecting commercial cups can deter them from nesting in undesirable places.

FOCUS ON
Condo Colonies
PURPLE MARTINS THRIVE ON COMMUNAL LIVING

A colony of purple martins flourishes in its elevated communal home, which includes a multi-unit "apartment house" and hanging gourds. A single pair will nest inside each individual unit.

Purple martins (*Progne subis*) are sociable, migratory birds, the largest of the American swallows, family Hirondinidae. Males display glossy, iridescent blue-black plumage, and both sexes have slightly forked tails, and long, tapered wings. They hunt high in midair, scooping up insects over water or fields.

For years, purple martins in the East have been facing the same loss of breeding sites as other cavity nesters: dead trees are no longer left standing, but are considered nuisances and felled. These birds are also challenged at remaining sites by competitive house sparrows and the introduced European starling. When this loss of nesting sites caused eastern populations to suffer in the 20th century, bird lovers began erecting multi-unit birdhouses or hanging clusters of nesting gourds to help purple martin populations rebound.

Today, eastern purple martins are one of three American species—along with barn

Attracting New Tenants

Mature purple martins typically return to the same nesting site year after year. If you are placing a new house in your yard, you need to attract first-year breeding martins with mottled plumage—which don't arrive until four weeks or so after their seniors. So either delay placing the house outside until a month after you first see martins or keep the holes plugged up until then to keep out starlings, sparrows, and other birds that might claim the units. You can also pipe taped martin songs into your yard to attract new birds.

swallows and chimney swifts—that have adapted to nesting almost exclusively in human-supplied structures.

Purple martins reward their "landlords" with their chortling, gurgling songs and chatty, neighborly behavior. They also perform a dramatic homecoming display when approaching their birdhouses, tucking in their wings and diving at great speeds toward their nests.

THE PROPER LOCATION

Ideally, martin houses require clear flyways. Try to locate them in the center of your largest open area, at least 30 feet from human habitations and 40 to 60 feet from trees. It's important to keep the birdhouse from twisting on the pole—if the orientation of the entrances shifts, the birds may abandon their nests. If you don't have a large open space, but still want to encourage purple martins, perhaps a local school or park has the proper setting; donate a house to them and offer to maintain it.

FINDING THE RIGHT HOUSE

Several types of martin houses can be purchased in garden centers or ordered online, including houses with varied numbers of units and hanging gourds. It's important that the homeowner can access the house's interior to clean the compartments and do nest checks, so the house should raise and lower easily using a pulley or winch system.

Martin houses need a minimum of four cavities; from 6 to 12 is optimal. The best materials are aluminum, UV-resistant plastic, and untreated wood like cypress or cedar. White, which reflects summer heat, is the desired color. Recommended pole height is 12 to 18 feet. Poles should be set in concrete at least one foot below the ground. Entrances holes can range from 1¾ to 2¼ inches. To deter starlings, place the hole flush with the compartment floor. It's also wise to install predator baffles around the pole.

Nesting gourds should be thick and not allow light to filter into the interior.

Purple martins reward their "landlords" with their chortling, gurgling songs and chatty, neighborly behavior.

(left) A male purple martin eats his insect dinner on a condo perch. Males do not attain their shiny purple-black coloring until they are three years old.

(right) A female and a juvenile seem to be having an argument outside their unit. Mated martin pairs are very protective of their territory, but individuals are still loyal to the whole colony. Members often fly off together to explore the surrounding area.

Mourning Dove

Zenaida macroura

Favorite plants

- pine nut
- sweetgum seed
- pokeberry
- globe amaranth
- corn
- buckwheat
- canary grass
- fountain grass

These gentle, taupe-colored birds are familiar sights to both city and country residents—perched in pairs on telephone wires, their graceful silhouettes are pleasing to the eye, and their soft cooing is both soothing and plaintive. These members of the Columbidae family have pointed tails, which distinguish them from the other members, like rock doves, that have fanlike tails. Along with a large tail, they have small heads and plump bodies.

Doves that breed and live across the entire United States and into central Mexico are year-round residents, but the populations from north-central Canada migrate during colder weather. Because they avoid flying over any large bodies of water, they typically winter in coastal Mexico or Central America.

The mourning dove—or the Carolina turtledove, as it was once known—forages for seeds in woody undergrowth or below bird feeders. These birds seek out a variety of open or semi-open habitats, including prairies, farms, light woods, and urban areas. They are powerful, arrow-straight fliers with speeds up to 55 miles per hour. During take-off and landing, their wings make an unusual whistling noise, a form of sonation—sounds produced by a bird other than vocalizations.

With an estimated population of more than 350 million, this species is one of the most abundant in the continental United States. It is also the most popular game bird in the nation, with more than 20 million hunted annually, including young birds, which are served as squab in restaurants. Yet, this dove is such a prolific breeder that its population numbers rarely diminish; in warmer climates a mated pair might raise six broods annually. This is feasible because the parents don't depend on special resources as food for their young—they consume their normal diet of seeds and regurgitate "pigeon's milk" from their crop linings to feed their offspring.

The male begins courtship with a noisy flight followed by an elegant circling glide, after which he struts past the female, puffing out his chest and cooing. Pairs

usually form monogamous bonds. The male offers the female a choice of nesting sites and allows her to build the nest, although he will gather the necessary materials—twigs, pine needles, and grass—and then stand on her back and pass them to her. She will locate the nest on a branch of an evergreen, orchard tree, mesquite, or cottonwood—or in the gutter of a house. She lays two white eggs, and incubates them for two weeks. The hatchlings mature in 12 to 15 days.

KEEP DOVES GROUNDED
Mourning doves prefer feeding on or near the ground and are quite happy scavenging among the grass and bushes for seeds that have fallen from feeders. You can cater to them by scattering millet on the ground or stocking ground or platform feeders with millet seeds.

Basics

LENGTH
11 to 13 inches

WINGSPAN
17 to 19 inches

WEIGHT
4.5 to 6.0 ounces

LONGEVITY
1 to 3 years in the wild; oldest in captivity was 31.

VOCALIZATION
Call is *woo-OO-oo-oo-oo.*

DISTRIBUTION
Across the United States and into Mexico year-round; some Canadian birds winter in Central America.

(opposite page) A mourning dove. French zookeeper Charles L. Bonaparte (nephew of Napoleon) coined its genus name to honor Princess Zénaide, his wife. The bird's specific name, *macroura,* means a "large tail," which it has.

(top) A nestling dove. This bird will probably have many siblings—mourning doves might raise up to six broods in a single breeding season.

similar species: *white-winged dove*

The tidy, taupe white-winged dove (*Zenaida asiatica*) of the Southwest is similar to the mourning dove, but has more uniform plumage and white crescents along its wings. As common now in cities as it once was in desert thickets, it forages on the ground for waste grain and seeds. Lure them into backyards with birdbaths; feeders stocked with sunflower seeds, milo, corn, and safflower; and berry-bearing shrubs.

A white-winged dove eating saguaro fruit. In the Sonoran desert, nesting doves are dependent on the growing cycle of the saguaro cactus—ingesting its pollen, nectar, fruit, and seeds.

Rock Pigeon

Columba livia

Favorite plants

- corn
- oat
- cherry
- elm
- poison ivy

Also known as rock doves—or simply pigeons—these flocking, nonmigratory members of the family Columbidae are arguably the most accessible and adaptable birds on earth. An introduced species in many regions—they were brought to the New World by Europeans in the 1600s—pigeons are now found on six continents. They often nest on ledges on the tall buildings of large cities, which replicate the rocky ledges where they breed in the wild.

Pigeons are stout-bodied birds, with small heads, short legs, and slender bills topped with ceres, a waxy band that contains the nares—or nostrils.

With little fear of people, they are easily domesticated. Carrier pigeons have partnered with humans in wartime and commerce, and homing pigeons are used to compete in the international sport of pigeon racing, where proven winners can sell for thousands of dollars.

Neolithic humans likely domesticated the rock doves that shared their caves, and many early cultures encouraged them by providing dovecotes. These birds not only offered a means of communicating and a food source, their droppings were valued as fertilizer and, later, as an ingredient in gunpowder. In religious symbolism, pigeons represent peace and good will or are messengers from God.

City or "feral" birds exhibit a range of colors, and are possibly examples of a phenomenon discovered through research with silver foxes in Russia—that when animals lose their fear of humans and no longer require the camouflaging coloration of the wild, their fur or feathers become much less uniform. Although the plumage of many city pigeons is identical to wild pigeons—called blue, an iridescent purple-green head with a pale gray body and darker wing bands—urban birds also occur in shades of black, brown, taupe, cream, and red; some are checkered, similar to blue with spots on the wings, or splotched with white.

City life is not without its perils, and metropolitan pigeons are at risk from traffic and window collisions, poisoning, predation by rats, and deadly strikes from the peregrine falcons and red-tailed hawks that also nest in skyscrapers and who number pigeons among their favorite foods.

Pigeons feed on seeds, grains, and fruit, as well as a lot of "people food" thrown away in cities. Outside urban areas, they frequent farms and rocky cliffs.

They reproduce almost all year long, feeding their young with regurgitated

Inspiring Genius

British naturalist Charles Darwin studied and kept pigeons after returning from his voyage on the *Beagle*. His observations about the great variety of breeds and the many differences between captive and wild specimens helped him formulate aspects of his theory of evolution.

"pigeon's milk" or "crop milk." Males court by selecting a nesting site, then sitting and cooing to attract females. The loosely constructed, flimsy nests of twigs or straw are used repeatedly, becoming a sturdy, albeit feces-molded, pot over time.

PARLAYING WITH PIGEONS

Even those living in high-rise apartments can observe birds if they are willing to encourage pigeons. A small balcony scattered with seeds will invite these colorful visitors to drop in—but first ask if there are city ordinances against feeding pigeons. Yes, pigeons are often reviled as civic nuisances, but up close they are no less interesting than other wild birds and have gentle, inquisitive personalities. In the suburbs, pigeons are regular visitors at platform and hopper feeders offering cracked corn or dried peas.

Basics

LENGTH
11.8 to 14.2 inches

WINGSPAN
19.7 to 26.4 inches

WEIGHT
9.3 to 13.4 ounces

LONGEVITY
15 years in captivity, 5 or 6 years for feral birds

VOCALIZATION
Song is a rolling series of deep coos, often made while strutting.

DISTRIBUTION
Worldwide after introduction of species

(opposite page) An urban pigeon looks down on the green park scenery from its window perch in an abandoned building.

(left) A curious suburban pigeon takes a break from feeding on seeds to check out the photographer.

(right) Same species, different colors. The more acclimated pigeons become to humans, the more their plumage will vary.

White-breasted Nuthatch

Sitta carolinensis

Favorite plants

- beech
- hickory
- oak
- hawthorn
- sunflower
- corn

This small acrobat of the North American woodland has the ability to maneuver in all directions—including upside down—on tree trunks and limbs while hunting for beetles and their larvae. White-breasted nuthatches move with a staccato, stop-and-start motion that makes them easy to identify. From a distance, they might look similar to small woodpeckers, but nuthatches do not brace themselves with their tails against the tree, as woodpeckers do.

The adult male displays dapper blue-gray plumage, white cheeks, a pale chestnut belly, and black collar and cap. It has a stocky body, oversized head, truncated tail, and strong bill and feet. Females are slightly duller and wear a gray cap, although some may show a black cap, especially west of the Rocky Mountains.

Slow and Steady

The ability to probe into tree bark from any angle like a nuthatch can is certainly an advantage, allowing it to locate food that would otherwise be out of reach. But some birds use a more methodical approach to gleaning, such as the brown creeper (*Certhia americana*). This little woodland bird starts near the base and then slowly spirals up large tree trunks in search of insects. The only North American member of the Certhiidae, or treecreeper family, it is found in coniferous and mixed forests.

These nuthatches belong to the family Sittidae. They inhabit most of North America and in the East prefer old-growth deciduous woodlands and, occasionally, coniferous forests. You can frequently spot them in orchards, parks, and suburban gardens. In winter, they forage at feeders. They are easy to find, even in dense woodlands, if you listen for their continuous nasal yammering.

Their diet consists mainly of insects, including beetles, weevil larvae, ants, and caterpillars (including gypsy moths and tent caterpillars), and spiders. They will also eat seeds and nuts and crops like corn.

After breeding, pairs stay together, although females have to tolerate males pushing them away from foraging sites. Instead, they keep a lookout while their mates feed. They nest in hollow, decaying trees and prefer oak, beech, and hickory, which also provide sustaining seeds. The male now does sentry duty, keeping a keen eye out for predators while the female lines the nesting cavity with fur, bark, and dirt, and then constructs a cup of grass, shredded bark, and feathers. She lays five to nine creamy, speckled eggs and incubates them for two weeks. The babies develop relatively slowly and are not ready to fledge for 25 or more days.

MAKING NUTHATCHES HAPPY

These energetic clowns need little encouragement to come to feeders, especially in colder weather, when they flock with other snowbirds. They love large seeds like sunflowers and peanuts and will feast on suet. They are known for stashing seeds in bark caches for later use and will often make many repeated trips to the feeder to "stock up." They might also breed in nesting boxes if you provide them.

Basics

LENGTH
5.1 to 5.5 inches

WINGSPAN
7.9 to 10.6 inches

WEIGHT
0.65 to 1.06 ounces

LONGEVITY
Record is 9 years.

VOCALIZATION
Contact call is a repeated, squeaky *nit;* excited call is *kri-kri-kri-kri;* the courting male's call is *qui-qui-qui.*

DISTRIBUTION
Most of North America, from southern Canada to northern Mexico

(opposite page) A white-breasted nuthatch hopping down a tree trunk. The name *nuthatch* probably derived from the birds' habit of lodging hard-shelled insects or seeds into cracks in tree bark in order to hull them with their strong bills.

similar species: *red-breasted nuthatch*

This active, plump little songbird (*Sitta canadensis*) of the northern and western woodlands boasts a cinnamon chest and black or gray eye line and is slightly smaller than its white-breasted cousin. Red-breasted nuthatches flock with kinglets, chickadees, and woodpeckers in the canopy and investigate tree trunks for insects and larvae. Their honking calls of *yank-yank* are reminiscent of miniature tin horns.

A red-breasted nuthatch nibbles on sunflower seeds. It will readily come to a seed or suet feeder.

Eastern Kingbird

Tyrannus tyrannus

Favorite plants

- blackberry
- mulberry
- elderberry
- cherry
- serviceberry
- nightshade
- sassafras fruit

Tyrant flycatchers, the Tyrannidae, are the largest family of birds, with more than 410 species worldwide. (They were named after Old World flycatchers, but are not related to them.) They are found throughout North and South America and exhibit many variations in size, shape, coloring, and patterning. They lack the complex vocal capabilities of most other songbirds.

There are 13 species of kingbirds, and the eastern kingbird is the most numerous in the East, ranging from New England to Florida and west to the Rockies. Big-headed and wide-shouldered, this bird has an upright posture and a squared-off tail. Its mole gray color, with a white belly and throat, gives it the aspect of a sedate businessman, yet when it is agitated, it flashes a bright crown of orange-red.

As the name implies, kingbirds are peerless hunters and fearless defenders of their territory, venturing out to harass encroaching crows, raptors, and great blue herons. To appear more intimidating during an attack, they raise their crowns and open their mouths wide—a behavior called gaping. They hunt by sight—perching on wires or fence posts to scan the landscape and sallying out to snatch insects on the wing or fluttering low over grassy fields. Their diet includes beetles, bees, wasps, grasshoppers, bugs, and flies. They may also hunt small frogs, dispatching them the way they tackle large insects: smacking their prey against a branch and swallowing it whole. In late summer, they add berries to their menu.

Eastern kingbirds breed in open habitats such as shrub-dotted grasslands, pastures, fields, meadows, and urban yards, and they are often abundant along the edges of wetlands, in quaking aspen groves, beaver ponds, newly burnt forests, and on golf courses. In fall, they migrate through eastern Mexico to the forests of South America, where they form large flocks and switch their diet to fruit.

Courting males perform aerial stunting, including up-and-down swoops, zigzags, and backward somersaults. The female builds a large, sturdy nest in an exposed tree using twigs, dried weed stems, bark, and found materials such as cigarette butts, plastic strips, and twine. The interior is lined with soft plant fibers. Males guard females at this time, possibly to prevent them from finding new mates. Females lay two to five pale eggs with a ring of spots that can take 14 to 17 days to hatch. Although the offspring are ready to fledge in 17 days, parents tend them for up to seven weeks. This generally limits their reproductive output to one brood a year.

IT'S THE BERRIES

Eastern kingbirds will be encouraged to visit your yard if you provide several varieties of berry bushes, especially those that fruit in late summer or early fall, when the birds are bulking up for migration.

Basics

LENGTH
7.5 to 9.1 inches

WINGSPAN
13 to 15 inches

WEIGHT
1.2 to 1.9 ounces

LONGEVITY
Record is 10 years, 1 month.

VOCALIZATION
Call is a stuttering *zap* that sounds like an electric spark.

DISTRIBUTION
Breeds across central United States to East Coast; winters in South American forests

(opposite page) A dapper eastern kingbird. Both its genus and species names come from the Latin for "tyrant" or "despot," most likely in reference to its aggressive behavior—even to members of its own kind.

(left) The bright scarlet patch in the crest is usually only visible when the bird displays during courtship or when it is agitated.

(right) An adult comes in for a landing to dine on berries. During the fall migration period, fruit will make up the bulk of its diet.

(bottom) A juvenile sits calling from its perch on a branch. It is much duller and paler than the adults of the species, with pale brownish gray feathers. Its parents may tend to it for more than a month after it fledges.

Eastern Phoebe

Sayornis phoebe

Favorite plants

- blackberry
- mulberry
- elderberry

This small, stocky flycatcher, with its alert, upright posture is a member of the Tyrannidae, the tyrant or New World flycatchers. The eastern phoebe has the honor of being the first banded bird in America—in 1804, naturalist John James Audubon attached silver thread to the leg of an eastern phoebe so he would recognize the bird when it returned to breed each year.

Phoebes are easy to spot when roosting in low trees or on fence posts, where you can often observe them pumping their long tails. The adult plumage is a warm gray above with a cream-colored belly and some tan shading on the chest. The black bill is short and thin. The head, which the bird "styles" by puffing up the crown feathers or flattening them completely, may appear too large for the round body.

similar species: *eastern wood-pewee*

The eastern wood-pewee (*Contopus virens*) is a migratory flycatcher of the eastern woodlands that can be heard rasping out *pee-a-wee!* all summer long. Similar to the phoebe in size and appearance, it is a grayish olive in tone and displays a slight crest and dual white wing bars. The wood-pewee hunts by watching from the foliage for insects to appear and then sallying out to strike.

This bird sings throughout the day; it begins before dawn, and you can still hear it after sunset.

Phoebes breed throughout the eastern United States and migrate to the Gulf states and Mexico in the fall. (They have the northernmost winter range of any flycatcher.) They are one of the earliest birds to come north in spring—their rasping calls of *fee-bee* are a sure sign that winter is waning—and one of the last to leave in fall. Some southern populations remain in their territory year-round.

They favor open woodlands or farm meadows, especially those near water, but will happily set up housekeeping in a park or yard. They are skilled hunters, watching from a tree branch and then flying out to catch insects in midair or hovering over foliage to forage. They sometimes stalk prey on the ground. In addition to flying insects like wasps, beetles, dragonflies, butterflies, moths, flies, midges, and cicadas, they consume ticks, spiders, and millipedes. Their diet is augmented with occasional fruits, berries, and seeds.

These birds prefer to nest in protected nooks. The female builds a cup of mud lined with moss and grass under a girder, beam, or eave. She lays two to six white, possibly speckled, eggs. These will hatch in 15 to 16 days, and the hatchlings will be ready to fledge in about 20 days. Unlike most songbirds, returning phoebes will reuse the same nest—unless a barn swallow has moved in before them. Conversely, phoebes will appropriate the nests of barn swallows or robins.

WHAT PHOEBES WANT

Phoebes are not fans of backyard feeders, but they will investigate yards that offer secure outbuildings for nesting—or even commercial nesting boxes—and maybe a berry bush or two.

Basics

LENGTH
6.5 to 7 inches

WINGSPAN
10.2 to 11 inches

WEIGHT
0.6 to 0.7 ounce

LONGEVITY
Record is 10 years, 4 months.

VOCALIZATION
Note is a sharp *chip* or *peep;* call is a raspy rising and falling *fee-bee.*

DISTRIBUTION
Breeds in the central and eastern states, migrates to Mexico; some remain in the South year-round.

(opposite page) An eastern phoebe returns to its perch after sallying out for a fly.

(left) Phoebe fledglings. These flycatchers originally nested on rock outcroppings, but most have become "urbanized" and prefer bridges, decks, and barns.

(right) Phoebes are loners, and, unlike most songbirds who must learn from other birds, will sing a perfect song even if raised in isolation.

Northern Mockingbird

Mimus polyglottos

Favorite plants

- multiflora rose
- mulberry
- hawthorn
- blackberry
- holly

Mockingbirds are nature's entertainers, known for complex musical offerings that string together a series of themes and mimic other birds, dogs, frogs, and even cell phones or car alarms. It is not uncommon for them to sing at night—and full moons seem to compel them. They continue to learn new songs as they mature, and older adults may have as many as 200 phrases in their repertoire. Some males actually have a separate set of songs for spring and fall.

Valued for these songs, mockingbirds were sold as caged birds from the late 1700s to the early 1900s, which severely depleted northern populations. Not only have they since bounced back, it's also possible that these birds have increased their range due to the widespread cultivation of multiflora roses, whose berries are a mockingbird favorite.

These slender, medium-sized birds, of the family Mimidae, have a flitting manner and show gray-brown plumage above a pale gray belly and two white wing bars. They have small heads and long legs and round, wide wings that make the tail appear especially long in comparison. In flight, patches of white on the wings and tail edges may flash brightly.

They are easily observed in towns and cities, where they sit on telephone wires, fences, or high branches of roadside trees, but they also seek out farms, hedgerows, second-growth woods, low grasslands, and, in the West, dense thickets. They are highly territorial toward any birds that stray into their nesting areas and will also threaten cats, humans, and even raptors.

These birds eat by running down insects on the ground or by swooping out of foliage to capture prey in the grass. They consume a variety of insects and even small lizards on occasion. They will also explore gardens for fruit trees or berries.

Northern mockingbirds nest in early spring; they apparently recognize their previous nesting spots and will return year after year. Males court females by singing and with displays of leaping and wing flashing. The male builds the foundation of

the nest in a dense tree or shrub, combining leaves, grass, and weeds on a base of twigs, and the female lines it with moss, hair, and plant down as well as refuse such as plastic, tin foil, and shredded cigarette filters. She will then lay three or four greenish or pale blue eggs with brown splotches that incubate for 12 to 13 days. Both parents feed the hatchlings. Pairs may produce two or three broods a year.

ENCOURAGING MOCKINGBIRDS

These lively birds are often seen in yards, hunting for insects in the grass, but they don't regularly come to feeders. You might tempt them with hulled sunflowers seeds, sliced fruit, and peanut hearts on a ground or platform feeder, and suet in a cage feeder. You can also keep them happy by supplying fruit trees and berry bushes.

Basics

LENGTH
8.3 to 11 inches

WINGSPAN
12.2 to 15 inches

WEIGHT
1.6 to 2 ounces

LONGEVITY
Record in the wild is 14 years, 10 months.

VOCALIZATION
Song is a series of long phrases repeated three times, includes mimicry; call is a loud, harsh *tchack* or *chair*.

DISTRIBUTION
Coast to coast in United States, south to Mexico

(opposite page) Mockingbirds maintain a high public profile—they are the official bird of five states and can be found in book titles, popular songs, and poetry.

(top) A juvenile northern mockingbird. Fledglings leave the nest in about 12 days, although they will not be proficient fliers for at least another week.

similar species: *brown thrasher*

Brown thrashers (*Toxostoma rufum*) are handsome, leggy birds that favor dense underbrush, but they will sing lustily from treetops or fence posts. Their plumage is a ruddy brown with a pale, deeply speckled breast and two black-and-white wing bars. They have bright yellow eyes and a downward-curved bill. Most brown thrashers summer in the central to northeastern United States and winter in Texas; other populations in the Deep South remain year-round.

Like those of mockingbirds, the songs of brown thrashers have a wide variety of musical phrases.

Gray Catbird

Dumetella carolinensis

Favorite plants

- holly
- cherry
- elderberry
- blackberry
- dogwood
- winterberry
- serviceberry
- grape

The mewing cry of the gray catbird, one of the most recognizable voices in North America's eastern and central woodlands, easily accounts for its common name. Like mockingbirds and thrashers, gray catbirds string together the songs of other birds and create their own unique compositions. Yet, by far, the sound most bird-watchers first learn to recognize is the catlike call.

The gray catbird, family Mimidae, is a medium-sized songbird that gives the initial impression of a slender robin. The body is a uniform ash gray with a black cap and a patch of warm red under the tail. They are leggy birds, with fairly long tails and long, rounded wings.

These birds breed throughout the central and eastern United States and across southern Canada, and in winter they depart for Central America and the Caribbean. Some populations in the coastal South do not migrate. They are not brash like their mimic cousins, but prefer the safety of the underbrush in tangled vines and dense thickets—their genus name, *Dumetella*, means "small thicket." They even avoid flying over open terrain; look for them gliding low over small shrubs and trees. They frequent woodland edges, streamside groves, overgrown fields, and hedgerows. In their tropical winter habitats, they spend more time in actual forests.

Catbirds consume a mixed diet of insects and berries. They are energetic foragers, fluttering constantly through tree branches in search of prey, including many types of beetles, ants, caterpillars,

grasshoppers, crickets, and other insects, as well as spiders and millipedes. In the garden, they are drawn to strawberries, blackberries, cherries, and grapes and may put a dent in your raspberry crop.

The male sings loudly to mark his territory and more softly during courtship. An interested female will answer with an equally quiet response. It is she who builds the nest in a dense thicket with materials supplied by her mate. It is typically a bulky cup composed of twigs, weeds, and leaves, maybe string, and lined with soft grasses or hair. She lays three or four turquoise eggs, some with red spots, which hatch in about two weeks. Both parents tend the nestlings, which take up to two weeks to fledge.

CATBIRD CUISINE

These personable birds dine on native fruit trees and shrubs such as winterberry, dogwood, and serviceberry, as well as many berry bushes. In winter they may visit cage feeders stocked with suet and raisins and platform feeders featuring oddities like cornflakes, cheese, and doughnut crumbs. They like to roost in small shrubs planted near deciduous trees. Catbirds love bathing, so adding a birdbath can draw them to your yard.

Mimics Among Us

The Mimidae are not the only avian mimics: parrots, corvids, mynahs, and bowerbirds also have this ability. This vocal replication relies on their complicated syrinx, the vocal organ at the base of the trachea, which is able to produce a wide range of tones, pitches, and sounds—and can be controlled by air pressure from each lung separately! The greatest challenge occurs when birds attempt to recreate the sound of cell phones, power saws, and human speech.

Basics

LENGTH
8.3 to 9.4 inches

WINGSPAN
8.7 to 11.8 inches

WEIGHT
0.8 to 2 ounces

LONGEVITY
Record is 17 ears, 11 months.

VOCALIZATION
Assemblage of musical and mechanical sounds with no repetition of phrases; call is a mewing cry; note is *kwut*.

DISTRIBUTION
Breeds throughout central and eastern United States; winters along the Gulf Coast to Central America

(opposite page) A gray catbird. Catbird songs, unlike those of mockingbirds and thrashers, do not repeat musical phrases, and the riffs will contain a random *meow* every so often. These softly warbled tunes can last up to ten minutes.

(top) A young gray catbird with the characteristically unkempt look of a fledgling. Its parents will continue to feed it for up to 12 days after it has left the nest. Catbirds will typically raise two broods a year.

Common Grackle

Quiscalus quiscula

Favorite plants

- corn
- oat
- rice
- sunflower
- sweetgum
- oak

With its iridescent head, sleek body, strutting, long-legged gait, and imposing size, the common grackle is an impressive visitor to suburban lawns, especially when viewed in a flock. These social, noisy, members of the Icteridae, or New World blackbirds, have slightly elongated bodies; long, dark bills; yellow eyes; and wedge-shaped tails. Males appear in several colorations: a bronze race, with a gleaming blue-black head and metallic brown back, and a purple race, with an iridescent purple head and dull purple back. There is also a "Florida" grackle with a green back and purple belly. Females look similar to males, but are less glossy.

These birds prefer open and semi-open terrain, such as woodlands, forest edges, marshes, swamps, palmetto hammocks, hedgerows, prairies, farms, cemeteries,

similar species: *boat-tailed & great-tailed grackles*

Two large species of grackle frequently flock with common grackles: the boat-tailed grackle *(Quiscalus major)* of the eastern shoreline and the great-tailed grackle *(Q. mexicanus)* of the Southwest and the Great Plains. The boat-tailed grackle has an iridescent black body, usually more blue-green, and a long tail that it folds into a v-shape—similar to the keel of a boat. The great-tailed grackle also has an iridescent black body, but is more blue-purple and has a tapered tail nearly as long as its body.

The boat-tailed grackle is a bigger bird than the common grackle, with a larger bill and longer tail.

parks, and suburban yards. They are year-round residents in the south-central and southern states, but are migratory in the Northeast, the Plains states, and Canada. The latter are short-distance migrants, wintering in the central or southern states, depending on their place of origin.

These unfussy omnivores will feed on seeds, crop grains, wild fruit, and berries, and they hunt for beetles, caterpillars, grasshoppers, frogs, minnows, mice, and other birds. They forage mostly on the ground or in shallow water and will often pick at refuse. At bird feeders they will hang awkwardly from hoppers or platforms, scattering seeds willy-nilly.

Male grackles puff up their feathers during courtship or to intimidate intruders. They also chase after females in the air, singly or in pairs. After mating, female grackles build bulky cuplike nests of twigs, leaves, grasses, corn husks, paper, string, cloth, and other discarded materials. They situate them high in dense conifers or in shrubs near water, rarely in barns, birdhouses, or tree cavities. Females lay from one to seven pale eggs that will hatch in 11 to 15 days. The babies are able to fledge in 10 to 17 days. Grackle pairs may nest in large colonies, and once breeding season ends, these gregarious birds form flocks numbering in the millions, typically with other Icterids.

GRACKLE FARE

Grackles are so attracted to backyard feeders that you might want to come up with ways to deter these potential food hogs. They will dine at ground, large hopper, and platform feeders and eat almost anything you provide, including sunflower seeds, cracked corn, millet, milo, peanut hearts, peanuts, oats, safflower, and sliced fruit. Suet in cage feeders is also popular.

Basics

LENGTH
11 to 13 inches

WINGSPAN
14 to 18 inches

WEIGHT
3.3 to 4.3 ounces

LONGEVITY
Record is nearly 23 years.

VOCALIZATION
Call is a *chuck* or *chack;* song a repeated, creaking *chewink* or *oo whew whew.*

DISTRIBUTION
Year-round in south-central and southern states; migratory east of the Rockies through northeastern United States and Canada

(opposite page) A common grackle. Their lustrous feathers come in a wide variety of colorations.

(left) An intense-looking grackle. These clever birds show little fear of humans.

(right) The upper bill of a grackle is made for scoring the hulls of acorns. At feeders, grackles might try to intimidate smaller birds.

Red-winged Blackbird

Agelaius phoeniceus

Favorite plants

- sunflower
- ragweed
- cocklebur
- corn
- wheat

The red-winged blackbird is an active, noisy wetland resident of such great numbers that it is possibly the most populous bird in North America. This abundance has made it one of the most studied wild birds in the world.

Red-wings are New World blackbirds, members of the Icteridae family that show some color. The male is a familiar sight along marshy lanes and reedy highway verges—jet black with red-and-yellow shoulder patches, called epaulets, on its wings. The female is far less showy: a streaky black-brown with a buff throat. They are wide-shouldered birds that exhibit a hunched posture when perching. Birders recognize them sight unseen by their musical songs and metallic *chacks*.

They breed in cattail marshes, either saltwater or fresh, and other watercourses,

but are also found in grassy prairies and overgrown farm fields. Their year-round range extends across the United States, although some populations in southern Canada migrate to western Mexico. In late summer and early fall, blackbirds form enormous flocks—sometimes reaching a million birds or more—along with grackles, starlings, and cowbirds. The red-wings separate from the flock each day to feed—flying as far as 50 miles away to forage—and then reconvene in the evening.

Red-winged blackbirds eat seeds, waste grain, fruit, and berries, as well as insects and spiders. They also prey on small animals such as frogs, mollusks, worms, and snails. They are adept at using their sharp conical bills to pry open aquatic plants to get at any insects hiding inside.

They breed in loose colonies among marshy reeds or on open grasslands. Males court by singing from a prominent stalk, widening their tails, and displaying their epaulets. Nesting females will wind stringy plants around several upright stems and then weave a platform of vegetation. Upon this base she adds decaying wood, wet leaves, and mud to create a cuplike nest. To avoid predation on their eggs and fledglings, she may locate it over water in dense foliage. In wetlands she will situate the nest in cattails, bulrushes, or sedges and in uplands, in goldenrod, blackberry, willows, or alders. She might also build a nest in wheat, barley, or alfalfa fields. She lays two to four pale blue-green eggs, which incubate for 11 to 13 days. The babies will be ready to fledge in two weeks. Adult red wings and their young are especially at risk from raptors, although males will challenge larger birds or even humans that disturb the nest.

RALLYING RED-WINGS

During migration or in cold weather, these birds will gladly visit ground, platform, hopper, and tube feeders to dine on black-oil and hulled sunflower seeds, cracked corn, oats, millet, milo, and peanut hearts.

Basics

LENGTH
6.7 to 9.4 inches

WINGSPAN
12.2 to 15.7 inches

WEIGHT
0.9 to 1.0 ounce

LONGEVITY
Record in the wild is more than 15 years.

VOCALIZATION
Call is a throaty *chack,* or a slurred *tereeee;* the male's song is *conk-a-lee;* the female's a scolding *chit-chit-chit-chit-cheer-teer-teer-teer.*

DISTRIBUTION
Year-round in the United States; some breed in northern Canada and migrate to Mexico.

(opposite page) A male red-winged blackbird. Depending on his level of confidence, he may boldly display his colorful shoulder patches or shyly hide them within his plumage.

(top) Red-wings dining at a backyard seed feeder. You are mostly likely to see them in the colder months.

(bottom) Red-wings in their nest. This species is polygynous, meaning that the males mate with multiple females in one season—as many as 15! Female red-wings will also breed with males other than their mate and lay eggs of mixed paternity.

(right) A female balances herself between two reeds.

Baltimore Oriole

Icterus galbula

Favorite plants

- raspberry
- crabapple
- trumpet vine
- mulberry
- cherry
- orange
- banana

The Baltimore oriole not only brings a blaze of color to eastern treetops in the spring, but its whistling song also fills the woodland, signaling that winter is past. It is a slender, medium-sized blackbird, slightly smaller than a robin. The male's vivid orange or yellow body shows black points on the head and wings, with a single white wing bar. The female has a grayish head and back, an orange-yellow breast, and two white wing bars. This bird was named not for the city of Baltimore but for the colors on the coat of arms of the 17th-century founder of the Maryland colony, George Calvert, first Baron Baltimore.

These orioles forage high in trees, seeking insects such as beetles, crickets, grasshoppers, moths, flies, and spiders, and snails and other invertebrates. They consume many pests, including tent caterpillars—which they whack against a tree trunk to remove the protective hairs—and gypsy moth caterpillars. They also relish nectar, berries, and fruit, preferring the darkest and ripest specimens. Some orioles feed by gaping—stabbing their closed beaks into ripe fruit, then opening them and lapping up the juicy interior with their brushy-tipped tongues.

They are found in open woodlands, forest edges, orchards, and wetlands, and because they have adapted to human habitations, you will frequently see them in parks and suburban yards. Breeding season is spent in most of central and eastern North America, except for the coastal South. In fall, these birds migrate to Florida, Central America, the Caribbean, and the upper tip of South America.

Orioles are typically monogamous. Courting males display by singing and chattering while branch hopping or bowing with wings dropped to show off their colorful backs. The female responds by fanning her tail and chattering. It is the female that builds the distinctive nest, a tightly woven pouch of grass, bark strips,

wool, and horsehair, lined with a layer of springy fibers and one of downy vegetation. This pouch hangs from the branch ends of maple, willow, cottonwood, or apple trees. (In the last century, Dutch elm disease decimated the elm trees in which these birds commonly nested.) The female lays three to seven pale gray eggs, which incubate for 11 to 14 days. The hatchlings are fed a diet almost exclusively of insects—rich in protein for fast-growing babies—and will fledge in two weeks.

BALTIMORE ORIOLE DESSERT BAR

These birds will happily respond to offerings of sliced oranges on platform feeders, jelly in a saucer, suet in a cage feeder, or nectar in special oriole feeders that are similar to hummingbird feeders. A variety of berry bushes will also bring them to your yard.

Basics

LENGTH
6.7 to 8.7 inches

WINGSPAN
9.1 to 12.6 inches

WEIGHT
0.79 to 1.48 ounces

LONGEVITY
11 years in the wild

VOCALIZATION
Song is a clear, piping whistle; call is a *wink*.

DISTRIBUTION
Breeds in central and eastern North America; migrates south as far as South America

(opposite page) A male Baltimore oriole in bright breeding plumage. This species is the state bird of Maryland and also the inspiration for the Baltimore Orioles baseball team.

(top) A female seems to be telling her mate to back away from the jelly. These orioles are famous for their sweet tooth and will readily come to feeding stations stocked with dishes of jelly or slices of fresh orange.

similar species: *Bullock's oriole*

From 1983 to 1995, the Bullock's oriole (*Icterus bullockii*) of the American West and the Baltimore oriole of the East were listed as one species (renamed the northern oriole). Genetic evidence has now shown them to be distinct, but nonetheless they do hybridize where their ranges overlap. Like the Baltimore, the male Bullock's oriole is a flashy bird—a deep yellow-orange with ebony wings, back, and tail tips, and white wing patches, along with a black cap and throat and black lines through each eye.

A male Bullock's oriole gathers nesting material from a mulberry tree.

European Starling

Sturnus vulgaris

Favorite plants

- cherry
- holly berry
- hackberry
- mulberry
- tupelo
- Virginia creeper
- sumac
- blackberry

This now-ubiquitous hoarse-voiced suburban songbird was not originally native to North America. In 1890, a misguided organization intent on bringing all of Shakespeare's bird species to this country imported and released 100 European starlings in New York City's Central Park by. As a result, there are now more than 200 million starlings in the United States.

Starlings, family Sturnidae, are compact birds, with short necks and stubby tails. In flight, their long pointed wings and pointed bills give them the appearance of a star, hence their common name. Their speckled black and brown plumage is not very refined, yet, in spite of their motley looks and being categorized as pests—primarily for impacting bluebirds and red-headed woodpeckers that also breed in cavities—

they are hardy and intelligent and possess a raffish charm. Starlings spend hours serenading their neighborhoods with a sputtering song interspersed with clever mimicry of other birds—they are cousins to the talking mynah bird.

Starlings consume insects, including beetles, grasshoppers, flies, and caterpillars, as well as invertebrates, foraging on the ground in groups, zigzagging through the grass. Berries, seeds, and nectar are also favorites.

Adaptability has certainly helped these Europeans conquer new worlds: they breed in cities, suburbs, parks, farms, meadows, and open groves. And though they tend to avoid dense forests or deserts, they will nest in buildings found in these habitats. Their range extends from

coast to coast in the United States and well north into Canada. In fall, they are short-distance migrants: southern populations remain in their territories year-round, while northern birds will generally head to warmer states.

Sociable and gregarious by nature, they gather into enormous flocks in the fall and winter. Starling flocks are renowned for flying in complex, tight-knit formations—called murmurations—creating breathtaking patterns as they surge and bank in total synchronization.

After the male establishes his territory, he chooses a nesting cavity and advertises the site to prospective mates by waving his wings. Both sexes furnish the cavity, but males often bring in scrap materials that the females promptly discard. The female lays three to six bluish eggs, which hatch in 12 days. The hatchlings, which are tended by both parents, are ready to strike out on their own in 21 to 23 days.

STARLING SNACK ATTACKS

What foods don't starlings enjoy at a bird feeder? They eagerly snap up sunflower seeds, whole or hulled, cracked corn, fruit, millet, milo, oats, peanut hearts, peanuts, and suet. Needless to say, they will flock to every type of feeder except nectar feeders.

Basics

LENGTH
7.5 to 9.1 inches

WINGSPAN
12 to 17 inches

WEIGHT
2.0 to 3.6 ounces

LONGEVITY
Record in the wild is 15 years, 9 months.

VOCALIZATION
Call is a descending *whee-ee;* song is squeaky and rasping, often imitative.

DISTRIBUTION
Across the United States and central Canada; northern birds may migrate south.

(opposite page) An adult European starling. Flocks of starlings might feed on valuable fruit and sprouting crops, but they are also beneficial to agriculture because they devour many destructive invertebrates.

(top) A starling parent perches outside a nesting box to feeds its young.

(bottom) Flock mates huddle together on a fence rail in a winter garden. During the colder months of the year, their bills are a brownish black; in summer, the female's bills will turn a lemony yellow, while the male's will turn bright yellow with a blue-gray base.

American Crow

Corvus brachyrhynchos

Favorite plants

- corn
- apple
- sumac
- wild cherry
- dogwood
- Virginia creeper
- juniper berry
- pumpkin seeds

These intelligent, vocal birds were once actively hunted as pests; attempts at eradication included dynamiting their roosts. Like magpies, American crows withstood the onslaught and eventually adapted to life in and around cities. They are now a familiar sight in both country and urban settings, gleaning agricultural fields as crows have done for millennia or perched on billboards and highway overpasses haranguing motorists.

Crows are bold, energetic corvids with enough size and heft that they fear very little, even large raptors. They are sturdy and long-legged, with thick necks and short tails. Their feathers, legs, and heavy bills are a uniform black. The plumage usually has a matte appearance, but post-molt feathers may be glossy.

They have made themselves at home in many habitats besides their native open woodlands and riverbanks: agricultural sites, parking lots, cemeteries, parks, campsites, vacant lots, athletic fields, suburban yards, public beaches, and garbage dumps. They are not migratory per se, living as year-round residents across most of North America, but some flocks that breed in Canada travel short distances south during colder weather.

Crows are omnivores that will eat almost anything. Their diet includes insects, earthworms, spiders, snails, frogs, small reptiles, grains, seeds, berries, and fruit, as well as fish, pet food, garbage and carrion. They sometimes steal chicks from nests, so they can become the object of mobbing. Crows, in turn, will mob eagles or large hawks. They are often seen feeding from road kill, but their bills are not constructed to rend skin or flesh like those of true scavengers.

Courting males display for females by puffing up, bowing, and singing a rattling song. Mated couples will then perch together and preen each other's feathers. Both sexes construct a large, bulky nest of sticks, twigs, bark strips, and weeds, lined with soft plant fibers and feathers. The preferred location is an evergreen tree or large shrub some distance off the ground. The clutch consists of three to nine pale greenish eggs that hatch in 16 to 18 days. The nestlings may take up to 40 days to fledge, but fortunately many crow families include "helpers"—offspring from several previous broods—that aid in raising the young and perform other nesting chores.

COAXING CROWS TO FEED

They are unfussy eaters, but crows are not big fans of feeders. To encourage them to visit your yard, try placing sunflowers seeds, cracked corn, oats, peanut hearts, and fruit on ground or platform feeders. Scattering whole peanuts or loose grain on your lawn might also tempt them.

(opposite page) An American crow struts off with a peanut. These omnivorous birds eat a vast variety of foods.

(top) In flight, crows flap their wings using a steady rhythm, with little gliding in between strokes.

similar species: *common raven*

These massive, powerful sooty black birds with their guttural croaks are more solitary than their crow cousins. Yet, common ravens *(Corvus corax)* often seek out humans—ravens were known to follow Native American hunting parties and wagon trains heading west hoping for scraps. Considerably larger than crows, they also have thicker bills and longer, thicker tails. Ravens range across northern North America and throughout the American West. Bright and inventive, ravens use tools and frequently confound scientists with their problem-solving abilities.

Beyond their great size, ravens are distinguished from crows by the shaggy feathers above their substantial beaks and their feathery throat pouches.

Clever Corvids

CROWS & THEIR KIN EXCEL AT PROBLEM SOLVING

A juvenile raven working on a fence nail. This curious raven had fallen when the branch he was on broke. He stayed two days on this fence with the parents continuously calling and scolding him as he explored his surroundings.

Researchers have long pondered whether "lower" animals and birds are capable of problem solving and using tools. These cognitive skills require a level of intelligence and calculation that was previously thought to exist only in primates and whales and dolphins. But recent studies have shown that corvids—crows, ravens, jays, and magpies—are not only the most intelligent birds, but their brain-to-body mass ratio is also equal to that of great apes and cetaceans—and

only slightly lower than humans. Bearing out these startling findings, crows' innovative tool-making abilities exceed those of chimps, and their problem-solving abilities are comparable to those of a five- to seven-year-old child.

Among other accomplishments: European magpies are able to recognize themselves in mirrors; captive blue jays use scraps of paper to retrieve seeds scattered outside their cages; urban crows utilize car traffic at crosswalks to crack nuts; Israeli crows employ breadcrumbs to lure fish; and New Zealand crows fashion fish hooks from twigs. Crows and scrub jays not only watch where other birds cache food, in order to steal it, they also make false caches to confuse birds that might want to rob them—thus predicting future consequences based on their own larcenous behavior. In the lab, crows knew enough to drop stones into a test tube half filled with water until a floating piece of meat rose high enough to snatch. They rarely bothered with the tube of sand with an equally tempting treat halfway up.

These behaviors, like those of primates, indicate the use of such mental tools as imagination and the anticipation of possible upcoming events to solve current problems. Scientists believe that the reason certain animals become "smart" is not due to physical needs, but is based on social ones—the necessity for developing the intelligence and understanding to navigate the complex group requirements of the tribe, troop, pod, or flock.

CORVIDS UP CLOSE

If corvids are native to your region, why not encourage these bright, garrulous birds to visit your yard? Keep ground feeders or lawns stocked with sunflower seeds and peanuts (the latter is a particular favorite of crows and jays). If there are not ample branches around your property for roosting, install horizontal wooden crossbars on raised poles—crows, in particular, are naturally sociable and in winter will roost together in the thousands along waterways or in woodlands. Remove any hanging bells or wind chimes that might startle cautious birds. A decoy crow or two from a fish and game shop will also bring corvids down to investigate.

Crows' innovative tool-making abilities exceed those of chimps.

(left) A hooded crow *(Corvus cornix)* looks over a ring dropped on the sidewalk. It is true that corvids are attracted to small objects, but they do not steal shiny trinkets just because they like them, as folklore insists, but rather they investigate anything that might be edible.

(middle) Among the smartest of birds, the magpie is also one of the few animals to recognize its own reflection.

(right) Along with the usual vocalizations, researchers have noted that ravens also use gestures to communicate, such as pointing with their beaks to indicate an object or holding up an object to get a flock mate's attention.

Black-billed Magpie

Pica hudsonia

Favorite plants

- elderberry
- black currant
- blackberry
- blueberry

This large, striking member of the crow family, also known as the American magpie, is a widespread resident of western rangelands. Its history with humans in this country is a long one—magpies followed bison-hunting Native Americans for scraps and pilfered from the Lewis and Clark expedition.

The bird's slender body is an inky black with white shoulders, a white belly, and iridescent blue-green flashes on the wings and the long, diamond-shaped tail. In flight, magpies glide gracefully, showing the white markings on their primary feathers. Like other members of the Corvidae, magpies walk upright, taking actual steps, rather than hopping from place to place as smaller birds do.

Many people find these garrulous magpies intriguing and entertaining, but

The yellow-billed magpies (*Pica nuttalli*) of the oak woodlands of California's Central Valley, which crosses the range of the black-bills, are found nowhere else in the world. They are identical to black-bills, except for the yellow bill and streak around the eye. Like all magpies, they are highly intelligent birds that roost together in flocks, and they react to the death of a flock mate in a curious manner: exhibiting grief, standing vigil, and holding "funerals," during which they place grass stems beside the body.

Magpies are often maligned as thieves of jewelry and other shiny treasures, but a recent study showed that they were actually deterred from feeding by the presence of shiny objects.

early in the last century, farmers and ranchers hunted black-bills as pests; populations also suffered when birds ingested poisoned bait left for predators. Their numbers are now stable, and the species has a range that extends across the western states, barring the arid Southwest and the Pacific coastline, and into Canada as far north as Alaska. They are not generally migratory, but some mountain birds relocate to protected lowlands during harsh weather. Their preference is for semi-open terrain—fields, conifer groves, streamsides, forest edges, sagebrush plains, farm country, and suburban areas. They avoid dense, unbroken forests or treeless grasslands.

Black-bills are omnivores, but they consume more insects than their corvid cousins, foraging on the ground for beetles, grasshoppers, and worms, and they will pick ticks off deer, elk, and moose. They eat seeds and berries as well as hunt small rodents and scavenge carrion, most often in large groups.

Once mated, magpies remain monogamous throughout the year. Both partners help to construct a very large domed—or "bushel basket"—nest typically made of twigs and located in the tops of trees. Some nests can take a month to complete, and if they disagree on location, each bird in a pair may begin a nest on its own. Females lay from one to nine tan or olive brown speckled eggs, which will hatch in 16 to 19 days. Parents share in the task of raising their young, which is a good thing, because the nestling period can last up to a month. Outside breeding season, these magpies commonly form flocks.

BRIBING BLACK-BILLED MAGPIES

These personable birds have wide-ranging appetites and will often come to large yards with platform or ground feeders stocked with sunflower seeds, cracked corn, fruit, millet, milo, peanut hearts, and peanuts. They also visit suet feeders.

Basics

LENGTH
18 to 24 inches

WINGSPAN
24 inches

WEIGHT
0.071 to 0.212 ounce

LONGEVITY
4 to 6 years; record is 9 years, 4 months.

VOCALIZATION
Call is a nasal *mag-mag-mag* or *yak-yak-yak* or a whistle.

DISTRIBUTION
Year-round from central California north to southern coastal Alaska and throughout much of the West

(opposite page) Its crisply defined color-blocked plumage of black and white gives the black-billed magpie an elegantly understated appearance.

(bottom) A black-bill finds a perch on the back of an elk in Rocky Mountain National Park. These magpies dine on the ticks they pick off deer, elk, and moose.

Blue Jay

Cyanocitta cristata

Favorite plants

- oak
- beech
- elderberry
- dogwood
- cherry
- blueberry

Both a goofy clown and an occasional predator of small birds and their eggs, this lanky, brash blue bird bugles raucously from suburban tree lines and hungrily haunts bird feeders. It's not surprising that some bird-watchers appreciate their high visibility, and others find them obnoxious.

Members of the Corvidae, or crow family, blue jays display large erect crests and delectable coloring: cerulean blue above, white below, with a black collar band, and wing primaries and tails banded with sky blue, black, and white. The tail is long and broad, the wings rounded, and the bill is heavy and black.

Blue jays are native to North America. When their numbers dwindled in the past century due to the clearing of eastern forests, these resilient birds adapted to city and suburban life, even scavenging at refuse bins. They live year-round in the central and eastern United States, as well as across southern Canada, although some northern populations migrate short distances to warmer regions. They can be erratic migrants, however, migrating one fall, remaining in their territory the following fall; then migrating again the third year. Researchers can find no reason for this lack of consistency.

They prefer dense conifer forests and oak woodlands when acorns are plentiful—their fondness for acorns is believed to have helped spread oak trees across North America after the last glaciers receded. Outside breeding season, jays inhabit orchards, woody verges, picnic grounds, and yards. Their diet includes insects, soft arthropods, small vertebrates like frogs and mice, and nuts and seeds. They may also prey upon injured birds or nestlings. Jays have a neat trick of holding nuts and seeds with their toes and pecking them open.

Jays maintain complex societal and family connections. Courting males put on aerial displays and feed females. Pairs typically mate for life, with both sexes building the cuplike nest of twigs, grass, and mud lined with rootlets. Look for them located high up in a tree crotch or on a

thick branch. The female lays two to seven bluish or brownish eggs: the male provides food for her while she incubates the eggs and for the nestlings after the eggs hatch in 17 to 18 days. Baby jays fledge in 17 to 21 days, but are prone to wander from the nest a few days before they can fly.

BLUE JAY WAY

Blue jays need little encouragement to drop in. They like peanuts (whole or shelled), sunflower seeds, corn cobs, cracked corn, millet, milo, suet, fruit, and mealworms and will approach most types of feeders. If they bully smaller birds, set up separate jay feeders with large treats away from your other feeders. Jays also enjoy cavorting in shallow birdbaths.

Basics

LENGTH
9 to 12 inches

WINGSPAN
13 to 17 inches

WEIGHT
2.60 to 3.26 ounces

LONGEVITY
7 years; record is 17 years.

VOCALIZATION
Call is a harsh *jeer* or musical *queedle-queedle*. The "whisper song" consists of quiet clicks, whirs, and liquid notes.

DISTRIBUTION
Year-round in central and eastern United States and across southern Canada; northern birds may migrate south.

(opposite page) An inquisitive blue jay takes a break from feeding to observe its human company.

(top) A blue jay gorging on peanuts. Blue jays will stuff food in their throat pouch and carry it to a cache, where they stash it to eat later.

similar species: *Steller's jay*

A slightly larger cousin of the blue jay, the Steller's jay *(Cyanocitta stelleri)* is the only crested jay found west of the Rockies. Coloration is variable—most birds are a brilliant blue with darker barring, but the blackish brown head of the northern birds softens to deep blue in the South. They noisily forage high in the canopy for pine seeds, acorns, berries, and fruit and hunt insects and rodents. They are named after German naturalist George Wilhelm Steller, who first recorded the species in 1741.

Steller's jays sport long, shaggy black-brown crests and have blue "eyebrows" above each eye.

Downy Woodpecker

Picoides pubescens

Favorite plants

- sunflower
- elderberry
- blackberry
- huckleberry
- holly

Petite and acrobatic, this woodland resident is frequently seen hanging off suet feeders during the colder months. The smallest of North America's woodpeckers and a member of the family Picidae, which also includes sapsuckers, piculets, and wrynecks, downy woodpeckers are widespread across the continent, except in the very cold north or driest desert habitats.

Their plumage features a broad white stripe down the back, black-and-white checks across the wings, and a black eye line bisecting white cheeks. The male displays a red head patch. These birds are roughly the size of a nuthatch, with the typical woodpecker physique—compact body, wide shoulders, erect posture, and a strong, straight bill, which in the downy appears small in comparison to the body.

Little Drummer Bird

Woodpeckers can be quite vocal, with shrill cries that resound through the woodland, but they do not sing in the sense that other birds do. They use a different tactic to establish territory or attract a mate: they hammer forcefully on trees with their powerful bills. When you hear this staccato drumming, which can carry great distances, you might assume that they are feeding. The truth is, woodpeckers are surprisingly quiet when excavating bark for insects or grubs.

Although these diminutive woodpeckers are found in wilderness areas like deciduous forests, second-growth woodlands, willow stands, and river groves, they have also adapted to less rural habitats like orchards, parks, picnic groves, vacant lots, and suburban yards.

They are for the most part nonmigratory and tend to flock with small songbirds such as chickadees and nuthatches, especially during cold weather. They are particularly noisy in spring and summer with their whinnying calls and frequent drumming on trees. They feed in the foliage of the canopy or cling precariously to slender weed stems, dining on beetles and their larvae, ants, and caterpillars—and pests like corn earworm, tent caterpillars, bark beetles, and apple borers. Roughly one quarter of their diet consists of plant matter like berries, grains, and seeds, especially acorns. In winter, downies will excavate tree bark for grubs—exploring with distinctive up, down, and horizontal movements.

Males and females feed in separate territories, but during breeding season males drum on hollow trees to attract a mate, or males and females may glide together, like butterflies, with slow, graceful wing beats. Both sexes excavate the nesting cavity in a dead or dying tree, a job that can take up to three weeks. Lichen or fungi may obscure the entrance. The female lays three to eight white eggs and incubates them for 12 days. Both parents feed the nestlings, which are ready to fledge in 18 to 21 days. A juvenile's plumage mimics the grown downies', except that the juveniles possess a much larger red cap than the adult male's patch.

GETTING DOWN WITH DOWNIES

These small "flying checkerboards" will reward you with frequent feeder sightings, especially if you supply suet cages. They also enjoy hulled and black-oil sunflower seeds, mealworms, peanut hearts, peanuts, and safflower in hopper and platform feeders. And make sure that they always have a source of fresh water in the winter.

Basics

LENGTH
5.5 to 7.1 inches

WINGSPAN
9.8 to 12.2 inches

WEIGHT
0.71 to 1.16 ounces

LONGEVITY
4 to 11 years in the wild

VOCALIZATION
Call is a descending whinny; note is a flat *pick*.

DISTRIBUTION
Most of North America except northern Canada and the deep Southwest

(opposite page) A male downy woodpecker. The small red patch at the back of the head helps distinguish it from the female.

(left) A female downy feeding on a selection of mixed grains and seeds.

(right) This brave downy is barely bigger than the hand that feeds it. Offerings of seeds such as black-oil sunflower can help you attract these comical birds.

Hairy Woodpecker

Picoides villosus

Favorite plants

- serviceberry
- cherry
- plum
- holly
- oak acorns

The hairy woodpecker may look like a scaled-up version of the downy woodpecker—with nearly identical checked plumage and a red crown on the male—but the two species are not closely related. Their similarity is considered an example of convergent evolution, when different animals independently develop the same useful traits, in this case dappled woodland camouflage.

The plumage of these medium-sized woodpeckers includes a wide white back stripe, contrasting black-and-white barred wings, and white cheeks with a black eye line. The tail is strong and pointed, supplying a brace for hammering, and the bill is proportionately larger than that of the downy, nearly the length of the head. Hairies feed by hitching up and along substantial tree branches in search of

insects like the larvae of wood-boring beetles, ants, caterpillars, bees, wasps, and spiders, along with berries, nuts, seeds, and sap. In flight, they exhibit the typical woodpecker undulations.

Hairy woodpeckers are not migratory, but remain year-round residents of mature woodlands across North America and into Central America. Their loud, sputtering calls echo over open pine, oak, and birch stands, mixed forests, river groves, prairies, southern swamps, and recently burned tracts, as well as more developed settings such as cemeteries, parks, and suburban backyards—and any place infested with bark beetles.

Males and females lead separate lives once breeding season ends, but in spring they frequently pair up with their mate from the previous year, with the female's winter turf determining the location of the nest. Courting couples drum together as a mating ritual, and females will also tap at symbolic nesting sites. Both sexes help excavate a nesting cavity—in tall deciduous trees in the East, in aspens and dead conifers in the West. The female lays three to six white eggs, which both birds take turns incubating. When the babies hatch in 16 days, both parents

feed them. Even after their offspring fledge, usually within 30 days, the parents continue to tend them.

WHAT HAIRY WOODPECKERS WANT

These striking, patterned birds will investigate yards and gardens that offer feeders stocked with black-oil and hulled sunflower seeds, mealworms, peanut hearts, peanuts, and safflower and suet in hanging cage feeders. Also, any dead or dying trees on your property are potential homes to nesting hairy woodpeckers—and then, subsequently, to wrens, chickadees, nuthatches, and even flying squirrels.

The Sapsucker Story

Sapsuckers belong to the woodpecker genus *Sphyrapicus*, which comprises four species: the red-naped (*S. nuchalis*) of the Rocky Mountains and the Great Basin; the red-breasted (*S. ruber*), which breeds from Alaska down along the West Coast; the Williamson's (*S. thyroideus*), found from Mexico north to British Columbia; and the sapsucker shown below, the yellow-bellied (*S. varius*), which ranges across Canada and the Northeast, with a discreet population in the Appalachians. These are slender black-and-white birds, with red markings on the head or chin. They feed by creating a series of holes in tree bark and lapping up the oozing sap. Insects trapped in the sap become food for their young. Sapsuckers can damage delicate trees, like birch, and many foresters consider them pests.

Basics

LENGTH

7.1 to 10.2 inches

WINGSPAN

13 to 16.1 inches

WEIGHT

1.4 to 3.4 ounces

LONGEVITY

4 to 11 years in the wild; more than 15 years in captivity

VOCALIZATION

Call is a rattling sputter; note is a sharp *tweek*.

DISTRIBUTION

Year-round across North America, as far north as Alaska, and south to Central America

(opposite page) A male hairy woodpecker checks out the stump of a newly cut tree. The hairy woodpecker's appetite for insects has helped control pest outbreaks such as those of codling moths in orchards or severe bark beetle infestations in live trees.

(top) A female at a backyard suet cage feeder. These woodpeckers prefer dining on suet or sunflower seeds.

Red-bellied Woodpecker

Melanerpes carolinus

Favorite plants

- hawthorn
- silver maple
- oak acorns
- hackberry
- grape
- mango
- orange

This denizen of America's eastern and central woodlands is one of three continental woodpeckers—the downy and the hairy being the other two—that regularly visit bird feeders. Red-bellies are so mild mannered around humans, they can seem almost tame.

The common name might be misleading for novice bird watchers, because it is the male's bright red cap—or red nape in the female—that is more visible in the field than the orange-red patch on the belly. The back and wings have a distinctive black-and-white barred pattern, but the cheeks and undersides are a light gray or buff, making this bird paler in overall appearance than other woodpeckers.

Red-bellies produce a variety of noisy vocalizations, including a rolling call that helps to identify them when they are feeding

in the foliage. They also create a clatter while drumming—hammering on hollow trees, aluminum roofs, and metal gutters.

They live year-round in the central and southern states and have extended their range to the Great Lakes and New England. This latter adaptation occurred after numbers began declining in the early 20th century. They are found in deciduous forests, in mixed woodlands, along rivers, and in swamps, as well as open areas— forest edges, clearings, farms, orchards, suburban yards, and city parks.

These birds forage on tree trunks for insects and arthropods, but can also take prey on the wing. Occasionally they hunt small reptiles, birds, or minnows. In some seasons, half their diet is made up of plant materials, including acorns, pine cones, nuts, seeds, berries, and fruit. They are considered beneficial by farmers and foresters because they consume many harmful insect pests, including the destructive emerald ash borer.

Males protect their territory with antagonistic displays—posturing with the wings, slow floating flights, and puffing up the head feathers. Courtship includes ritual drumming and the preliminary excavation of several nesting holes in soft-wood trees such as elm or willow. The female selects which nest the pair will complete. Drilled holes are then placed nearby to warn off intruders. The female lays four or five white eggs, which hatch in 12 to 14 days. Both parents feed the nestlings, sometimes for weeks after they fledge, usually in 22 to 27 days. Southern pairs may produce up to three broods a year.

RED-BELLY REST STOP

Bring these lively birds to your yard by providing suet in a cage or stocking a large hopper or platform feeder with sunflower seeds, cracked corn, sliced oranges, mealworms, peanut hearts, peanuts, or safflower. Red-bellies will also sip nectar water from hummingbird feeders.

Basics

LENGTH
9 to 10.5 inches

WINGSPAN
15 to 18 inches

WEIGHT
2.6 ounces

LONGEVITY
12 years on average, up to 20-plus years in the wild

VOCALIZATION
Call is a *thraa-thraa-thraa* and *chur-chur-chur;* song is *chiva-chiv-a* or a low *grr-grr* during courtship.

DISTRIBUTION
North from the South and the Great Plains to southeastern Canada and New England

(opposite page) Although its common name is red-bellied woodpecker, the male of the species is known for its sleek red head and bold black-and-white striped back.

(top) The female red-belly has a red nape and reddish feathers around the base of her bill. They are frequent visitors to backyard feeders.

similar species: *red-headed woodpecker*

It may appear similar to the red-bellied woodpecker, but the red-headed woodpecker (*Melanerpes erythrocephalus*) displays a full cowl of crimson over the head and large color blocks of black and white on the body. The call is a shrill, raspy *queeah!* Its year-round range extends throughout the East, from southern Canada to the Gulf States. Red-heads feed on insects, seeds, and berries. Sadly, numbers are declining due to loss of dead trees for nesting and traffic fatalities while chasing after insects.

A denizen of open forests and wetlands, the red-headed woodpecker will also visit suburban yards.

Northern Flicker

Colaptes auratus

Favorite plants

- dogwood
- sumac
- cherry
- grape
- wax-myrtle
- elderberry
- sunflower
- thistle

A northern flicker's speckled brown coloration seems the antithesis of the striking black-and-white plumage so often associated with the Picidae. When it flies, however, this woodpecker displays bright color on the upper primary shafts and lower wings and tail. Categorized as red-shafted in the West and yellow-shafted in the East—the two color morphs were once considered separate species—these birds interbreed where their ranges cross. Flickers also show a black bib on the breast and a white rump; the male sports a bright red nape and red malar stripes (mustaches) in the west and black malars in the east.

Flickers are abundant throughout North America, from Alaska to Nicaragua, but have suffered some loss of nesting sites taken over by starlings. Populations in

Alaska and Canada are migratory in winter—rare for woodpeckers—moving east, then south along the Atlantic coast. Although stateside flickers tend to remain residential, red-shafts in the western mountains may head south or simply seek lower altitudes.

These birds feed in open country, so they avoid unbroken tracts of forests. They are found in open woodlands, fields with scattered trees, swamps, marsh edges, city parks, and suburbs. Some western birds inhabit mountain forests up to the tree line.

Northern flickers perch upright on branches like other woodpeckers but in general do not use their long bills to probe for insects in trees. Instead, they hunt on the ground, foraging in the dirt for beetles, caterpillars, and snails and lapping up ants or termites with their long barbed tongues. They may go aerial for flies, butterflies, and moths. They also feed on many fruits and berries, as well as nuts and seeds.

Courting males call, drum, swing their heads, and spread their wing and tail feathers to impress a potential mate. Both sexes excavate a nesting cavity in a dead pine, willow, quaking aspen, or cottonwood tree a safe distance above the ground. Females lay five to eight white eggs and share incubation duty with males. Nestlings hatch in 11 to 16 days and are fed by regurgitation. They take about a month to fledge, although the adults continue to nurture them, eventually leading them to foraging sites.

FLICKER FEEDER PICKS

Flickers will visit platform or hopper feeders stocked with black-oil and hulled sunflower seeds, cracked corn, millet, peanut hearts, peanuts, and safflower, as well as suet in cage feeders. These birds frequently dig for insects on suburban lawns, sometimes flying up abruptly from the grass and startling unwary humans with their flashing wings.

Basics

LENGTH
11 to 12.2 inches

WINGSPAN
16.5 to 20 inches

WEIGHT
3.9 to 5.6 ounces

LONGEVITY
9 years 2 months for yellow shafts; 8 years, 9 months for red shafts

VOCALIZATION
Call is a loud, squeaking *wicka-wicka-wicka* or a piercing *ki-ki-ki-ki;* note is a sharp *peough.*

DISTRIBUTION
Across the North American continent

(opposite page) A male northern flicker displays the red-shafted coloration found in the western states. When he is at rest, just the red on the underside of the tail is visible.

(top) A red-shafted flicker in flight shows the red shafting between the flight feathers, which glow orange against the bright sunlit sky.

(left) A female searching in the grass for food. Northern flickers will climb up the trunks of trees to hammer on wood, but they prefer to forage on the ground.

(right) A northern flicker—displaying the chrome yellow shafts and black malar stripes of the eastern color morph—dines at a suet feeder on a snowy afternoon. These birds are frequent guests in yards that offer winter nourishment.

Those Elusive Woodpeckers

ATTRACTING THESE UNIQUE BIRDS TO YOUR YARD

An imposing pileated woodpecker *(Hylatomus pileatus)* accepting the offerings at a suet feeder. In winter, when the insects they feed on have died off, woodpeckers appreciate this high-energy food. You can help these vigilant birds relax by placing the bird feeder on a tree located in a quiet, sunny spot.

Woodpeckers belong to one of the most intriguing bird families: the Picidae. These active, acrobatic birds come in many sizes, from the diminutive downy to the imposing pileated. Their plumage is universally striking and often features splashes of bright red. As nonmigratory birds, they are available for observation throughout the year. Unfortunately, many species are shy or reticent to leave the safety of the woodlands where they dwell. Yet, if you follow these simple tips, you can bring these entertaining beauties to your yard during all four seasons, and you will discover that these birds are champs at exterminating destructive garden insect pests and grubs.

TEMPTING FOODS

There are several food options that will encourage woodpeckers to visit your property, including suet. Bird suet consists of hard cakes of beef and pork fat mixed with seeds, nuts, and berries and is typically provided in a cage feeder. (Avoid suet during hot weather, though, because it can melt and get on birds' wings.)

Many woodpeckers will investigate platform feeders stocked with sliced oranges or apples, which supply necessary nutrients and energy. Peanuts and black-oil sunflower seeds are protein sources that will attract red-headed and red-bellied woodpeckers. Small, high-protein mealworms—available at most pet stores—are the larvae of the beetle *Tenebrio molitor.* Place them on platform feeders with low sides. Mealworms will keep for weeks in a ventilated jar layered with rolled oats.

COMFORTING SPACES

There are several landscape modifications you can make that will encourage these birds to leave the safety of the woods.

Woodpeckers like the security—and potential food resources—offered by trees and shrubs with dense foliage. Make sure your landscape includes at least one clump of evergreens, such as arborvitae, and a few heavily leafed shrubs or deciduous trees. Evergreens will provide nuts and sap, and oak trees offer acorns; fruiting trees or shrubs will also be appreciated.

Woodpeckers enjoy drinking from and bathing in a birdbath situated in a secluded spot. A cold-weather alternative is to place a shallow bowl of water outside each morning as source of clean, unfrozen water.

If your property contains any old stumps or dead trees that are not a risk to buildings, leave them standing as potential sources of insects, roosts, and nesting spots for woodpeckers, including, possibly, the breathtaking pileated. You can create feeding poles by drilling large

Providing Distractions

Woodpeckers don't discriminate where they excavate for insects or nests—and your porch, deck, or house could be at risk. One solution is to distract them with alternative sources of food in dead trees or nesting boxes. You can also place decoy owls or hawks, hang windsocks, or string reflective disks on fishing line in the areas they are damaging to keep them at bay.

holes into a wooden pole and setting it upright in your garden. Fill the cavities with an ongoing supply of suet to encourage many varieties of woodpeckers to dine. Roosting boxes offer shelter during cold weather or nesting sites in the spring. Locate them near trees and set them high on poles in order to eliminate the threat of mammal predators.

You can bring these entertaining beauties to your yard during all four seasons.

(top) A female downy woodpecker. These tiny birds will cling to both suet and tube feeders.

(left) Orange halves are not just for orioles. Red-bellied woodpeckers are particularly fond of the juice of this fruit. Some woodpeckers will even sip the nectar from a hummingbird feeder.

(middle) A hungry hairy woodpecker clings to a peanut feeder. Look for feeders that allow woodpeckers to eat in the same position that they use while hunting insects.

(right) Along with feeders, a birdbath can attract woodpeckers to your yard, such as this golden-fronted woodpecker (*Melanerpes aurifrons*), which is a rare migrant into Texas.

Rufous Hummingbird

Selasphorus rufus

Favorite plants

- penstemon
- red columbine
- Indian paintbrush
- scarlet sage
- gilia
- lily
- fireweed
- nasturtium

These diminutive inhabitants of the Pacific uplands breed farther north than any other members of their family, Trochilidae, nesting from northern California to Alaska and the Yukon. Yet, as soon as the weather turns chilly, they make a beeline—hummingbird line?—for Mexico. Heading north in spring, they hug the lower western slopes of the Rocky Mountains for warmth. In the fall, they follow a more inland route over the Rockies, feeding on late-blooming wildflowers in mountain meadows, some at elevations of more than 12,000 feet.

Rufous hummingbirds breed in open areas, including woodland edges, brushy second-growth habitats, streamsides, thickets, parks, and yards, and in forests up to the tree line. In their Mexican wintering territories, they prefer shrubby

Hummingbirds occur only in the New World. It's easy to understand why these dazzling beauties fascinated European settlers when they first witnessed them darting around wild blossoms. Christopher Columbus mentions them in his writings, and scholars actually pondered whether they might be a cross between a bird and an insect; at one point they were even called flybirds. During later centuries, their iridescent feathers became fashionable as ornaments, a trend that has thankfully ended.

terrain, and oak-pine forests at middle to high mountain elevations.

In addition to their long-distance flying marathons—migratory journeys of 4,000 miles are not unusual—these birds are also known for their feisty attitude. Both sexes jealously guard their favorite browsing patches and will attack any hummer species that challenges them. They feed on plant nectar as well as small insects—plucking aphids off leaves or snagging gnats, midges, and flies in the air, where they maneuver with great skill.

In sunlight, the male's plumage causes it to glow like a living ember—a bright orange on the back and belly with an explosive pop of red-orange on the gorget. Some males show a greenish forehead. The female wears a coat and cap of greenish gold, with white undersides and a ruddy rump and tail; she may display a scaled-down orange gorget. Their bills are long and slender, their wings short, and their tails fold into a point.

A rufous male exhibits typical hummer courting behavior, flying high into the sky and then swooping down toward the female, creating a popping sound with his tail feathers at the bottom of the dive. One male often mates with several females. The female builds the nest, a cup of grasses, moss, spider webs, and plants, which she conceals in the limbs of a tree or in a vine. She will lay two white eggs, which incubate for 15 to 17 days.

These birds are still abundant, but their dependence on finding the right balance of conditions in each habitat makes them vulnerable to climate change, and their numbers have recently begun to decline.

ZEROING IN ON RED

Not only will these agile fliers sip happily at nectar feeders, some rufouses return to certain backyards seeking feeders they had used the previous year. They also appreciate any red trumpet-shaped or tubular blossoms in your garden.

Basics

LENGTH
2.8 to 3.5 inches

WINGSPAN
4.3 inches

WEIGHT
0.1 to 0.2 ounce

LONGEVITY
Record is 8 years, 11 months.

VOCALIZATION
Note is a thin squeal; song is a rapid, trilling *chippy-chip-zee*.

DISTRIBUTION
Breeds from the Pacific Northwest to Alaska and the Yukon, migrates along the Rockies, winters in Mexico

(opposite page) A male rufous hummingbird. Of all the western hummingbirds that occasionally visit the East, this long-distance voyager is the most frequently sighted.

(top) A female rufous hummingbird sipping nectar from a fuchsia blossom. Bright red tubular flowers are most likely to draw this sprightly hummer. Migrating birds might linger in your yard for only a week or two.

(bottom) A female tending her young. She feeds her offspring by regurgitation until they fledge, usually in three weeks.

Allen's Hummingbird

Selasphorus sasin

Favorite plants

- penstemon
- scarlet monkey-flower
- red columbine
- Indian paintbrush
- scarlet sage
- tree tobacco
- eucalyptus
- bottlebrush

Allen's hummingbirds may resemble the rufouses, but these lively, flashy denizens of the far West have a more southerly distribution, living and breeding along a narrow strip of both the California and southern Oregon coastlines. In spite of inhabiting this mild climate, these birds migrate to the foothills and mountains of Mexico. They also like early seasonal departures, heading to their southern range as early as May, making a rather languid migration ending with an August arrival. They may begin their northern migration in December, arriving in their breeding territory in January.

They are found in brushy canyons, moist coastal regions, chaparral, open oak woodlands, streamsides, and suburbs. While wintering in Mexico, they seek out forest edges and high mountain meadows.

similar species: *calliope hummingbird*

The calliope hummingbird (*Selasphorus calliope*) is another jewel of the West, with the male's vibrant green body, white chest, and burst of raspberry at the throat. The female is also greenish, but with rusty sides, and she lacks the colorful gorget. This tough little charmer is not only the smallest bird in North America, it is also the smallest long-distance migrant in the world, traveling from its mountain breeding grounds in the Pacific Northwest to Mexico and pockets of the American South. These birds feed on nectar and insects, often by "hawking"—flying out to catch their prey in midair.

The rich raspberry gorget of the male calliope sets it apart from its cousin, the Allen's hummingbird. This species was named for Calliope, the Greek muse of eloquence and epic poetry.

Allen's hummingbirds have compact bodies, with long bills. From below, the males' plumage shows the same coloring as the rufous—orange sides, white chest and a flashing red-orange gorget with elongated feathers wrapping the throat—but their backs and heads are a luscious, shimmering metallic green. The female and the immature Allen's hummingbirds are so similar to the female rufous—greenish back with rusty sides and pale belly—that observations of their migratory patterns require prior banding in order to differentiate the two species.

Allen's hummingbirds feed on nectar, preferring to hover over flowers and dip their bills deep into the blossoms, as well as tiny insects, and tree sap. They occasionally snatch spiders or trapped insects from spider webs.

Males court potential mates by flying back and forth in a swinging motion like a pendulum, and then performing a high, plummeting dive. During breeding season, the male and female seek different habitats: the male establishes territory in open, coastal scrubland, while the female nests in densely vegetated areas like forests. The nest is a cup made of grass or leaves, camouflaged by moss or bark held on with spider webs, and placed on a shrub branch. The female lays and incubates two white eggs, which hatch in 17 to 22 days. She also feeds the nestlings—in a nest that stretches to accommodate her growing young—until they fledge in 22 to 25 days. Males are not necessarily idle at this time—they are fierce defenders of their territory and have been known to chase off hawks and falcons.

ALLEN'S APPETITES

These lovely amber and green birds are attracted to hummingbird feeders, as well as gardens that offer them a range of red, tubular nectar-producing plants. Even though these birds have adapted well to suburban settings, their populations have recently begun showing some decline.

Basics

LENGTH
3.5 inches

WINGSPAN
4.3 inches

WEIGHT
0.1 ounce

LONGEVITY
4 years in the wild

VOCALIZATION
Call is a low *chup* or a brisk *zeee chuppity-chup.*

DISTRIBUTION
Breeds from southern coast of Oregon down to Baja California; winters in Mexico

(opposite page) A male Allen's hummingbird. These birds take their name from Charles Andrew Allen, an American naturalist and collector of the late 19th and early 20th centuries.

(bottom) A tiny female Allen's hummingbird briefly perches on an aloe vera leaf.

Anna's Hummingbird

Calypte anna

Favorite plants

- currant
- gooseberry
- manzanita
- eucalyptus
- nasturtium

Delicately colored and fast-moving, this bird is found year-round along the Pacific coast, from British Columbia to the Baja and inland as far as Arizona. It may be the only species of hummingbird seen in winter in these regions when others have flown south. On the other hand, some populations of Anna's hummingbirds may head to Mexico if it gets too cold.

Originally native to Southern California and the Baja, these birds increased their breeding territory substantially during the second half of the last century with the mass planting of exotic flowering trees in residential landscapes. They now have the northernmost year-round range of any hummingbird.

Anna's hummingbirds are commonly seen in woodlands, shrubby terrain, small waterways, chaparral, eucalyptus groves, savannahs, and coastal sage scrub, as well as in city parks and gardens. They are common in their range, and their numbers are on the rise as they increasingly adapt to suburban living.

The stocky male displays a bronze-green back, a pale gray chest, and a dark, forked tail, with a crown and throat of shimmering, iridescent magenta. In low light, the head and throat may appear dark red or even black. The female is green above and gray below, with a small magenta gorget.

In addition to feeding on flower nectar and tree sap, these hummers hunt tiny insects such as midges, whiteflies, and leafhoppers—and in a most unusual manner. Rather than trying to skewer flying insects with their sharp bills, they open their beaks wide and zero in on their prey. Anna's are also efficient pollinators: adults can shake their bodies 55 times per second in flight, distributing pollen as they go.

Courting males hover in midair, offer their scratchy metallic song, and then fly more than 120 feet in the air and plummet straight down toward the female, creating a loud popping noise with their tail feathers at the end, a form of sonation. (Males actually orient themselves so that the sun catches their iridescent feathers as they

dive!) Nesting begins in December or earlier, when the female builds a cup of plant fibers and spider webs in a vine or under eaves and lines it with plant down and feathers, often camouflaging the exterior with lichens. She lays two tiny white eggs, and when they hatch, in 14 to 19 days, feeds her young by regurgitating small insects. The nestlings begin to fly in around 18 to 23 days.

MANNA FOR ANNA'S HUMMINGBIRDS
Anna's hummingbirds enjoy sipping nectar water from hanging feeders, as do other hummers. They will also seek out both native and cultivated species of flowering plants in the garden.

Basics

LENGTH
2.8 to 3.5 inches

WINGSPAN
4.7 inches

WEIGHT
0.1 to 0.2 ounce

LONGEVITY
8.5 years

VOCALIZATION
Males produce a buzzy *chee-chee-chee.*

DISTRIBUTION
Year-round along the Pacific coast from British Columbia south to Baja California. Some birds migrate to western Mexico in winter.

(opposite page) Iridescent magenta feathers cover the head and throat of a male Anna's hummingbird. Nineteenth-century French naturalist René Primevere Lesson named this bird after Anna Masséna, Duchess of Rivoli.

(top) A female Anna's hummingbird feeds her young in their well-camouflaged nest.

similar species: *Costa's hummingbird*

The Costa's hummingbird (*Calypte costae*), one of the many hummers that inhabit southwestern Arizona, is a jewel of the desert—the male shows a metallic green back and flanks, black tail and wings, and iridescent purple cap and throat feathers. These birds prefer arid terrain, washes, and sage scrub and any open habitat with a wide cross-section of plants. They feed on nectar from agave, chuparosa (colloquial Spanish for "hummingbird"), and desert honeysuckle blooms and small insects.

The throat of a Costa's is a deep shade of purple compared to the bright magenta of the Anna's.

Ruby-throated Hummingbird

Archilochus colubris

Favorite plants

- trumpet vine
- bee balm
- honeysuckle
- cardinal flower
- columbine
- penstemon
- hollyhock
- foxglove

These tiny jewel-like creatures hover over blooming flowers and unfurl their long tongues to feed on the nectar within. As well as plant nectar, ruby-throated hummingbirds feed on a small insects and spiders, aiding gardeners by consuming destructive aphids.

Even when out of sight, they can be heard buzzing around the garden. They are bold by nature, often ignoring a human presence or comically dive bombing anyone they perceive as a threat.

Ruby-throated hummingbirds, which are members of the Trochilidae family, are the only hummingbird found east of the Mississippi. The males, which are smaller than the females, have an iridescent green upper body, a fiery red throat patch, or gorget, and a forked tail. Females lack the red throat and have a blunt tail.

These aerial acrobats flit and dart with lightning speed and great precision, their wings beating 40 to 80 times a second. Yet, in spite of their flying skills, their relatively small feet make it difficult for them to hop along branches as other birds do. Ruby-throats have one of the highest metabolic rates of any animal: their hearts beat up to 1,260 beats per minute, and they take 250 breaths per minute, even at rest.

These delicate, diminutive birds migrate long distances, spending the colder months in Mexico, Central America, and the West Indies. If they migrate over the Gulf of Mexico, ruby-throats could end up making a nonstop journey of up to 500 miles. In preparation for the journey, the birds will add up to a gram of body weight to sustain them during these long flights.

Ruby-throats do not pair bond after mating, so the female must build her nest alone in a protected tree or shrub. There, she lays two tiny white eggs and does all the parenting. On his part, the male will fiercely protect his territory.

ATTRACTING RUBY-THROATS

Many homeowners hang out red plastic or glass feeders filled with sugar water to tempt hummingbirds into their yards, but these little airborne bundles of energy will also feed wherever their favorite plants are in bloom. They prefer tubular-shaped flowers in bright red, orange, and pink colors, such as the trumpet vine or scarlet bee balm. They also enjoy running-water features in the garden and will happily take advantage of a bird bath.

Basics

LENGTH
2.8 to 3.5 inches

WINGSPAN
3.1 to 4.3 inches

WEIGHT
0.071 to 0.212 ounce

LONGEVITY
Record in the wild is 9 years, 1 month.

VOCALIZATION
Rapid, squeaky chirps as warning; courting males make a *tik-tik tik-tik* with their wings.

DISTRIBUTION
Eastern North America and the southern Canadian prairies to the Maritime Provinces

(opposite page) A male ruby-throat sips from a nectar feeder. These high-energy birds will flock to feeders spring through fall.

(left) A juvenile's red throat is just beginning to show.

(right) A female lacks the red throat of her male counterpart, but all ruby-throats have stunning metallic green backs.

similar species: *black-chinned hummingbird*

The male black-chinned hummingbird (*Archilochus alexandri*) of the West resembles its eastern cousin with its metallic green back and whitish belly. Instead of a ruby throat, however, this small fellow lacks any brilliant color other than a thin strip of iridescent purple bordering its chin—and even that tends to blend in with the black head unless seen in just the right light. Black-chins are widespread in the West, living in diverse habitats, from deserts to mountain forests.

Its chin patch of purple differentiates the black-chinned hummingbird from the ruby-throat.

PART TWO

BEES & Other Beneficial WILDLIFE

Creating a Habitat for Bees

(opposite page) A honeybee approaches a stalk of viper's bugloss, one of its favorite sources of nectar.

Bee Basics

THE ANATOMY & BIOLOGY OF THE BEE

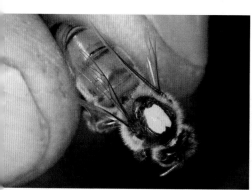

(left) A honeybee queen. Beekeepers often mark these essential bees so that they can easily spot them.

(middle) A drone bee surrounded by workers. The role of these large males is to mate with the queen.

(right) Workers buzz about a hive frame. Accounting for more than 99 percent of a hive's population, these bees perform nearly all the functions necessary to maintain a bee colony.

Bees are flying insects that are closely related to wasps and ants. There are more than 20,000 species found on every continent except Antarctica, divided into seven to nine families. Bees are typically a soft yellow or yellowish brown with dark stripes on the abdomen.

These stripes are significant, warning predators that this small insect will sting to defend itself or its home.

Bees' bodies are composed of three parts: the head, thorax, and abdomen. The head contains two antennae, which provide a sense of touch and smell; two large, faceted, compound eyes, which allow bees to simultaneously see up and down and from side to side; and three smaller eyes, which are sensitive to light and aid in orientation. The two powerful protruding jaws, or mandibles, are used to manipulate objects or repel invaders, not for eating. Bees suck their food through a tubelike tongue, or proboscis.

The armor-plated thorax is the site of the bee's breathing holes, called spiracles, along with two pairs of wings and three pairs of legs. The flight muscles are also located here, allowing bees to beat their wings more than 200 times per second. The forelegs are employed for overall grooming and cleaning the antennae; the hind legs contain transparent pollen baskets, which store this vital protein source during foraging excursions.

The abdomen, also armor-plated, contains such vital organs as the heart, the stomach, and the intestines. Other aspects of bee physiology are specialized for each of three castes: the queen, drone, and worker bees.

THE QUEEN

The queen bee is hatched from a special large cell in the birthing chamber and is fed only royal jelly during the larval stage. She is larger and longer than the other bees, with relatively short wings. Her abdomen contains both oviducts and spermathecae that store millions of sperm and ovaries that produce eggs.

THE DRONE

Drones are larger than workers and have enormous eyes, which are useful during the mating flight. They possess a male sex organ, the endophallus, for inseminating the queen, but they have no stinger. Several drones may mount the queen during the single mating flight, but the drones either die afterward or are ejected from the nest once they have fulfilled their role in reproduction.

THE WORKER

Worker bees are small and compact, but they are truly the backbone of the hive, performing a host of functions. There are glands in their heads that secrete royal jelly, enzymes in their mouths that help turn plant nectar into thick honey, scent glands that produce pheromones, and glands in their lower abdomens that produce flakes of beeswax used for building and maintaining the hive. Their abdomens contain a honey stomach that allows them to transport nearly their own body weight in nectar back to the colony. They also possess a stinger—a modified ovipositor with two barbed spears that inject venom into predatory insects or animals. Workers are female in gender but cannot reproduce. Yet, it is a worker bee's larva that is chosen to transform into a queen when the old queen dies or becomes infertile.

A honeybee's stingers are meant to ward off insect invaders, but if they pierce human skin, the barbed tips become embedded, and when the bee tries to flee, it loses part of its abdomen and dies. If a bee lands on you, don't try to brush it away—it may become alarmed and sting. Wait for it to move off once it has determined you are neither food nor a threat.

A honeybee drinking from a puddle shows its distinct anatomy, with a striped abdomen, nearly transparent wings, compound eye, and tubular proboscis.

A Brief History of Bees

BEES & BEEKEEPING THROUGH THE AGES

Straw skeps are still in use today, although most are now merely decorative or used only as temporary quarters for a hive that has recently swarmed.

Modern bees evolved over millions of years. It is believed they originated in the Far East—the earliest known specimen, a 100-million-year old bee trapped in amber, was recovered in Myanmar (formerly Burma). It is probable that, like wasps, bees were originally carnivores that consumed other insects. At some point bees switched to what was perhaps a more palatable alternative—sucking sweet nectar, a source of carbohydrates, from blooming flowers with their tubular tongues and collecting edible pollen, a source of protein, from the plant's interior reproductive organs.

That is when a curious thing occurred: the sticky, powdery pollen the bees picked up on their legs from the plant's male anther was transferred to the female stigma, either of that same plant or of other similar plants, replicating the fertilization process that produces fruit and seeds. Many plants are not great at self-pollinating, and cross-pollination is often left to the wind. Yet, once bees became an effective part of this process, flowering plants actually evolved many different enticing forms, colors, and markings to attract more bees and thus ensure more pollination . . . and more progeny.

THE SWEET LIFE

Bees not only play a key role in pollinating crops and garden plants, in the case of the widespread western honeybee *(Apis mellifera)* they also produce commercially valuable honey, beeswax, royal jelly, and propolis. Most bees prefer a solitary existence, like mining bees, which live in underground burrows. Honeybees, on the other hand, form large hive colonies with a complex social order. It is here they create hexagonal wax combs in which the nectar that foraging workers ingested in their "honey sacs" is then stored. House bees repeatedly remove this nectar, "chewing" it to break down the complex sugars into simple sugars more resistant to bacteria. As house bees continuously fan their wings, evaporation takes place, and the substance condenses into honey. This honey reserve is critical to the life of the hive—feeding the larvae and workers and helping colonies in temperate regions survive winters without flowers.

Some scientists rank the discovery and harvesting of honey just below the mastery of fire as a life-sustaining turning point in human history. It became a source of sustenance and in early civilizations was the only sweetener available for food and alcohol. Valued as an antiseptic for millennia, it was also used by some early cultures to embalm their dead. The ancient Egyptians began the custom of keeping bees at home, typically housing their hives in an upturned basket later called a skep.

During the Middle Ages, many villages in Europe maintained their own hives, and monasteries kept bees to provide the slow-burning, sweet-smelling beeswax favored for church candles. The Maya of Central America were expert beekeepers—their apiaries featured thousands of hives that likely housed the native stingless bee *Melipona beecheii*.

Beehives made from logs covered in straw at an outdoor museum. These types of hives replicate the natural environment in which bees build their hives. By the time hives such as these were in use in the 16th century, humans had been keeping bees for thousands of years. Bees were such a key part of early cultures that they were actually used as names—both the Hebrew Deborah and the Greek Melissa mean "bee."

A Honeybee's Life Cycle

BEE DEVELOPMENT FROM EGG TO ADULT

All bees go through four stages of metamorphosis, regardless of whether they are honeybees, bumblebees, or solitary bees: egg, larva, pupa, and adult. In most nests, this cycle is ongoing: the queen retains millions of sperm after mating and is able to lay 2,000 eggs per day—and up to one million in her lifetime. The following descriptions are based on honeybees, yet they also reflect many other species.

EGG

After mating with her drones, a young queen begins to lay her eggs in oval cells; in commercial hives workers keep growing larvae in place using royal jelly. The eggs are tiny, roughly half the size of a grain of rice. If the queen chooses a normal-sized cell, she lays a fertilized egg that hatches into a worker. A wider cell receives an unfertilized egg that becomes a drone. The workers that construct the cells determine their size, and therefore regulate the ratio of female workers to male drones in a hive. The eggs hatch in three days.

LARVA

Bee larvae are white and maggot-like—with a nervous system, digestive system, and an outer covering. Although tiny and helpless, they grow quickly, requiring a ready supply of food—sometimes eating as many as 1,300 meals a day. In some species, the larvae are parasitic and feed off paralyzed insects left by the mother; others feed on galls, figs, or pollen balls, also supplied by the mother. Honeybee

larvae are dependent on worker bee brood nurses that feed them a mixture of honey, pollen, and secretions, called bee bread, after an early diet of royal jelly. In six days, the larvae, now 1,500 times larger, are sealed into their cells with beeswax, where they weave silk cocoons and transform into pupae.

PUPA

This is the transitional stage when the bee develops into a recognizable adult. The wings, legs, and antennae begin to take form. The color of the eyes changes from pink to purple, and then black. The fine body hairs develop. Ten or 12 days later, the bee chews its way through the wax cap and emerges fully formed. The workers now quickly clean the cell so that it can be reused.

ADULT

Once the adult honeybee leaves its cell, it is ready to assume its duties, whether outside on the wing or inside the hive. It takes 16 days for queens to complete the cycle, 21 days for workers, and 24 days for drones. Worker bees typically live from 30 to 120 days, drones live 40 to 50 days, and a queen's lifespan is from two to five years.

Most bees have the means to survive cold weather. Honeybees cease collecting nectar and cluster together, shivering to keep warm. This keeps the center of the hive, where the queen resides, close to 80 degrees. Some species hibernate or burrow underground. Others species do die off, but only after the queen has laid a new batch of eggs that will hatch the following spring.

1 **egg-laying queen**
Supported by worker bees, the much larger queen bee lays eggs in the wax cells. Beekeepers become adept at spotting the queen, thus assuring that she is alive and reproducing, a sign that a hive is functioning well.

2 **workers feeding brood**
Worker bees act as brood nurses, keeping the hatched larvae fed. When the larvae reach full growth, the workers cap the cells with wax. Inside the cells, the larvae will spin cocoons and become pupae.

3 **emerging bee**
Inside the cell, a pupa transforms, with its wings, legs, eyes, and other parts of the body developing. Once this process is complete, it will emerge from the chamber by cutting the wax cover with its mandibles.

4 **new adult**
Nearly all the pupae will emerge as workers. These industrious bees perform just about every task in a honeybee colony: building and maintaining the hive; collecting nectar and pollen and turning it into honey; and taking care of the brood.

Hive Dynamics

HOW HONEYBEE COLONIES WORK TOGETHER

(top) Honeybees in the hive. These insects work together to ensure the well-being of the entire colony.

(bottom) Field worker bees flying in and out of a hive. Box hives allow beekeepers to move them from field to field to vary the crops the bees will pollinate.

In nature, honeybees will establish a hive in just about any dark, secluded space in which they can affix their wax combs: in a rock crevice, rotted-out stump, hollow tree trunk, or even under a deck, outbuilding, or porch. A modern commercial box hive replicates these conditions, including the darkness: honeybees work and thrive in a pitch black environment. Yet, regardless of the nest's location, a woodland grove or the yard of a professional beekeeper, hives function in much the same manner.

COLLECTIVE COOPERATION

The credo of any honeybee colony is that the whole hive benefits when everyone works together. The center of the hive, figuratively, is the egg-laying queen . . . and there can be only one. If several larvae are prepped as potential queens, the first one to emerge stings her rivals to death. After a "virgin" mating flight with her drones, 100 million sperm will be stored in her oviducts, enough to fertilize 2,000 eggs a day. If she becomes infertile or dies, the workers create a new queen, ready for her own virgin flight.

A hive contains a single queen and perhaps a 1,000 drones, but there might be as many as 60 times that amount of workers. And from the day they leave their pupal cocoons, most workers follow the same career path—first cleaning nesting cells; followed by acting as nurse bees, responsible for feeding voracious larvae; and then fanning the hive to keep it cool. At 12 days old, their bodies begin producing wax from the sugar found in nectar. It takes ten ounces of honey to yield one ounce of beeswax, which workers use to create a series of hexagonal cells called combs that store honey and pollen and house the birthing chambers.

At around 17 days, the workers take their turn as entrance guards, stinging or ejecting predators. Finally, month-old workers fly off to gather food as field bees. This may seem like a promotion after repelling invaders, but honeybees can travel 50 miles a day as they forage and repeatedly return to the hive with their booty. It's not surprising that most worker bees die from exhaustion.

RUNNING AWAY TOGETHER

If a hive becomes overcrowded, the colony will divide in a swarm. Workers will prepare a new queen, and soon after up to 60 percent of them will fly away with the existing queen. The swarm may rest on a tree trunk or building while scouts seek locations for a new hive.

Beekeepers happily re-home these bees, which can be quite docile at this time, by vacuuming them up. Many states protect honeybees, so if a swarm settles under or near your house, be sure to contact bee removal experts rather than exterminators. If food is scarce, an entire colony may abscond, abandoning the hive in search of better conditions.

DANCING IN THE DARK

Honeybees can let their hive mates know of the best places to forage . . . by dancing. When field bees discover a significant

new source of food, they communicate the location to other bees in the hive by performing a "happy dance"—either a circular dance that indicates that the food is less than 100 meters away or a figure-eight, abdomen-shaking waggle dance that tells the other bees that the source is more than 100 meters away. The length of the dance communicates the find's distance from the hive, left or right turns indicate direction, and the bee's odor reflects the type of plant.

A swarm of honeybees. When a colony becomes crowded inside its current hive, workers will begin to raise a new queen. The old queen will then leave the colony, followed by up to two-thirds of the workers and some of the drones. The workers cluster around her to protect her and keep her warm. While swarming, the workers do not have any brood or honey to protect, so they are usually very gentle and will rarely sting.

The Art of Beekeeping

MAINTAINING A HIVE HELPS KEEP HONEYBEES ALIVE

(left) A rural beekeeper in full protective gear removes a hive frame to assess the health of the hive.

(middle) Bees flying out and then later returning with pollen-filled pouches is a sign that your hive is functioning well.

(right) A bee hive sits in the middle of an urban rooftop garden. Honeybees are adaptable insects that can thrive just about anywhere: in the city, countryside, or suburban backyard, readily traveling for miles to collect nectar and pollen.

The worldwide decline of the honeybee population is making headlines. Large commercial beekeepers, in particular, are seeing population numbers drop. Yet, there is some good news—home beekeepers are having fewer problems and are maintaining a steadier number of healthy hives. Not only are these beekeepers harvesting pure, wild honey for their own use, they are also benefiting their local areas—honeybees pollinate crops and garden plants as far away as four miles. And more good news—once hives are up and running, they require very little care.

Almost anyone can keep bees, but before you rush out to buy the gear, you may want to educate yourself about what to expect. Check your local extension service, which may offer courses or can suggest a local beekeeper, one who can guide you through your first season and help you understand how to avoid potential problems. You should also check local laws—in many areas, especially urban ones, beekeeping is prohibited. In other regions, regulations limit the number of hives you can maintain.

A BEEKEEPER'S PRIMER

It is best to set up your hives after the last hard freeze in the spring and have your equipment in place before you order your bees. Basic equipment includes stackable hive boxes, called supers, and frames with wax foundations, which are imprinted with the pattern honeybees will create as they make the comb.

Next, you will require protective clothing—a zippered bee suit, veiled helmet, and gloves. Other necessary equipment includes a stainless steel smoker, frame grips, and other hand tools. Your initial financial outlay may be high, but once you are set up there will be few additional costs.

Situate the hives where the bees will have a clear flight path and face few disruptions from humans or pets. If possible, set them on bricks or concrete blocks to keep out rain or insect invasions, being sure, however, to keep them level from side to side, with the fronts angled just slightly lower than the rear. This will ensure that any rainwater drains out of the hives.

Ideally, they should be situated on a south-facing slope—to access warm morning light—and protected from prevailing winds by a hedge. If a natural water source is not nearby, supply a birdbath or water basin.

Once you've set up their new home, it is time to bring in the bees, which are available online. Each hive will need worker bees and an egg-laying queen. It takes three pounds of bees to fill a hive—that comes to as many as 12,000 bees!

A week after you've installed the bees, check to make sure that the queen is laying. A smoker can help you access the hive; smoke not only masks alarm pheromones, it also causes bees to panic—believing the hive is on fire, they gorge on honey. Bees with engorged abdomens usually can't sting. If the queen is laying and the bees are busily flying in and out of the hive, you can assume all is well.

Within a month, the brood will begin hatching, and the hive will then go on to reproduce rapidly during the warm summer months. When it is time for your first harvest, leave most of the honey for the bees to consume over the winter, taking only a bit for yourself in late summer.

A beekeeper uncapping the cells on a frame to harvest both the wax and the honey within. Each frame can hold more than six pounds of honey, so when you harvest, share some of the honey with your neighbors, who may have been skeptical about having bees buzzing in their area . . . a little good will can go a long way.

A Bee Garden

SELECTING & ARRANGING PLANTS TO ATTRACT BEES & OTHER POLLINATORS

tip

Learn the value of weeds. Instead of grabbing the herbicide to rid your lawn of dandelions and clover, let them flower and go to seed. Don't mow or uproot dandelions in the early spring, especially. These yellow blooms are some of the first plants to provide food for hungry bees before the fruit trees come into blossom.

Pollination is essential for a thriving garden—and a thriving ecosystem—and there are no better pollinators than bees. Home gardeners can do their small share to keep bee populations from waning by choosing plants that will welcome bees to the yard. There is a multitude of choices—bees will come buzzing for a host of plants, including

pollen- and nectar-rich species of native wildflowers, flowering vegetables and herbs, berry bushes and shrubs, fruit trees, and old-fashioned varieties of annuals and perennials. Larger trees, such as maple, willow, and black locust, also supply bees with food sources.

WHAT BEES NEED

Provide both food and water sources. When choosing plants for a pollinator-friendly garden, think native. Hardy, low-maintenance varieties are more likely to lure the local indigenous pollinators to your yard. Mix annuals, perennials, and

shrubs that bloom in succession so that nectar and pollen will be available throughout the growing season. In early spring, for example, the bell-shaped flowers of the snowdrop (*Galanthus* spp.) will give bees a source of food when it is otherwise scarce. Later in the year, the herb rosemary (*Rosmarinus officinalis*), with its long blooming season in most areas, can supply nectar well into winter.

Allow bees to collect the pollen and nectar they need by leaving the flowers on your plants and not deadheading them. Harvest herbs and vegetables for your own use, but still leave the plant

1 common foxglove
(Digitalis purpurea)
Bumblebees love foxgloves, and no wonder: the structure of the dramatic purple blooms was entirely developed by the visits of this insect.

2 scarlet bee balm
(Monarda didyma)
Showy scarlet red flowers brighten a garden, and bees—especially long-tongued ones—enjoy the tubular blooms of this aromatic herb.

3 zinnia
(Zinnia spp.)
A must-have in any garden designed to attract bees, as well as birds and butterflies. Its colorful, long-lasting flowers will produce nectar well into the fall season.

4 borage
(Borago officinalis)
Known as the bee herb, borage boasts cobalt blue flowers that sit atop a leafy mound of green foliage. In summer, the starry blooms will ooze nectar.

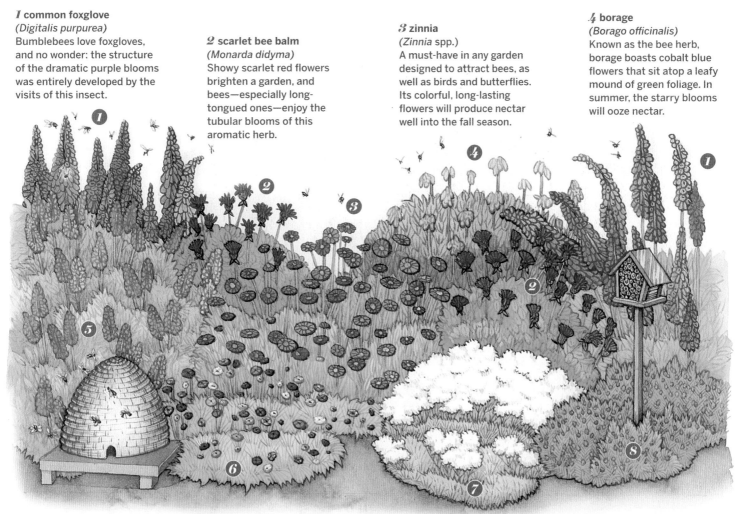

5 garden sage
(Salvia officinalis)
The sage family is a great choice for attracting bees and other pollinators. Garden, or culinary, sage attracts honeybees.

6 sweet William
(Dianthus barbatus)
This charming cottage garden favorite will lure bees with its variegated flowers—and its sweet perfume is heavenly.

7 common yarrow
(Achillea millefolium)
Its flat-topped clusters of tiny disk and ray flowers provide pollen for honeybees.

8 rosemary
(Rosmarinus officinalis)
This classic culinary herb will supply bees with an early-spring food source and keep them in nectar during the winter months.

intact, and uproot annuals only after the flowers are completely gone.

Providing a water source is essential: honeybees use water to make honey and cool the hive. It need not be elaborate—simply place a few stones or corks in a water-filled dish or shallow birdbath so that bees can perch on them. You can also create a bee water station by leaning a board underneath the slowly dripping faucet of a rain barrel.

Bees and other pollinators also need shelter to hide from predators, to protect them from the elements, and to give them a place to rear their young. You can let a bit of your yard and garden go native (see pages 22–23) or even erect artificial nesting boxes to encourage pollinators to set up housekeeping in your area.

And finally, avoid using pesticides, herbicides, or other chemicals whenever possible. Many of them—even the organic ones—are toxic, not only to bees and other pollinators, but also to yourself and your family members, your pets, and other backyard wildlife.

A bee-friendly plan
You can use this plan to begin cultivating a spot in your yard for bees and other pollinators. Many of the plants shown above will return each year and spread moderately. Though all are illustrated in bloom, not all species shown flower at the same time. Your goal is to create a succession of blooms that will supply bees with pollen and nectar for as many months as possible.

∿ TOP 10 ∾

PLANTS TO ATTRACT BEES

Cultivating a bee-friendly garden is easy—bees are attracted to a vast variety of plants, including annual and perennial flowers, wildflowers, herbs, and even lawn grasses. Plan a mix of species that blooms throughout the growing season to lure all kinds of beneficial pollinators.

1 LAVENDER (*Lavandula* spp.)
The highly scented, nectar-rich blooms of lavender draw both honeybees and bumblebees at the height of summer.

2 SNOWDROP (*Galanthus nivalis*)
These early-flowering blooms give honeybees a source of nectar when it is scarce. The single-flowered varieties are best for bees.

3 MARJORAM (*Origanum majorana*)
This fragrant culinary herb with small pinkish white flowers ranks as a favorite with honeybees, bumblebees, and other bees.

4 BORAGE (*Borago officinalis*)
The cobalt star-shaped flowers are the superstars of nectar producers; honey made from borage tastes especially sweet.

5 VIPER'S BUGLOSS *(Echium vulgare)*
This flower produces copious amounts of nectar and pollen May through September, providing vital winter stores.

6 APPLE *(Malus* spp.)
Honeybees love the nectar of apple blossoms and will flock to them in spring—also pollinating your fruit crop while they feed.

7 BEE BALM *(Monarda* spp.)
Its common name attests to its superb ability to attract all sorts of bees from petite honeybees to large black bumblebees.

8 COMMON FOXGLOVE *(Digitalis purpurea)*
These showy, bell-shaped flowers come with a large landing lip so that bumblebees can reach the nectar deep inside the blooms.

9 CLOVER *(Trifolium* spp.)
Many species of these flowers draw bees—red clover is a favorite of bumblebees, and white and alsike produce light, sweet honey.

10 COMFREY *(Symphytum officinale)*
All kinds of bumblebees and solitary bees, as well as honeybees, feed on these small nectar-rich bell-shaped flowers.

CHAPTER FOUR

Bees & Other Pollinators

. . . .

(opposite page) A bumblebee collects the pollen from an aster. These hardy blooms are favorites of many pollinators.

Know Your Bees

THE BEES MOST LIKELY TO VISIT YOUR YARD & GARDEN

(left) A western honeybee sips nectar from a thistle flower. These well-known "basic" honeybees are now distributed worldwide.

(middle) Its sparse abdomen hair helps distinguish the European dark bee, which has a deep, rich brown color.

(right) A Carniolan bee. These zealous pollen gatherers are known for their high honey production.

Although there are more than 4,000 native species of bees in the Americas, those that produced honey could not satisfy the needs of early settlers. By the 1600s, the more prolific honeybees from Europe were being imported to the New World, and bee husbandry sprang up in many towns. Not surprisingly, great numbers of these bees escaped their hives and became naturalized in the vast, fertile wilderness of their new home continent.

In the beekeeper's search for the perfect honeybee or hybrid, certain strains come into vogue, and others lose popularity. The stalwarts have been the bees that produced the most honey; the ones that best adapted to commercial hives; and those that proved most resistant to disease and parasites.

WESTERN HONEYBEE

Also known as the European and the common honeybee, *Apis mellifera* originated in Africa but soon spread throughout Eurasia. Early settlers introduced this foundation bee—and several subspecies—to the Americas.

EUROPEAN DARK HONEYBEE

Also known as the German black bee or simply the black bee, the European dark bee (*Apis mellifera mellifera*) also came to North America with the earliest European settlers. These bees are very dark and can be irritable when handled.

ITALIAN HONEYBEE

An important subspecies of the western honeybee, the Italian honeybee (*Apis mellifera ligustica*) was first imported to the United States in 1859, and it quickly became a favorite with beekeepers, which it remains today. These pale bees have lengthy brooding periods, are disease resistant, and are prolific honey producers.

CARNIOLAN HONEYBEE

Mild-mannered Carniolan honeybees (*Apis mellifera carnica*) originated in middle Europe and have long been a favored stock in the United States—they proliferate in the spring to take advantage of early bloomers.

BUMBLEBEES

These stocky, fuzzy members of the genus *Bombus* create small colonies, sometimes underground, and are important pollinators currently suffering a decline. Like honeybees, they display aposematic, or warning, color banding to indicate that the females will sting.

MINING BEES

Known for burrowing and reproducing underground, the *Andrena* genus includes more than 1,300 species of bees. Many mining bees are beneficial pollinators.

OTHER HONEYBEES

Other honeybees of note not covered here in depth are the Caucasian, the Buckfast, and the Russian honeybees.

Caucasian honeybees (*Apis mellifera caucasia*) are native to the Ural Mountain foothills. These docile, once-popular bees possess long tongues that allow them access to a wide range of flowers. Their honey crops can be low, however, and their overuse of propolis, a sticky resin called "bee glue," makes their hives difficult to manipulate. Beekeepers do harvest propolis, however, for its value in traditional medicine. Propolis is also harvested commercially to be used as an ingredient in waxes for stringed instruments, such as violins, and for automobiles.

Buckfast honeybees emerged when British hives were decimated in the 1920s by acarine disease, now believed to be caused by the ectoparasitic tracheal mite *Acarapis woodi*. Brother Adam of Buckfast Abbey, a Benedictine monastery in Devon, eventually developed a bee mainly from Italian stock mixed with other subspecies of *A. mellifera* that not only has excellent housekeeping skills to keep down the disease but is also a fine honey producer.

The Russian honeybee, a strain of *A. mellifera* from the Primorsky Krai region near the Sea of Japan, has survived decades of contact with the devastating ectoparasite *Varroa destructor* and is now being considered by American beekeepers for its resistance to the mite.

fact

Bees belong to the order of insects known as Hymenoptera, which is derived from the Greeks words *hymen* and *ptera*, meaning "membrane wings."

(left) A common eastern bumblebee (*Bombus impatiens*) collects pollen from red clover. This species of bumblebee is one of the most important pollinators used in North American commercial greenhouses.

(middle) A female yellow-legged mining bee (*Andrena flavipes*) on a forget-me-not flower. Although nearly all female mining bees have stingers, the stingers are usually too small to penetrate human skin.

(right) A Buckfast honeybee collects pollen from the center of a coneflower. This strain of bee was developed mainly from the Italian subspecies of the western honeybee. It was named for the Benedictine monastery in which it was bred.

Western Honeybee

Apis mellifera

Favorite plants

- crocus
- wintergreen
- lavender
- lobelia
- grape hyacinth
- borage
- apple
- aster

Western honeybees, also known as European or common bees, are not only renowned producers of honey, they are also highly valued pollinators of plants, trees, and crops. They are such exemplary performers that for centuries they have remained one of the most popular honeybees in the world. Commercially, western honeybees and a number of their races have become established components of the agricultural system of the United States.

In spite of their industrious natures, these are small bees, the workers averaging only a half inch in length. They are covered with numerous hairs, display black-and-yellow banding on the abdomen and, when seen from above, are "thread-waisted"—unusually narrow—between the thorax and abdomen.

Entomologists suspect the *Apis* genus might be a relatively late arrival to the biosphere—solitary bees populated every fertile continent on earth, but social honeybees were initially limited to the three continents of the Old World. In the case of *A. mellifera,* the species probably arose naturally in eastern tropical Africa about 10,000 years ago, gradually spreading to the temperate regions of Europe and then eastward to Asia and the Tian Shan range in China. An alternative theory suggests that the bees originated in Asia and spread westward. Wherever they sprang from, it was life in these temperate zones, with their shortened foraging seasons, that led western bees to hoard their food resources, which in turn made them outstanding honey producers.

As methods of animal husbandry advanced, western bees consistently proved their worth with bountiful honey crops and superior nest hygiene—which reduces the risk of disease and parasites. When Europeans first colonized North America in the early 17th century, the honey-deprived settlers quickly began importing their most reliable bees— including this bee and its dark cousin, *A. m. mellifera.* Eventually, millions of western honeybees cast off domesticity and spread across both North and South America—where they still forage today.

There are 28 recognized subspecies, or races, of the western honeybee, which are further divided into four branches based on region. The western honeybee was the third insect, after the fruit fly and mosquito, to have its genome mapped. One startling discovery: the genes that regulate their circadian rhythms resemble those of vertebrates more than those of other insects.

WELCOMING WESTERN HONEYBEES

Western honeybees are attracted to most nectar and pollen-rich garden plants, but make sure to have some spring bloomers for bees just emerging from their winter-bound hives—try planting crocus, lily of the valley, witch hazel, and flowering quince to restore these hungry bees.

Basics

SIZE
Worker, 0.5 inch

LONGEVITY
Worker, 6 weeks in summer, 4 to 9 months in cold weather; queen, 3 years

DISTRIBUTION
Worldwide, except Antarctica

(opposite page) A western honeybee sips on the nectar of white clover. The distinct separation between the thorax and abdomen gives rise to this bee's description as "thread-waisted."

(top) Two honeybees head to the center of a purple crocus. Western honeybees are sometimes called European honeybees, not because they originated there, but instead because it was settlers from Europe who first brought them to North America.

similar species: *Africanized honeybees*

An aggressive, heat-tolerant western honeybee subspecies, *Apis mellifera scutellata,* was introduced to Brazil from Africa in the 1950s. Careful crosses with docile local bees were intended to lessen their volatility. Several queens escaped quarantine, however, and began breeding with European bees, resulting in unstable hybrids that attacked and even killed humans. Today, these "killer bees" have reached the American South and Southwest, but cold winters have halted their spread farther north.

An Africanized honeybee, at left, is slightly smaller than the western honeybee, at right.

European Dark Bee

Apis mellifera mellifera

Favorite plants

- heather
- crabapple
- crocus
- borage
- marjoram
- hyssop
- hellebore
- rose

Also known as the German black bee and Western European honeybee, this subspecies of the western honeybee originally ranged from Britain to Eastern Europe and became domesticated during the modern era. It was likely the first honeybee imported to the New World when the native bees, with their meager output of honey, could not satisfy the needs of the colonists.

The European dark is a large and stocky honeybee, with brown and black stripes and distinctive black-veined wings. From a distance, the whole bee appears a rich brown or black. The head and thorax are abundantly hairy, yet the abdomen is relatively smooth. There are three main races: the brown *mellifera,* the black-and-yellow heather bee *lehzani,* and the *nigra,* which is black with dark wings. There are also regional breeds, such as the Alps black, Pomeranian brown, and the black Scandinavian.

These are hardy bees that endure cool, moist climates, overwinter well, and manage a decent yield of honey, even when foraging is poor. They have a strong pollen-collection drive, notable longevity in the worker and queen castes, and are possibly hardy against the *Varroa* mite. Dark bees are also effective hive guardians, repelling wasps and other invaders. On the minus side, they have a slow spring build-up and don't begin foraging as quickly as other races. Although they are generally considered easy to handle, some feral/domestic hybrids can be unpredictable, stinging without provocation.

As other honeybees gained popularity in North America and Europe, this bee fell out of favor. After nearly being wiped out by tracheal mites in the early 1900s, the dark bee was no longer commercially significant. According to the Honey Bee Restriction Act of 1922 and its subsequent amendments, it

is against the law to import these bees into the United States. Over time, the remaining descendants of the original dark bees brought to North America hybridized and became feral. Some of these wild colonies may have shown resistance to the *Varroa* mite outbreak in the 1980s.

WHERE ARE THE DARK BEES?
No original-strain dark bees are left in North America, but based on DNA sequencing analysis, a number of what is known as M lineage bees have been found in Arkansas, Louisiana, Mississippi, Oklahoma, North Carolina, and Missouri. Concerned breeders and research facilities abroad are dedicated to preserving and spreading the original stocks. Only a handful of colonies exist in Germany, but there are now populations of the *lehzani* in Norway, the *mellifera* in Poland and Belgium, and the *nigra* in the Alps. A hive of feral dark bees known as the British black—thought to have been wiped out by the Spanish flu in 1919—were recently rediscovered in a Northumberland church, exciting scientists and local bee breeders.

Natural Enemies

Some honeybee predators are bold enough to invade hives, while others simply attack bees on the wing. Insect threats include the Asian giant hornet, wasps, robber flies, dragonflies, some praying mantids, and the water spider. Other spider predators include fishing spiders, lynx spiders, goldenrod spiders, and the St. Andrew's Cross spider. Toads, anole lizards, American bullfrogs, and wood frogs also make meals of honeybees, as do bee-eating birds like common grackles, ruby-throated hummingbirds, and tyrant flycatchers. Mammals that prey on bees or their hives include bears, opossums, raccoons, honey badgers, and skunks.

Basics

SIZE
0.625 to 1 inch

LONGEVITY
Queen, up to 8 years; workers also live longer than other honeybees.

DISTRIBUTION
Feral hybrids in the American South; cultivated in Germany, Switzerland, Norway, Belgium, and Poland; feral stock in northern Great Britain

(opposite page) The birth of a European dark bee. Originally from Britain and Eastern Europe, this species first arrived in the New World in the 1600s with the earliest European settlers.

(top) Larger than the western honeybee, the European dark bee also has longer hairs on its thorax and a distinctive vein patterning in its wings.

Italian Honeybee

Apis mellifera ligustica

Favorite plants

- clover
- catmint
- angelica
- goldenrod
- lilac
- black locust
- snowdrop
- basil

This attractive honeybee exemplifies many of the positive qualities beekeepers have sought for centuries: it is docile in the hive, a tireless forager, and a honey-making machine. A subspecies of the western, this bee is believed to have originated in continental Italy—south of the Alps and north of Sicily—and probably survived the most recent ice age on the Italian peninsula.

Italian honeybees are generally pale, with brown and yellow bands on the abdomen. Among the different strains, there are three color varieties—workers with three abdominal bands are leather colored; those that are bright yellow are called goldens, and those that are pale yellow are cordovans. They tend to be on the small side with shorter body hair compared to the darker races.

similar species: *Sicilian black bee*

The hardy Sicilian black bee (*Apis mellifera siciliana*) is descended from an African strain and has been cultivated in Sicily for thousands of years. In the 1970s, the Italian honeybee's preeminence threatened the Sicilian bee, which was abandoned commercially and faced extinction. Thanks to the efforts of entomologist Pietro Genduso, as well as concerned beekeepers and farmers, these bees are seeing a revival.

The efforts of small-scale beekeepers across the globe might help to prevent the decline of bees.

Introduced to North America in 1859, these little workhorses quickly usurped the European dark bee that had been introduced by colonists centuries earlier. Among their many advantages, the Italians showed resistance to European foulbrood—a key factor in their replacing the dark bees. They are very hygienic and keep their hives clean, which helps combat disease and parasites; the pale queens are easier to locate than those of darker races; they don't overuse propolis; and workers produce pure white caps over their honey stores, ideal for harvesting commercial crops.

Italians begin brooding in early spring and continue into the fall, creating populous hives capable of gathering substantial amounts of nectar. The downsides are that they continue to brood even when nectar is scarce and these large hives require more honey to sustain them in fall and winter. Other drawbacks include a tendency to drift to other colonies and a strong instinct to rob hives during a dearth of nectar, which can spread disease.

With their Mediterranean origins, Italian honeybees have trouble withstanding cold temperatures—they don't form tight winter clusters inside the hive like western honeybees and so need to compensate for the heat loss by consuming precious reserves. They also don't perform well in humid tropical heat or in cool maritime regions. There are reports that when they hybridize with dark bees, they may become aggressive. Nevertheless, the pale Italians are now the most widely distributed honeybees in the world.

These are the most popular commercial honeybees in the United States—in part due to their willingness to enter supers—the stacked wooden hive boxes that contain the honey frames. Some beekeepers split their hives and introduce Italian queens, which supposedly increases a colony's robustness, to the new ones. These bees also do well in the temperate climates of Australia and New Zealand.

ITALIAN HONEYBEE BANQUET

These vigorous foragers seek out annual and perennial garden favorites, flowering herbs, wildflowers, and many types of berry bushes, as well as fruits and vegetables. They also favor maples, willows, black locusts, and sumacs.

Basics

SIZE
0.5 inch to 0.625 inch

LONGEVITY
Workers, 6 weeks on average; queens, 3 to 5 years

DISTRIBUTION
Worldwide, except Antarctica; prefer temperate climates without extremes of heat or cold

(opposite page) Italian honeybees in the hive, with the queen marked with a blue dot. These relatively gentle bees are known as good "beginner bees" for those new to beekeeping.

(bottom) An Italian honeybee sips the nectar of a thyme flower. This bee is also known as the Ligurian bee, from a region in northwest Italy that supposedly produces the tastiest honey. Another kind of honey from Italy, *millefiori*—meaning "thousand-flower"—combines all the flavors of the Tuscan fields and is considered one of the most healthful varieties.

Carniolan Honeybee

Apis mellifera carnica

Favorite plants

- clover
- stonecrop
- live-forever
- bee balm
- yarrow
- buckwheat
- cherry
- parsley

The Carniolan, a subspecies of the western honeybee, is another large, dark honeybee that might be mistaken for the European dark bee. That dark bee is no longer found in this country, however, so if the population of a pale Italian hive begins to turn dusky one season, the new queens have most likely been consorting with Carniolan drones during their mating flights.

These bees have deep grayish bands or spots on their abdomens—they are also known as gray bees—relieved with bands of gray or brown. They may appear as long as European dark bees, but their abdomens are more slender. Their tongues are quite long, adapted for feeding from clover, and their body hair is very short.

Carniolan honeybees, or Carnies, are native to Eastern Europe—Slovenia,

Croatia, southern Austria, Bosnia and Herzegovina, Serbia, Hungary, and Bulgaria. They first naturalized in and adapted to a region called Carniola, now in Slovenia, as well as in the Alps of southern Austria, the Dinarides region, the southern Pannonian plain, and the northern Balkans.

These bees are enthusiastic gatherers. Other pluses in the hive include early-morning foraging; flying out even in cold or wet weather; searching far afield for resources; a quick response to changes in nectar or pollen availability; the ability to survive winters on small stores because the queen stops laying in fall; and an explosive brood build-up in the early spring. They are extremely gentle to work with and so can be maintained in relatively populated areas. Their sense of direction is superior to the Italians, and, although they use propolis, they do not slather it everywhere as Caucasians do. Carniolans also crossbreed well and are resistant to brood diseases. And even though they have a tendency to swarm and will stop brood rearing if resources dwindle, the Carniolan is the second most popular

Breeding Bee Hybrids

Today's domestic honeybees are not simply subspecies of that original western honeybee. Modern bees comprise strains and hybrids that have been carefully developed and selectively bred for certain qualities, among them: supporting the hive, sustaining honey production, and interacting peaceably with their keepers. Hybrid bees, such as 'Midnite' and 'Starline', also exhibit what is known as hybrid vigor, a hardiness and resistance to disease that can be maintained throughout successive generations by controlled breeding.

domestic bee in North America, after the Italian. It is also one of the most widely distributed of all the *Apis mellifera* subspecies worldwide.

THE RETURN OF THE CARNIOLAN

Recently, new supplies of Carniolans honeybees have been imported to the United States in hopes of refreshing the limited gene pool in this country. Unfortunately, some hybridizing that has occurred between Carniolans and other subspecies has resulted in isolated examples of aggressive bees.

Beekeepers are also looking into a Russian Carniolan bee that was specially engineered in the 1990s from "Yugo" stock to have a natural resistance to *Varroa destructor* and tracheal mites. These bees make an excellent choice for apiarists who are losing bees to these parasites or for novice beekeepers seeking hardy, gentle bees that are likely to have few problems with infestation.

Basics

SIZE
0.5 to 1 inch

LONGEVITY
Workers live up to 12 percent longer than other subspecies.

DISTRIBUTION
Cultivated worldwide, except Antarctica

(opposite page) A Carniolan honeybee feeding on a cherry blossom. Its name comes from Carniola, a region now in Slovenia. Its specific name, *mellifera,* is Latin for "honey bearing."

(top) A colorful Carniolan apiary in Slovenia. There has been a recent push to re-introduce these bees into the United States. Carnies are less likely to drift to other hives and are also less prone to robbing honey than their Italian cousins.

FOCUS ON
Guardians of the Garden
BENEFICIAL INSECTS PROVIDE NATURAL PEST CONTROL

Ground beetles are voracious predators of many of your garden's soil pests. *Calosoma scrutator*, often called the caterpillar hunter, is one of the largest and most attractive of these beetles in North America. Like many other ground beetles, it hunts at night, searching for its favorite soft-bodied larvae.

Insects are not necessarily harmful presences in your yard or garden: many are exceptionally helpful. Consider the diminutive hunters that feed on destructive aphids, cutworms, grubs, beetles, and mealybugs or the parasitic predators that lay their eggs on or inside insect pests, which become a food source for the parasites when they hatch. Nurturing these garden benefactors is a major reason homeowners need to avoid commercial pesticides, many of which do not discriminate between bad bugs and good ones. A healthy garden should literally be crawling with battalions of these soil soldiers, who perform their duties so well, both day and night, that serious insect infestations never get a chance to occur.

Some "assassin" insects or their larvae prey on a range of garden invaders; others are the natural enemies of specific harmful insects. Both cases are examples of biological controls—living organisms employed to control pests, either by

Sending Out an SOS

In the 1980s researchers discovered that plants were actually capable of sending out distress calls, in the form of chemical alarm signals using volatile organic compounds, or VOCs, when attacked by harmful insects. Beneficial insects pick up these "cries" for help and quickly respond by targeting the predators. Incredibly, adjoining plants often produce the same alarm generated by the plant in peril.

predation, parasitism, or other natural mechanisms. Many of these insect helpers will make a home in your garden if you offer them a balanced habitat with the right plants—especially perennials that supply nectar for energy and pollen for protein to support egg development.

BRING ON THE BUGS

Nocturnal blue-black ground beetles target slugs, cutworms, cabbage maggots, and other pests that live in the soil—one beetle larva can eat more than 50 caterpillars. Attract them with perennial plantings or white clover.

Bright, spotted lady beetles—also called ladybugs or ladybirds—eat aphids, mites, and mealybugs. Their voracious larvae are even more effective. Entice them with coreopsis, angelica, dill, fennel, and yarrow.

Orange and black soldier beetles will eat a number harmful insects, but occasionally beneficial ones, too. They seek out catnip, hydrangea, and goldenrod.

Aphid midges are tiny, long-legged flies that resemble mosquitoes. Their larvae feed on more than 60 aphid species, which they paralyze with toxic saliva. Aphid midges seek out pollen-rich plants.

Slender, tan damsel bugs, or nabids, feed on aphids, leafhoppers, small caterpillars, moth eggs, thrips, and others. Some gardeners use a fine net to harvest damsel bugs from alfalfa fields and then release them on their own plants.

The female braconid wasp injects her eggs into aphids and moth and beetle larvae so that her own larvae might feed on them. Braconids seek out small-flowered plants like dill, parsley, and yarrow.

Lacewings may look ethereal, with their large gossamer wings, but they and their hook-jawed larvae—referred to as aphid lions—help control aphids, caterpillars, scales, thrips, mealybugs, and whiteflies. They are drawn to coreopsis, angelica, cosmos, and sweet alyssum.

Tachinid fly larvae burrow into host caterpillars and feed on them from the inside. The flies are attracted to herbs like parsley and dill, as well as sweet clover.

The praying mantid, with its signature "praying" forelegs, is a fierce hunter, stalking moths, grasshoppers, crickets, and flies, but these fascinating insects will devour whatever they can catch—including both harmful and beneficial insects.

A healthy garden should literally be crawling with battalions of these soil soldiers.

(*left*) A lady beetle feasts on aphids. There are about 30 genera in this insect's family, the Coccinellidae.

(*right*) A tomato hornworm covered in wasp eggs. A braconid wasp has injected her eggs into this destructive larva of the five-spotted hawk moth. When the eggs hatch into larvae, the caterpillar will be eaten.

Bumblebees

genus *Bombus*

Favorite plants

- foxglove
- comfrey
- viper's bugloss
- rosemary
- clover
- wood geranium
- cornflower
- rhododendron

Bumblebees are among the most familiar garden pollinators. Doddering along from blossom to blossom with their fuzzy bodies, legs packed with pollen and wings buzzing softly, they seem both personable and comical. By nature, they are placid creatures and rarely confrontational, even going out of their way to avoid human contact. If threatened, however, they will sting.

Native to most temperate or semitropical zones, these bees prefer cool, open, flower-rich grasslands with one long adverse season—usually winter. They have large, rounded bodies that are covered with soft hair—long, branched setae—called pile. Their coloration is aposematic: contrasting color bands that warn animals an insect may sting. Most bumblebees are black with buff, yellow, or orange markings.

They feed on nectar, lapping it up with their long tongue, or proboscis, which folds under the head during flight. There are more than 250 species worldwide, with roughly 50 found in North America.

These are social insects, like honeybees, that form small colonies of perhaps 50 to 400 bees with one queen. It is she who searches in spring for a nesting site beneath the ground or in a tangled clump of grass, flying in a zigzag close above the lawn. Once the queen is settled, she lays her eggs; newly hatched workers begin gathering nectar and pollen to feed her and also start tending the nest. Unlike the neat precision of honeybee hives, bumblebee nests are haphazard, often having dead bees or grubs near the entrance. Clearly, these bees live as casually as they fly. Workers also make honey, but it is not edible by humans.

In summer, the queen produces a new generation of workers and, finally, in late summer, new queens and drones. After mating, only the fertilized queens survive—they will hibernate underground during the winter and emerge the following spring to begin the process anew.

BRINGING THE BUMBLEBEES
Bumblebees sample the bounty of each passing season—in early spring feeding on apple, pear, plum, and cherry blossoms,

California poppies, bluebells, and pussy willow, followed in late spring by foxgloves, geraniums, honeysuckle, roses, salvia, and wisteria. They will sample from herbs like chives, oregano, and mint and fruit such as raspberries, strawberries, and blueberries. Summer favorites include viper's bugloss, sunflowers, delphinium, snapdragons, lavender, hollyhocks, cosmos, and cornflowers. In early fall, they feed on pumpkins, melons, and zucchini. Due to their varied tastes, they are able to pollinate flowers, herbs, vegetables, shrubs, fruit trees, and agricultural crops.

These busy pollinators will become garden regulars if you provide them with nest boxes. Typically 15 to 25 inches in diameter, the boxes feature one entry hole and two or three for ventilation, which require a net covering to keep out ants. It helps if your garden is set up for long-term or staggered blooming times—bumblebees require nectar from March to September.

Basics

SIZE
Worker, 0.25 inch to 1 inch; queen, 0.75 inch to 1.25 inch

LONGEVITY
One season or less; fertilized queens overwinter and lay eggs in spring.

DISTRIBUTION
Temperate to tropical zones worldwide, except Africa or Australia; introduced to New Zealand, spread to Tasmania

(opposite page) While sipping nectar, a common eastern bumblebee *(Bombus impatiens)* can dust itself in the flower's pollen. This species ranges through eastern North America, along with the western desert areas, California, and Oregon.

(top) An American bumblebee *(Bombus pennsylvanicus)* drinks nectar from oregano blossoms. This species is one of the bumblebees most often encountered in eastern North America.

similar species: *stingless bees*

The Meliponini—tiny, stingless bees—are a sister tribe to the Bombini and are found in the tropics. Pre-Columbian peoples cultivated them for their honey, but their output is low by modern standards. Still, these bees are vital pollinators of tropical plants, especially of the vanilla orchid, source of the vanilla bean. The vine blooms just one day a year and has a hidden source of pollen that only these bees know how to access.

A stingless bee. These bees are "stingless" because their stingers are simply too small to deploy.

Masters of the Night

BATS EXCEL AS INSECT PREDATORS & PLANT POLLINATORS

Lesser long-nosed bats (*Leptonycteris curasoae*) pollinate night-blooming cacti, such as the saguaro and organ pipe, and they also pollinate century plants and other agaves.

For thousands of years, humans have feared bats, mostly due to superstitions and folklore that equate them with evil. The reality is that bats are amazingly beneficial creatures, pollinating hundreds of commercially significant plants, spreading fruit seeds, and consuming multitudes of harmful insects.

There are more than 1,300 species of bats, all belonging to the order Chiroptera, Greek for "hand wing." The majority of bats are small, nocturnal, globally widespread mammals—warm-blooded vertebrates with fur that nurse their young. They are, notably, the only mammals that have the ability to actually fly, using wings that are elastic membranes spread between elongated digits.

There are two basic suborders: megabats, such as fruit bats, that can weigh up to four pounds and eat fruit, nectar, or pollen; and microbats, which primarily eat insects but also feed on nectar, pollen, fish, frogs, and blood. Megabats hunt visually, but microbats navigate in the dark using echolocation, emitting ultrasound "chirps" to avoid colliding with obstacles. Even though bats originated 50 to 60 million years ago, research indicates that they had the ability fly before they evolved the necessary organs to echolocate.

Pollinating bats are particularly drawn to white or pale flowers with large, bell-shaped blossoms, many of which bloom at night. These blossoms often contain copious amounts of fruit- or musk-scented nectar that bats find irresistible. Nearly 500 species of tropical fruit, such as mango, banana, guava, cacao, and agave, depend on bats for pollination. Bat species that feed on whole fruit play a key role in seed dispersal and reforestation.

Bats in Tight Spaces

If you want to encourage bats, wooden bat houses offer a warm, safe haven and even a place to reproduce. These houses replicate the narrow space between a tree and its bark where bats typically roost. Commercial houses can be ordered online, purchased from garden shops, or constructed from plans. The best location is near water and vegetation, in a spot with plenty of warming sunlight, and placed a minimum of 15 feet above the ground. Hang them on a tree or building—wood, stone, or brick that retains heat is an ideal mounting site; metal siding is not. If your yard is plagued by mosquitoes or other flying pests, it won't take much to bring these nocturnal hunters to your property. A supply of bat houses should keep them there.

These voracious hunters can consume mosquitoes, midges, gnats, and other flying pests at a rate of 600 per hour.

There are more than 40 bat species in the United States and Canada, all of them insectivores except for three flower-eating species that migrate to the Southwest from Mexico—the Mexican free-tailed bat, lesser long-nosed bat, and Mexican long-tongued bat. A number of native bats are known to visit suburban yards in search of food— these voracious hunters can consume mosquitoes, midges, gnats, and other flying pests at a rate of 600 per hour.

Like honeybees, bats are beset by a mysterious ailment that is depleting populations at a startling rate. Labeled white nose syndrome—for the powdery fungal growth that appears on the nose and wings—it results in loss of fat stores, damage to wing membranes, and death. It is found in the mines and caves of more than 25 states and has resulted in a death toll exceeding six million bats—so far. There is currently no cure.

(top) A Mexican long-tongued bat *(Choeronycteris mexicana)* enjoys a midnight snack at a hummingbird feeder. These migratory bats spend summers in southern Arizona and winters in Mexico, where they are important pollinators of several species of cactus.

(bottom) A little brown bat *(Myotis lucifugus)*. This common North American bat is an effective insectivore, devouring many backyard flying nuisances, such as mosquitoes, moths, gnats, wasps, and midges.

Mining Bees

genus *Andrena*

Favorite plants

- pussy willow
- viburnum
- dogwood
- goldenrod
- aster
- apple
- violet
- blueberry

Mining bees—also known as digger bees, ground bees, and mud bees—are reliable pollinators, a welcome backup at a time when honeybees might not be around to do the job. Mining bees also aerate suburban lawns and parkland with their many-branched nesting tunnels. They prefer woodland edges, meadows, prairies, and old agricultural fields.

They are members of the widespread *Andrena* genus, which has more than 1,300 species. Their coloration is often dark—brown or black with whitish abdominal bands and smoky wings. Color variations include red and metallic blue or green. Small and fuzzy, with featherlike hair—useful against the chill of early spring—they have large heads and short tongues. Females, which are larger than males, can be identified by a broad patch of velvety hair above the eyes known as the facial foveae.

Their life cycle differs radically from social bees. In March or April, adults emerge from underground hibernation to seek a mate. Males die soon after mating, while the now-fertile female excavates a nesting burrow in sandy or dry soil near a shrub or low tree for protection from the weather. After carving out multiple birthing cells, she places a ball of pollen and nectar inside each one before depositing an egg and sealing the chamber. She may lay up to 30 eggs during her six- to eight-week lifespan. When the larvae hatch, they feed off the food supply, spin a cocoon, and pupate into adults, remaining dormant inside their cells until the following spring. Some adults emerge in fall and their offspring hibernate as pupae.

Certain mining bees form large subterranean communities—called aggregations—of adjacent burrows with hundreds of branches. One telltale sign of mining bees is a pencil-wide hole in the ground with a small "volcano" of dirt around it; another sign is a quantity of tiny bees buzzing over the lawn. The latter is often of concern to homeowners, but

Solitary Bees

Honeybees may be the rock stars of the bee world, but the vast proportion of bees on earth—90 percent—are solitary bees, including the mason bees, such as *Osmia bicornis* shown below, and the mining, carpenter, and leafcutter bees. The earmark of a solitary bee is that every female is fertile and constructs a nest by herself. In effect, she is both queen and worker in her own private burrow. Solitary bees tunnel into rotted wood, soft mortar, or dry soil; some live in human-supplied houses that use bamboo tubes as tunnels. They are also known for being oligoleges, bees that gather pollen from a narrow spectrum of species or only one species.

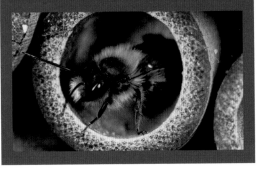

mining bees are no threat—the females' stingers are too small to harm humans, plus they are too busy prepping their nests to harass people. And, at most, they are only active for six weeks. The ultimate message is to leave these bees alone and let them get on with their work.

MAKING MINERS AT HOME

Mining bees appreciate a flower-rich habitat of native plants, especially ones that offer them lots of nectar and pollen in the spring, when the females are carrying food back to their nests. Like bumblebees, mining bees are "buzz" pollinators, vibrating a flower with their wings to make the pollen shower down over them.

Basics

SIZE
0.25 to 0.75 inch

LONGEVITY
Most species pupate in summer and hibernate as adults. The females then spend six weeks nesting and laying eggs before dying.

DISTRIBUTION
Most of Northern Hemisphere; some parts of Southern Hemisphere

(opposite page) An early mining bee *(Andrena haemorrhoa)* feeding on blooming willow. These bees visit a wide variety of plants, especially spring-blossoming shrubs and flowers like dandelions.

(left) A long-lipped andrena bee *(Andrena barbilabris)* warily emerging from her underground burrow. If you need to use your lawn while miners are active, simply sprinkle them with a hose. Never resort to pesticides or insecticides. Recent tests show that even low doses of nicotine-derived pesticides can wipe out entire populations. The andrenas may be the next group of bees we need to start worrying about.

PART THREE

BUTTERFLIES & MOTHS *in the Garden*

CHAPTER FIVE

Creating a Habitat
for Butterflies & Moths

· ·

(opposite page) A mourning cloak butterfly drinks the nectar of a pink-and-white dahlia.

Butterfly & Moth Basics

THEIR HISTORY & ANATOMY

(left) An extreme closeup of a swallowtail shows its segmented body, three pairs of legs, wandlike antennae, compound eyes, and long proboscis, which it uncurls to drink nectar from a flower.

(middle) The tubular veins radiating from the base of the wing form a different pattern in each genus; taxonomists use this as their main criteria when classifying butterflies.

(right) Two zebra longwings mating. Each butterfly species has a unique genital configuration, with only the correct male "fitting" the corresponding female.

Few things in nature are as picturesque as butterflies, with their colorful wings and delicate, graceful manner of flitting from blossom to blossom. Even children who flee from most bugs find themselves fascinated by these "self-propelled flowers," as author Robert Heinlein called them. It's no wonder many gardeners work to attract butterflies—they are more than ornamental, they are also valuable pollinators.

Moths are the seldom-seen aerial denizens of the night—flying, feeding, and mating after the sun has set. For creatures of the darkness, however, some moths are extraordinarily beautiful, boasting rich colors and striking patterns that rival the loveliest butterflies.

SCALED WINGS

Butterflies and moths belong to the order Lepidoptera, the second most populous order after beetles. The name derives from the ancient Greek for "scaled wing." There are a total of about 180,00 species—160,00 of which are moths—in 126 families and 46 superfamiles that live on every continent except Antarctica. Moths are the evolutionary ancestors of butterflies, with fossil records going back 150 million years. When certain moths successfully adapted to living in daylight and evolved brighter colors, they became butterflies. Modern species of both groups display a range of wing colors and patterns—from drab leaf browns to the exquisite hues of the tropics—that provide camouflage, mimicry, warnings to predators, and mating lures.

Anatomically, both butterflies and moths have segmented bodies made up of a head, thorax, and abdomen, covered with an exoskeleton of chitin, a type of protein, and connected by flexible tissue. The head features two compound eyes—which produce a mosaic view of the insect's surroundings—a long, coiled, tubular proboscis, and two antennae that act as information sensors. These are typically clubbed—having small balls on top—in butterflies and fringed in moths. At the base of the antennae lies the Johnston's organ, which helps determine orientation and balance during flight. At the front of the head lie the bristling labial palpi, which contain olfactory sensors and possibly act as dust filters for the eyes.

The thorax is home to breathing spiracles, two pairs of wings, powerful flight muscles, and three pairs of long legs. The legs contain a number of sensors that pick up warning vibrations, as well as detect the correct plants for egg laying. The abdomen houses more spiracles, the tubular heart, and the digestive and reproductive tracts.

PROVIDER OR PEST?

Butterflies have been recognized as beneficial pollinators for years, but it is only recently that moth researchers concluded that they, too, contribute to the pollination of a wide cross-section of plants around the globe. Conversely, the caterpillars of many butterflies and moths are voracious plant-eating menaces that can wreak agricultural destruction. Considering that females can produce from 200 to 30,000 eggs in one day, the overall beneficial and detrimental effects of these creatures need to be weighed and evaluated. In some cases, endangered species cannot afford to have their caterpillars eradicated as pests.

tip

Handle with care: the minute scales on the wings and body of a butterfly can be hairlike, bladelike, or variable in form, and are usually powdery, meaning they may rub off if the insect is handled roughly.

A distinct difference between the anatomy of butterflies and moths is the structure of the antennae. A butterfly's are most often club-shaped with a long shaft and a bulb at the end. A moth's are saw-edged or feathery, as on the cecropia moth below. Extremely sensitive to odors, the antennae allow the moth to detect food sources and potential mates.

A Butterfly's Life Cycle

THE METAMORPHOSIS FROM CATERPILLAR TO WINGED INSECT

The notion of a grotesque or ungainly caterpillar transforming itself into a glorious, graceful butterfly has been universally embraced as a symbol for change or reinvention. This imagery is so inspiring that it has frequently been used in literature, poetry, art, and even advertising to indicate any transfiguration.

Butterflies and moths, like many other insects, are holometabolous, meaning that they must go through complete metamorphosis to become adults. Complete metamorphosis requires four stages—egg, larva, pupa, and adult, or imago—and can take one month or as long as a year. The following descriptions are based on the monarch butterfly, but are valid for many other lepidopterans.

Mating—and procreating—is a butterfly's primary job in life, and most are ready to do so when they are three to five days old. Male butterflies court by flapping their wings, sending minute scales containing pheromones to the female's antennae. Pairs typically mate near the plant that will feed their offspring— in this case, milkweed. The male uses claspers at the tip of the abdomen to attach to the female, and the two can remain interlocked for up to 16 hours.

FROM EGG TO CATERPILLAR

The female normally deposits only one cylindrical egg the size of a pinhead under a milkweed leaf, but she may lay as many as 700 in a month. In three to eight days, the caterpillar hatches and begins its quest to eat as much as possible in the

shortest time possible, which is why it has been born on the exact plant it needs to do this. The body is cylindrical, with a well-developed head, mandibles, multiple pairs of legs and prolegs, with hooks for grasping, and simple eyes. Caterpillars' exoskeletons do not stretch as they grow—in stages called instars—so they molt their skins several times. Depending on species, caterpillars are varied: smooth or hairy, spiked or knobbed, wildly colored or a plain green, fierce looking (for show) or even poisonous (for real).

SPINNING A COCOON

Once a caterpillar has matured—in about two weeks—it spins an anchor mat on a milkweed leaf with silk from a spinneret on its head. It then hangs by a stem, or cremaster, attached to this silken anchor and sheds its skin a final time. As the larva pupates, it already contains all the cells it needs to form an adult body, legs, and wings. Many moth caterpillars spin a silk cocoon to protect the pupa. These cocoons are often camouflaged and placed in concealed locations, sometimes underground. The butterfly pupa has no covering and is called a chrysalis—from the Greek *chrysos,* for gold.

A BUTTERFLY EMERGES

In ten days, the adult monarch butterfly emerges, head down, waiting for its wing veins to inflate with fluid, called hemolymph, from its swollen abdomen. In an hour or two, the now-slim monarch is ready for its first flight.

1 **egg to caterpillar**
An adult butterfly will lay her eggs on the plant its larvae—or caterpillars— need to eat to survive. For monarchs, this is milkweed.

2 **caterpillar**
A caterpillar does little other than dine on the milkweed plant while it grows.

3 **caterpillar to pupa**
Once it has matured, a caterpillar sheds its skin and becomes a chrysalis. During this pupal stage, the adult butterfly forms inside.

4 **pupa to adult**
An adult butterfly emerges after about two weeks.

5 **adult**
The butterfly is soon ready to fly off, visiting nectar plants. It will reach sexual maturity in three to five days, ready to begin a new cycle.

A Butterfly Garden

SELECTING & ARRANGING PLANTS TO ATTRACT BUTTERFLIES

tip

Butterfly houses furnish these vulnerable insects with a place to shelter from wind and harsh weather or to simply rest at night. The narrow slots on the front allow access to butterflies, but keep birds and other predators from entering. These houses—many of which are decorated with floral or rustic motifs—are meant to be hung in your garden, near a source of nectar.

The ideal wildlife garden is a place of natural variety that engages the senses—offering the sweet songs of nesting birds, the contented buzzing of foraging bees, and rewarding views of brightly hued butterflies as they light on blooms to feed. In order to complete this sensory trio, you need to tempt butterflies to spend time exploring your garden; otherwise, they are there—and gone flitting away—in no time.

Providing plenty of sunlight is key when creating a landscape in which butterflies will want to linger. Butterflies need to maintain a body temperature from 80 to 100 degrees and prefer sunny areas with low wind and flat rocks on which they can warm themselves.

DOUBLE-DUTY PLANTINGS

A butterfly garden should offer two types of plants: host plants and nectar plants. Host plants like milkweed, hollyhock, dill, and sunflower support eggs and caterpillars. Nectar plants like butterfly bush, lilac, purple coneflower, and Joe-pye weed, supply adults with food. If you research which species are native to your region and what plants they prefer—for instance black swallowtails lay their eggs on members of the parsley family—you will know the appropriate plants to buy. If possible, opt for native flowers and shrubs, the plants butterflies are predisposed to feed from. Butterflies can also be lured closer by certain foods, such as very ripe fruit and nectar in feeders.

Make sure to include a water source—butterflies prefer to drink water from

1 meadow blazingstar
(*Liatris ligulistylis*)
Imposing height makes these purple stunners easy targets for monarchs and other butterflies that enjoy their nectar for many weeks during late summer.

2 spotted Joe-pye weed
(*Eutrochium maculatum*)
Beginning in late summer, flat clusters of tiny purplish pink flowers bloom atop this tall plant, which monarchs flock to until the early fall.

3 cutleaf coneflower
(*Rudbeckia laciniata*)
Masses of yellow flowers bloom late on this giant coneflower, producing a sweet nectar just as monarchs need to fuel up for the fall migration.

4 four o' clock
(*Mirabilis jalapa*)
These very fragrant, old-fashioned flowers will lure moths and other nocturnal pollinators with long tongues. During the day, you might also see hummingbirds flitting about them.

5 bleeding heart
(*Dicentra* spp.)
The heart-shaped flowers of this plant droop from arching stems in spring. This charming species is the host plant for swallowtail and painted lady caterpillars.

6 swamp milkweed
(*Asclepias incarnata*)
The host plant of the monarch caterpillar, swamp milkweed produces globes of pink flowers that are a summer nectar source.

7 pearly everlasting
(*Anaphalis margaritacea*)
This early-blooming northern plant is often the first host plant to receive butterfly eggs, such as those of the American lady, each season. Its nectar will also attract other species.

8 New England aster
(*Aster novae-angliae*)
These prolific fall bloomers provide butterflies with nectar at a time of the year when most sources are scarce.

sunken birdbaths or shallow saucers filled with wet pebbles or sand. Male butterflies engage in "mud puddling"—feeding from a patch of damp soil, where they acquire the minerals and salts they need for successful mating. Create a homemade mud puddle by placing damp soil in a dish, adding some table salt, and placing a flat rock in the center.

PLANNING & RECORDING
It helps to sketch out a plan for your new garden, bearing in mind the blooming period and sunlight requirements of your chosen plants and their eventual height. With butterflies, as with other wild visitors, staggered bloom times are appreciated, especially at the end of the growing season when resources are scarce. Don't forget to keep a photo journal of which butterflies you have observed on which plants and what activities they engaged in—females laying eggs, for instance, or pupae hatching or adults feeding. That way you'll know which plants were successful when it comes time to update your butterfly garden next spring.

A butterfly-friendly plan
You can use this plan to begin devising a garden area that will welcome butterflies in all stages of their life cycle. Many of the plants shown above will return each year and spread moderately. Though all are illustrated in bloom, not all species shown flower at the same time. Your goal is to create a succession of blooms that will supply adults with nectar for as many months as possible and to provide plants that will support reproduction.

PLANTS TO ATTRACT BUTTERFLIES

Choosing plants to attract butterflies is not just about finding lovely blossoms that supply the adults with nectar. Butterflies also need host plants for their eggs and larvae. A mix of annual and perennial flowers, shrubs, and herbs should thrive in most gardens while giving butterflies what they need.

1 MILKWEED (*Asclepias* spp.)
As well as being the host plant for monarch larvae, milkweed attracts adult swallowtails, fritillaries, skippers, and hawk moths.

2 LANTANA (*Lantana* spp.)
Butterflies frequent the efficient nectar-producing blooms of this ornamental favorite, which comes in many colors.

3 ALPINE ASTER (*Aster alpinus*)
This prolific fall bloomer with its pastel-colored daisy-like flowers supplies nectar for butterflies and foliage for caterpillars.

4 LAVENDER (*Lavandula* spp.)
Whether you want to attract butterflies, bees, or hummingbirds, no pollinator garden is complete without this fragrant herb.

5 LILAC (*Syringa vulgaris*)
The heavenly scent of lilac's spring blossoms will enchant your senses and those of butterflies, which will feast on its nectar.

6 PHLOX (*Phlox paniculata*)
Summer-flowering phlox bears scented clusters of nectar-rich blooms in a variety of colors, from white to pink to red.

7 SPOTTED JOE-PYE WEED (*Eutrochium maculatum*)
This towering perennial allows easy viewing of the butterflies and other pollinators that will flock to its puffy late-summer blooms.

8 BUTTERFLY BUSH (*Buddleia davidii*)
This butterfly magnet is great for urban gardens, where its growth can be controlled, but as a nonnative spreader, it can be invasive.

9 FRENCH MARIGOLD (*Tagetes patula*)
With its long blooming period, this low-growing plant with flowers of blended red, yellow, and orange is a great summer nectar source.

10 DILL (*Anethum graveolens*)
Plant this delightfully airy culinary herb for its kitchen uses and its role as a host plant for black swallowtail butterflies.

CHAPTER SIX

Butterflies & Moths

· · · · · · · · · · · · · · · · · ·

(opposite page) A queen butterfly—a cousin of the more familiar monarch—sips on the nectar of a zinnia.

Know Your Butterflies & Moths

THE BUTTERFLIES & MOTHS MOST LIKELY TO VISIT YOUR YARD & GARDEN

(left) A cabbage white butterfly on a French marigold. The widespread white group of butterflies may lack the drama of other flashier families, but they still have a delicate beauty.

(middle) A silver-bordered fritillary sips nectar from a wild orchid. The fritillaries take their name from the checkerboard design that appears on their wings.

(right) An American copper. Coppers are very active butterflies, fluttering their richly patterned wings as they patrol for mates, look for food, or vigorously defend their territory.

Here is a brief overview of the butterfly families explored in this chapter. These butterflies have been chosen because of their widespread distribution in North America and, of course, their beauty.

SWALLOWTAIL BUTTERFLIES

Forty species of the large, colorful butterflies of the family Papilionidae are found in North America. The long "tails" on the hind wings of most of these butterflies, which resemble the long, pointed tails of swallows, give this family its common name.

SULPHURS & WHITES

Both sulphurs and whites belong to the large Pieridae family, which includes about 1,100 species. These butterflies are white, yellow, or orange in coloration, often with black spots.

BRUSH-FOOTED BUTTERFLIES

The Nymphalidae is the largest family of butterflies with about 6,000 species worldwide. They are called brush-footed butterflies for the brushlike set of hairs on the forelegs or four-footed butterflies because they are known to stand only on their four hind legs while curling up the other two.

• *Milkweed Butterflies* The subfamily Danainae lay their eggs on various milkweeds on which their larvae will then feed. Four species are found in North America, including the monarch.

• *Satyrs & Wood-Nymph* The numerous members of the widespread subfamily Satyrinae are typically brown with paler markings.

• *Checkerspots & Crescents* The subfamily Melitaeinae contains mostly small- to medium-sized orange-brown butterflies with black or dark brown markings. They are often weak fliers. This group is distributed only in the Northern Hemisphere and the American tropics.

• *Anglewings, Tortoiseshells, Thistle Butterflies & Buckeyes* The Nymphalinae is a worldwide subfamily of medium-to-large butterflies with 26 species in North America.

• *Greater & Lesser Fritillaries* Part of the subfamily Heliconiinae—the Heliconians or longwings—both greater and lesser fritillaries are commonly found in North America. They are typically orange with black spots on the upper side of both wings and often appear checkered—hence the name, which comes from the Latin word *fritillus,* meaning "chessboard."

• *Admirals* The subfamily Limenitidinae comprises medium-to-large woodland butterflies, with 26 species in North America.

GOSSAMER WINGS
The Lycaenidae is the second largest family of butterflies, with approximately 4,700 species.

• *Hairstreaks* Found worldwide, the Theclinae is the largest subfamily of gossamer-winged butterflies, with about 90 species in North America.

• *Coppers* Typically metallic red or orange, the butterflies of the subfamily Lycaeninae occur mainly in the Northern Hemisphere, with about 20 species found in North America.

• *Blues* There about 40 species of the Polyommatinae in North America. The males of this subfamily are almost always blue.

SKIPPERS
There are about 300 species of the small-to-medium-sized butterflies of the large family Hesperiidae in North America.

SATURNIID MOTHS
The moths of the family Saturniidae are medium to very large in size—this family includes the largest moths found in North America.

• *Giant Silkmoths* The Saturniinae, or saturniines, are often striking moths, some with bright colors and distinctive eyespots.

• *Royal Moths* The subfamily Ceratocampinae is called royal or regal moths. Caterpillars of these moths tend to be large and robust with knobs, horns, or other features that make them a favorite at zoos and educational centers.

OWLETS
Owlets are members of the superfamily Noctuoidea, which includes about 70,000 described species, the largest number for any lepidopteran superfamily. It contains both the Erebidae and Noctuidae families, among others. The Arctiinae, a large and diverse subfamily of the Erebidae, numbers around 11,000 species worldwide, including the brightly colored tigers.

SPHINX MOTHS
The medium-to-large moths of the Sphingidae family are commonly called sphinx, hawk, or hummingbird moths—and some can actually be easily mistaken for hummers.

tip

You can learn a lot just by observing a butterfly. There are three Ps of butterfly behavior: puddling, lapping up salts and minerals from mud; patrolling, males actively seeking females to mate with; and perching, basking in the warm sun.

(left) A silver-spotted skipper. This family gets its name for the fast, intense flight of its members, which makes it appear as if the butterflies are skipping from flower to flower as they seek out nectar.

(middle) A garden tiger moth. These members of the Arctiinae subfamily are perfect examples of the extraordinary colors and patterns of moths.

(right) Called the royal walnut or regal moth, this gray-green and orange moth is a member of the royal moth subfamily.

Eastern Black Swallowtail

Papilio polyxenes

Favorite plants

- milkweed
- Joe-pye weed
- purple coneflower
- bee balm
- zinnia
- phlox
- dill
- fennel

The Papilionidae family, with their signature lobed wings, comprises more than 550 species of swallowtails. Many of its members are tropical, but the family is represented on every fertile continent. Swallowtail larvae are known for a defensive scent gland on the head called the osmeterium. The genus name, *Papilio,* comes from the Latin for "butterfly," while the specific names honor mythological Greek figures. The eastern black was named for Polyxena, the daughter of Trojan King Priam.

Also known as the American or parsnip swallowtail and the celery worm, the eastern black swallowtail ranges from the Rocky Mountains to the eastern states and across southern Canada, and from Arizona into northern Mexico in the Southwest. It prefers open wetlands,

Nature's Mimics

To avoid ending up as dinner for predatory wildlife, butterfly and moth larvae have developed a few methods of camouflage. Some can squirt noxious odors, while others can take on undesirable forms. The larvae of swallowtails are superb mimics. The spicebush larvae, for example, use two types of mimicry—early brown larvae look like bird droppings, while during the final instar, large "eyes" on the yellow-green caterpillar's head give it the appearance of a tiny green snake. Both of these forms are common among the swallowtails. Other caterpillar species grow long hairy tufts, spines, or hornlike projections that are barbed with venom. Some larvae take on the appearance of unripe berries, leaves, or bark to deter hungry birds.

prairies, pine savannahs, woodlands, fields, weedy lots, roadsides, and gardens.

The black ground color creates a striking contrast with the two rows of yellow wing spots, bright on the male, subdued on the female, and the red bull's-eye circle on the inner edge of the hind wing. Females show powdery blue on the lower wings between the spots. The underwings are identical on both sexes: yellow spots on the front wings, and large orange spots separated by powder blue on the hind wings.

Males emerge early to establish a territory for courtship flights and mating. After mating, the female lays rounded, pale yellow eggs singly on plants in the

Apiaceae, also known as the carrot, parsley, or celery family, on new foliage or flowers. The larvae are stout and when agitated their hornlike scent glands pop out and emit a penetrating odor. These caterpillars start out black with a white saddle—mimicking bird droppings—and gradually become lime green with black transverse bands with yellow spots, which is perfect camouflage on sun-dappled leaves.

Swallowtails pupate in a "heads up" position—the cremaster attaches to a plant stem on a silk pad, and a silken girdle holds the upright pupa in place. Summer broods typically have green or tan pupae. Late season pupae are often deep brown; they will overwinter and hatch in the spring. Summer-bred adults emerge in 9 to 18 days. Black easterns live longer than many other temperate-zone butterflies, possibly up to a year.

BRING IN BLACK EASTERNS
If you want these black beauties in your garden, offer host plants like parsley, celery, dill, and fennel, and preserve any Queen Anne's lace on your property. Nectar plants include zinnia, purple coneflower, and bee balm, as well as butterfly bush and milkweed.

Basics

WINGSPAN
2.8 to 3.7 inches

SEASONS
Broods from May to June; July to August; possible third brood in the South

DISTRIBUTION
Across the United States east from the Rockies; into Arizona and northern Mexico; across southern Canada

(opposite page) An eastern black swallowtail feeding on a zinnia. This species tends to fly close to the ground, making it easy to identify.

(left) Two stages of the larva feeding on celery, one of the many members of the Apiaceae this species uses as a host plant. These caterpillars often eat highly toxic members of this family, such as poison hemlock, but are able to detoxify their deadly chemicals.

(right) Their graceful silhouette helps make the swallowtails favorites with collectors and nature lovers.

Giant Swallowtail

Papilio cresphontes

Favorite plants

- azalea
- bougainvillea
- lantana
- Japanese honeysuckle
- goldenrod
- dame's rocket
- sweet pea
- swamp milkweed

Measuring five inches or more in diameter, this imposing black-and-yellow swallowtail is sure to get noticed in the garden. It is often seen sipping nectar from flowers or lapping water from mud puddles. Its range extends across the central and eastern United States and south from Ontario to Florida. It is also found throughout the Southwest, Mexico, Central America, and beyond.

The giant swallowtail is an elegant butterfly, with dorsal wing surfaces in black or deep brown that feature a diagonal yellow bar across the upper wings. A series of spots travel from the outer edge of the crossbar down toward the tail and end at a red mark. The underwing is yellow, bisected with a lacing of black, light blue, and red, and the body is a buttery pale yellow.

similar species: *palamedes swallowtail*

The titanic black-and-yellow palamedes swallowtail butterfly (*Papilio palamedes*) can approach six inches in diameter. Its vivid yellow marking are closer to the outer edge of the black wing than those of the giant swallowtail. It prefers swampy woodland edges in the American South. In spite of its size, it often makes lazy flights high into the treetops. Eggs are laid and larvae feed on magnolia, sassafras, and members of the laurel family, hence its other common name, the laurel swallowtail.

A palamedes feeding on penta blooms displays its vibrant orange, yellow, white, and blue markings.

Adults feed on wildflowers and native plants like goldenrod and swamp milkweed and prefer deciduous or mixed forests. Courting males patrol pine woodlands or citrus groves, cruising with slow, strong, gliding wingbeats, seeking interested females. Wooing and mating typically occur in the afternoon. Although the female lays her brownish eggs, which look like orange peel, one at a time on the surface of a leaf, she may produce a total of 300 or 400. The larvae are considered an occasional pest of citrus trees in the South. Called orangedogs or orange puppies, the caterpillars feed mostly at night and can damage young groves, quickly defoliating small plants. They will also dine on prickly ash and hop plants.

The smallest larvae instars are dark with white saddles—total bird poop clones!—and have setae, or stiff hairs, in knobs along their bodies. As they mature, they lose the hairs, develop a swollen thorax, and become a mottled dark brown and white, at which point they resemble small, scaly, lumpy snakes. These larvae pupate upright at a 45-degree angle, attached to a twig or branch at the posterior and held in place with a silken girdle. In 10 to 12 days, a spectacular adult will struggle free and take flight. Larvae from late broods may overwinter as pupae and emerge in the spring.

GIANT APPETITES

Bring these oversized stunners to your yard by offering host plants such as citrus trees, prickly ash, hop trees, and common rue, along with nectar plants like lantana, swamp milkweed, zinnia, and azalea. Giant swallowtails also find a homemade mudslide quite tempting.

Basics

WINGSPAN
4.0 to 6.3 inches

SEASONS
First-brood adults emerge in May; second by August; southern populations may have three broods.

DISTRIBUTION
East from the Rockies; south from Ontario to Florida; in the Southwest ranges into Mexico

(opposite page) A giant swallowtail feeding on dame's rocket. This swallowtail's specific name is taken from the Greek figure Cresphontes, king of Messene and a great-great grandson of Heracles.

(left) Disguised as bird droppings, the early caterpillars will certainly appear unpalatable to potential predators.

(right) An adult giant. From unsightly bird dropping look-alike to dazzling adult, the metamorphosis of these butterflies is remarkable.

Eastern Tiger Swallowtail

Papilio glaucus

Favorite plants

- aster
- daisy
- sweet pea
- lilac
- swamp milkweed
- Joe-pye weed
- calendula
- sunflower

The eastern tiger might just be the emblematic swallowtail—easily identified by its black-on-yellow stripes and sweeping wing projections. These butterflies also have a wide range—throughout the eastern half of North America and west to the Colorado plains and central Texas. A former Canadian subspecies, *Papilio glaucus canadensis*, was elevated to species status in 1991.

The male is yellow with black tiger stripes, but the female is dimorphic, possessing two color forms—one similar to the male and the other a darker morph with shadowy black stripes. Both female colorations feature a row of blue chevrons on the hind wing and an iridescent blue sheen on the hind underwing.

Eastern tiger swallowtails can be found in deciduous forest edges, river valleys,

Basics

WINGSPAN
3.1 to 5.5 inches

SEASONS
Two broods from May to September in North; three from February to November in South

DISTRIBUTION
East from Colorado to the Atlantic coast; south from Vermont to the Gulf Coast

broadleaf woods, parks, and suburbs, and they are frequently spotted flying high above the treetops. Their favorite nectar plants are red or pink with sturdy stems; they especially seek out flowers in the pea, aster, and dogbane families. Host plants include a number of trees: tulip, birch, ash, willow, and cottonwood.

These butterflies tend to be solitary, but courting males will scout the woodlands on the wing for prospective mates, focusing on areas where host plants grow. Females lay their round green eggs singly on leaves; they later turn yellowish with reddish spots before hatching in 4 to 10 days. The larvae are brown with a pale saddle—mimicking bird droppings—and turn green during the fourth instar. The color darkens during the fifth instar, just before pupating, when the caterpillar positions itself upright on a silken pad and attaches itself to its base plant by weaving silk around its midsection. The chrysalis is green or various shades of brown, and may be found on tree trunks, fence posts, or in leaf litter. Metamorphosis can take 9 to 11 days; in regions with cold winters, the pupae may hibernate.

FEEDING THE TIGERS

Lure these butterflies to your yard with host plants like wild black cherry, sweet bay magnolia, basswood, tulip tree, birch, ash, cottonwood, aspen, and willow. Nectar plants for feeding include garden favorites like lilac, aster, daisy, calendula, and sweet pea and wildflowers such as bee balm, milkweed and Joe-pye weed. Males also enjoy the chance to "mud puddle" for water, salts, and minerals.

(opposite page) A female eastern tiger swallowtail on milkweed shows the yellow morph coloration associated with this species.

(left) A male eastern tiger drinking. The males often congregate with other swallowtails at water sources like riverbanks, sipping from the water and mud to extract minerals, along with moisture.

(top) The eastern tiger caterpillar relies on protective mimicry. In its fifth instar, it takes on the look of a stubby green snake.

(bottom) A female in the black color morph can easily be mistaken for an eastern black tiger swallowtail.

similar species: *western tiger swallowtail*

The active western tiger swallowtail (*Papilio rutulus*) is common across most of the western United States, where it mates in canyons and on hilltops. It is distinguished from the eastern tiger, in part, by the underside markings on the forewing, which form bands instead of spots. The female is not dimorphic. It ranges in size from 2.75 to 4 inches and feeds on thistles, California buckeye, zinnia, and yerba santa.

A western tiger nectaring on lilac. Like eastern tigers, westerns are attracted to this fragrant shrub.

Clouded Sulphur

Colias philodice

Favorite plants

- dandelion
- marigold
- mistflower
- phlox
- grape hyacinth
- verbena
- lantana
- coneflower

The sulphurs and whites are part of the Pieridae family, which contains 1,100 species worldwide, mostly found in the tropics but also across North America. These are some of the first butterflies to appear in spring. They are generally white, yellow, or orange, often with black markings. The females display different patterns—and sometimes coloration—from the males, including a white form that is greenish white rather than yellow. It is believed that the buttery yellow shade of a Pieridae known as the common brimstone suggested the name "butter-coloured fly" to British naturalists.

The clouded sulphur butterfly, also called the common sulphur, is found across North America. They are part of the subfamily Coliadinae, the sulphurs. These butterflies do not sequester toxic chemical

Basics

WINGSPAN
1.50 to 2.75 inches

SEASONS
Three flights in the north, May to October; three in the south, March to November

DISTRIBUTION
Across North America—Alaska south to central Texas; quite prevalent in the East

compounds from their food plants in their bodies, making them popular fare with birds and other insectivores. They are, however, quite agile when pursued. Clouded sulphurs inhabit open areas such as meadows, alfalfa or clover fields, roadsides, and suburban lawns and are known to swarm at mud puddles seeking moisture and nutrients.

The male's dorsal wings are a lemon yellow, with solid black edging, while the female's edging shows yellow spots. The ventral hind wing on both sexes has a doubled silver spot edged with pinkish orange. In some populations, there is also a white morph of the female called alba.

Males patrol in search of receptive females, and the female, after mating, lays her pale yellow eggs singly on host plants. They will turn red after a few days and then gray just before hatching. The young larvae feed on legumes, especially clover,

but they are also cannibalistic and will eat one another. The green larva has two white stripes running down its body, which may contain bars of pink or orange. The chrysalis is green and hangs upright with a silk girdle. Just before eclosion, the emergence of the adult, the pupa turns yellow, with a pink "zipper." Three broods are usual for these butterflies, with the pupae of a third brood hibernating until spring in the North.

CATER TO CLOUDED SULPHURS

These butterflies are garden regulars and typically need little encouragement. Their main host plants are in the pea family: red clover, white sweet-clover, white clover, vetches, soybeans, alfalfa, and black locust. Nectar plants include many lepidopteran favorites like milkweed, coneflower, and butterfly bush. And don't forget the water sources and mud puddles.

(opposite page) A buttery yellow clouded sulphur nectaring on lantana.

(left) A pale alba morph of the clouded sulphur. The coloration of these butterflies is highly variable, with males and females showing different markings. Color also varies according to season, ranging from a cloudy white to a sulfurous green-yellow.

(middle) The black banding is noticeable on the male.

(right) Some clouded sulphurs have a green cast. The pigments responsible for the distinctive wing colors of the Pieridae are derived from waste products in the body.

similar species: *orange sulphur*

Also known as the alfalfa butterfly, the orange sulphur *(Colias eurytheme)* ranges from Canada to Mexico and will often interbreed with the clouded sulphur and other members of the *Colias* genus, producing hard-to-identify hybrids. It is a smallish butterfly, only 1.8 to 2.25 inches in diameter, and the male's upper wings are orange or deep yellow with solid black edges, while the female's upper wings show spots in the border. The orange sulphur caterpillar can be a pest in alfalfa fields.

Orange sulphurs gather on rocks to puddle, taking in salt and minerals.

Cloudless Sulphur

Phoebis sennae

Favorite plants

- bougainvillea
- cardinal flower
- hibiscus
- lantana
- morning glory
- zinnia
- cosmos
- penta

An attractive yellow butterfly with pink markings, the cloudless sulphur—also known as the cloudless giant sulphur—is primarily found throughout the American South, although it often travels north to Nebraska, Iowa, Illinois, and even New Jersey and Canada. It is also widespread in South America, as far south as Argentina, and throughout the West Indies.

Cloudless sulphurs prefer open spaces: their habitats include meadows, glades, overgrown fields, seashores, scrub lots, watercourses, road edges, and gardens.

The male and female are sexually dimorphic—presenting different markings or colorations. The adult male's dorsal wings are a lemon yellow with no markings; the female's are yellow or white with narrow black-spotted borders and an

similar species: *great southern white*

A delicate, medium-sized butterfly, the great southern white (*Ascia monuste*) is found along the Gulf Coast and the Mississippi Valley. Although both sexes are normally a creamy white with gray zigzags along the wing edge, in the wet season, the females turn pewter gray. Some populations may migrate along the Florida coast, but they only make a one-way trip in their lifetime. The larvae favor hosts in the mustard family, such as cabbages and radishes, as well as nasturtiums. Adults feed on many flowering species, including saltwort, lantana, and verbena.

A great southern white rests on a leaf, showing the tips of its antennae, which are pale blue.

irregular black spot on the forewing. Her upper ventral wing also has an irregular spot, while both sexes have two pink-edged silver spots on the ventral hind wing. Both the male's ventral wings are finely laced with deep pink.

Climate determines their breeding season, which can run from midsummer to fall in cooler regions. In the semitropics or tropics, cloudless sulphurs will breed all year long. Males fly rapidly as they search for potential mates near nectar plants. Females show receptivity by flicking their wings and then closing them. After mating, the female lays a pitcher-shaped white egg, which soon turns pale orange. In six days, it produces a hungry larva that will only feed on the leaves, buds, and flowers of the cassia tree or on American or wild senna, a perennial legume with a branched stem and multiple yellow blooms.

The larva's first instar is yellow and shrimplike, giving way to a green body with two yellow side stripes speckled with aqua and dark blue spots. Larvae that feed on flowers only show black bands across a yellow body. The mature larva attaches to a branch with both a cremaster and a central silk line and forms a bulging chrysalis—pointed at each end and humped in the center—that can be yellow or green with pink stripes. In several weeks, the adult butterfly will be ready to emerge.

SET THE TABLE FOR SULPHURS

If you want to attract these lively yellow pollinators to your garden, try long tubular blossoms like cardinal flower, hibiscus, and morning glory or annuals like cosmos and zinnia. Also, consider their host plant, American or wild senna, which is often used to landscape wildlife gardens.

Basics

WINGSPAN
1.9 to 2.8 inches

SEASONS
Broods midsummer to fall in temperate regions; year-round in warm regions

DISTRIBUTION
From the Deep South to Argentina and the West Indies; often found north to the Great Lakes

(opposite page) A cloudless sulphur nectaring on a zinnia. These flowers are one of the favorite blossoms of many butterfly species.

(left) A cloudless sulphur caterpillar. Its black bands indicate that its diet consists of flowers only. These caterpillars create a tent from a leaf on the host plant, where they hide from predators during the day.

(right) This dainty butterfly's genus name is derived from Phoebe, the sister of Apollo, a god of both Greek and Roman mythology. The specific name relates to its larval host, wild senna.

Cabbage White Butterfly

Pieris rapae

Favorite plants

- mustards
- dandelion
- red clover
- aster
- mint
- common sage
- sweet pea
- tickseed sunflower

Just as introduced birds will often usurp the territories and food resources of natives, so too do introduced butterflies affect indigenous species. The cabbage white butterfly, one of the most widespread in North America, was accidentally introduced to Quebec around 1860. By the time of the San Francisco earthquake in 1906, it had reached the American West Coast. It eventually challenged the native checkered white in many of its habitats. Fortunately, it is this continent's only introduced butterfly.

Also known as the small white, small cabbage white, or simply the white butterfly, it can be found on every fertile continent. The larvae feed on members of the mustard family and are considered a pest on cabbage, broccoli, kale, and

cauliflower. The sexes are similar: the dorsal wings are white with a black or gray tip on the forewing. The female shows two black spots on this wing, while the male shows only one. The underwings are yellowish green or greenish gray.

At present, cabbage whites range throughout North America, from southern Canada to northwest Mexico, except for desert regions and the Gulf Coast. They seek out open terrain in most settings: country fields, suburban picnic groves and yards, and abandoned lots or weedy riverbanks in cities.

Males court females by zigzagging up and down in front of them. The female lays a single, yellow, ridged egg on the underside of a host plant leaf. The caterpillar, also known as the imported cabbageworm, is grassy green with a narrow yellow stripe. Born hungry, it will

consume its own egg before feasting on the host plant. The larva anchors the leaflike chrysalis with both a cremaster and a silk girdle. Late broods overwinter inside the chrysalis. Cabbage white adults are among the earliest butterflies to emerge in spring, and they will continue to fly until the first hard frost of winter.

DINING WITH THE WHITES

These butterflies are not fussy eaters and will explore gardens featuring their favorite mustard family host plants, as well as wildflowers like dandelions, composites like asters and daisies, leafy greens like arugula and winter cress, herbs like sage and mint, legumes like clover and vetch, and sedums like 'Autumn Joy'.

(opposite page) A cabbage white nectaring on cow vetch, which is a member of the Fabaceae, the legume or pea family—a favorite food source for this butterfly.

(top) Caterpillars of this species prefer to feed on members of the mustard and cabbage family (Brassicaceae). The mustard oil in these host plants makes the larvae distasteful to birds.

(bottom) Mating cabbage whites. During courtship, a male will sometimes catch the closed wings of a female and fly short distances with her dangling beneath him.

similar species: *checkered white*

Although the checkered white *(Pontia protodice)*, a small white butterfly with gray markings, is still widespread, competition with the cabbage white has resulted in some population loss. During mating, males are able to pass along protein nutrients to the female that aid in egg production. These butterflies feed on composites, like daisy and aster, hibiscus, lantana, and cardinal flower, as well as legumes and mustards. Its host plants include mustards and cabbages (family Brassicaceae), along with caper.

The female has gray spots with mustard to yellow-green slashes that give it a checkered appearance.

Monarch

Danaus plexippus

Favorite plants

- milkweed
- Joe-pye weed
- coneflower
- ironweed
- aster
- marigold
- zinnia
- cosmos

Is there an observer of nature who doesn't admire the monarch? It is familiar to us in many forums: flitting through gardens or inside butterfly enclosures; in the classroom, where its life cycle becomes a teaching tool; and in documentaries about its curious affinity for milkweed and its marathon migrations. It also happens to be one of the most beautiful of the North American butterflies.

The monarch is a milkweed butterfly, subfamily Danainae, which lay their eggs exclusively on milkweed plants. There are roughly 300 species worldwide, with four in North America. The milkweeds belong to the Nymphalidae, the brush-foots, which is the largest family of butterflies with more than 6,000 species. As the common name suggests, some species have brushlike hairs on their forelegs.

The monarch's striking wing coloration—intense black veining surrounding fields of bright orange and black borders dotted with white—signals to predators that this butterfly is poisonous (due to its larval diet of milkweed). The veining on the male's wings is narrower than the female's and may be paler, and he is typically larger. There are two populations in North America, the western and eastern; it is the latter that migrates to Mexico and the Southwest in winter.

Monarchs love to bask in the sunlight; they frequent agricultural fields, meadows, prairies, urban lots, suburban gardens, riverbanks, and roadsides—or anywhere they can find host plants during breeding season. In the fall, migrating populations need access to nectar for energy. Females lay single cream-colored or pale green eggs on the underside of new milkweed leaves. The larvae then go through five growth periods, or instars, and during the second instar develop their distinctive banding of white, yellow, and black. When it is ready to pupate, the caterpillar hangs upside down by its hind legs, sheds its skin, and forms a green, gold-flecked exoskeleton. The "newly minted" adult emerges from this chrysalis in about two weeks.

MEALS FOR MONARCHS

These butterflies will seek out a range of plants, including lilac, clover, dogbane, lantana, and thistle, as well as fall perennials like goldenrod, aster, coreopsis, and sunflower. Don't forget to supply several varieties of host plants, such as common milkweed (*Asclepias syriaca*), swamp milkweed (*A. incarnata*), and showy milkweed (*A. speciosa*). You can also concoct a fruit cocktail that will tempt monarchs and other species. Just place slices of orange, grapefruit, cantaloupe, strawberry, peach, kiwi, apple, nectarine, watermelon, or banana outside in a sunny location. Keep in mind that they prefer mushy, overripe fruit.

Basics

WINGSPAN
3.5 to 4.5 inches

SEASONS
One to three broods in the North; four to six in the South

DISTRIBUTION
From North America, it has spread to Cuba, Hawaii, the South Pacific, Australia, India, North Africa, and South Africa.

(opposite page) Monarchs nectaring on asters. These butterflies cover fields of asters during fall migration.

(top) Overripe fruit in a shallow pan can attract butterflies to your yard.

(left) A monarch nectaring on milkweed. Most species of milkweed contains cardiac glycosides, poisons that are stored in the bodies of both the caterpillar and adult monarch. These chemicals are distasteful to birds and other vertebrate predators.

(right) A monarch chrysalis is a lovely gilded jade green.

Monarch's Milk

Nothing benefits monarchs more than a steady supply of milkweed, and so you may want to join the concerned gardeners across the country who are cultivating this host plant. Because wildflowers can be capricious about taking root, make sure your milkweed will thrive by sowing collected seeds into a mulched bed in the fall or starting them indoors under a grow light before transplanting them outdoors.

Preserving the Monarch Butterfly

LOCAL AND MULTINATIONAL SUPPORT AIDS THREATENED MIGRATORS

Scores of monarch butterflies cluster together on pines and eucalyptus trees during their migration to overwinter in Monarch Grove Sanctuary, Pacific Grove, California.

Most butterflies live only a short time; some barely a week or so. But certain populations of monarch butterflies live long enough to migrate south in the fall and begin the journey home in spring. Eastern monarchs continue to breed in summer—and it is the later broods that are destined for something special. In August or October, newly emerged adults take part in a massive migration, traveling thousands of miles to wintering spots in central Mexico and the Southwest. During this journey, the butterflies enter

diapause, a state in which their bodies store lipids, carbohydrates, and proteins.

Those that reach the Mexican forests will carpet tall trees in aggregations that may contain a million butterflies or more. When it's time to seek water, they cascade down toward the ground en masse, in black and orange ripples, before taking flight. They come out of diapause around February, and many will mate before leaving. As the females travel north, they lay eggs along the way, and when these butterflies emerge, they continue the trip

Monarchs in Space

In 2009, monarchs may have made the ultimate migration when their larvae, along with those of painted ladies, were transported to the International Space Station in their own habitat aboard the space shuttle *Atlantis*. There, they were expected to complete metamorphosis as part of an educational experiment monitored by school children on earth. As the first adult monarch emerged from its chrysalis and floated gently in the weightless environment, the astronauts reported that they were "happy parents."

How monarchs find their familial "turf" is one of nature's mysteries.

home. Oftentimes, the butterflies that arrive at the original breeding ground are several generations removed from those that left in the fall. How monarchs find their familial "turf" is one of nature's mysteries.

A STAGGERING DECREASE
Monarchs have been completing this perilous journey for eons without any serious problems. During the past decade, however, conservationists began noticing a sharp decline in their numbers. Many gardeners simply stopped seeing these beauties. Most significantly, observers in Mexico were reporting that the number of hectares (1.65 acres) the butterflies occupied had dropped severely—from 27.5 in 2003 to 1.65 in 2013.

Researchers cite three factors behind this crisis: deforestation and illegal logging in the monarch's Mexican habitats; recent bouts of severe weather, attributed to climate change; and loss of critical milkweed plants to herbicides.

But things are looking up for these valuable pollinators. Thanks to a 2014 summit between the United States,

Canada, and Mexico—and subsequent steps taken to foster monarchs—the wintering population in Mexico is expected to quadruple in 2015 to nearly four hectares. The ultimate goal is to reach six hectares by the end of the decade.

(top) Scores of monarchs cluster together. In Mexico, they use oyamel fir trees; in California, eucalyptus. They somehow know and use the same trees year after year.

(bottom) A tagged monarch, Many organizations use tagging to track these butterflies and study their migration patterns. Tagging is now a popular educational project for student and wildlife groups.

Queen Butterfly

Danaus gilippus

Favorite plants

- milkweed
- butterfly weed
- zinnia
- late boneset
- ragwort
- heliotrope
- mistflower
- shepherd's needle

The elegant and regal queen butterfly makes a perfect consort for the monarch and is another of North America's spectacular brush-foots. These moderately large butterflies inhabit the Deep South—Florida to Texas to Southern California—and the tropical lowlands of the West Indies, as well as Central and South America. They are also regularly sighted on the Great Plains and sometimes along the Atlantic seaboard. Their preferred terrain is open land: meadows, fields, and marshes. They will also investigate the edges of hammocks and forests, but rarely enter them.

At a glance, the queen butterfly may be mistaken for the monarch, but its coloring is more uniform, with less veining—the dorsal wings are a rich, ruddy chestnut with black borders, the forewing borders

Basics

WINGSPAN
2.8 to 3.75 inches

SEASONS
Broods in July and August in central states; year-round in Florida and Texas

DISTRIBUTION
The Deep South; the West Indies; Mexico to Argentina; occasionally the Great Plains

show two rows of white spots, and the apex is scattered with white spots. Both underwings are edged in black with double rows of spots, and the hind underwing is veined in black.

Males actively patrol for females, which are capable of mating up to 15 times daily. Male queen butterflies possess signaling organs called hair-pencils that emit pheromones to attract females—these chemicals may act as both an aphrodisiac and a tranquilizer. The odors can also repel competitive males of the same species. Hair-pencils are normally internal, but during courtship they are levered outside the abdomen. Females often pass over males with low hair-pencil levels. Both male monarchs and male queens have scaly black scent spots, called androconia, on their dorsal hind wings. In queens, these spots emit pheromones, but on the monarchs they do not—scientists are not sure what their purpose is.

The female lays a single, creamy, ovoid egg on the underside of a milkweed leaf; it will hatch in about four days. By the second instar, the larvae are vibrantly striped with yellow, white, and black. Even though they are quite similar to monarch caterpillars, they are darker overall and have two pairs of long, fleshy tubercles—or filaments. After four instars, the larvae are ready for pupating. The queen's chrysalis is a smaller replica of the monarch's celadon green case, even down to the golden flecks. Sometimes the chrysalis may be a soft pink. Adults generally emerge in two weeks.

PLEASING THE QUEEN
Luckily, adult queens are easily satisfied. They seek out nectar-rich plants—notably wildflowers like milkweed and shepherd's needle, overripe fruit, and even dung piles. Host plants include, of course, many species of milkweed, as well as dogbane.

(opposite page) A male queen butterfly nectaring on mistflower. The base color of the queen's wings may range from a deep orange to chocolate brown, but there are always rows of white spots against the darker wing borders.

(left) A queen butterfly feeding on pink boneset, one of this species' favorite sources of nectar.

(right) Queen caterpillars making a meal of a leaf. The larvae's main purpose is to eat as much as they can. A larva with a poor diet will result in a smaller adult butterfly; one that has ingested lots of nutritious foliage will metamorphose into a larger, healthier adult.

similar species: *soldier butterfly*

This largish, deep orange butterfly of subtropical North and South America is sometimes mistaken for the queen, but the soldier butterfly *(Danaus eresimus)* has slightly more veining. It is a slow-flying butterfly that can easily be approached for study in citrus groves, weedy watercourses, dry fields, and forest edges. Host plants include milkweed and the strangler vine.

This heat-loving butterfly is also called the tropical queen due to its resemblance to *Danaus gilippus*.

Northern Pearly-Eye

Enodia anthedon

Favorite tree sap

- poplar
- willow
- birch

This earth-toned butterfly is part of the Satyrinae, or brown family, which includes the satyrs and wood-nymphs. This family exceeds 2,400 species, making up more than half the brush-footed butterflies. The satyrs and wood-nymphs are small- to medium-sized butterflies with brownish, often drab, wings that typically show several eyespots—dark circles surrounded by a lighter color.

Weak fliers that avoid bright sunlight, these butterflies are more likely to be found in damp, shady woodlands than in dry, open fields. Their larvae feed on grasses, palms, and bamboos.

The northern pearly-eye ranges across North America, from central Canada east to New England and south to Mississippi and Alabama. Like most satyrs, it prefers marshy grasslands, waterways, and dense

similar species: *eyed brown*

A low-flying native of central and eastern North America, the eyed brown (*Satyrodes eurydice*) is found in open meadows, grassy prairies, and marshlands. It is pale brown in color with prominent eyespots, each with a light dot in the center and four yellow and dark brown rings around it. The forewing eyespots are smaller than the hind wing spots. Female eyed browns scatter their eggs among many host plants, although the caterpillars prefer to feed on members of the *Carex* genus, such as lake, wheat, bottle, or tussock sedge. Third- and fourth-stage larvae hibernate over the winter.

An eyed brown butterfly. As members of this species age, their color steadily lightens.

woods and is often seen on rural dirt or gravel roads. These butterflies are swift, but erratic, in flight. Their wings are slightly scalloped; the dorsal wings are a taupe or purplish brown, with deep brown eyespots at the borders. The ventral wings are also pale brown with a row of four black spots on the forewing and five or more on the hind. The orange clubbed antennae are tipped in black near the top.

Courting males perch facing downward on tree trunks or vegetation at the edge of open spaces to await passing females. After mating, females lay a single, green, barrel-shaped egg on the stem of some type of woodland grass. The "hairy" caterpillar is leaf green with green and yellow lateral stripes. The horns are red and the forked tail, a satyr trait, is pink. Third- and fourth-stage caterpillars hibernate over the winter in green pupae with cream-colored heads.

Populations of northern pearly-eyes have fluctuated in the past two centuries. During the late 19th and early 20th centuries, they dipped due to the heavy deforestation taking place in the eastern United States. Recent reforestation programs have once again provided these butterflies with their favorite habitat, and their numbers are now steady; some specimens even move outside their range and turn up in new areas.

PLANTING FOR PEARLY-EYES

Even though these butterflies do not feed on nectar, but instead dine in the woods on tree sap, rotting fruit, fungi, carrion, mud, and dung, northern pearly-eyes might come to shady gardens or yards near woodlands that provide larval host plants, including white grass, orchard grass, bearded shorthusk, Japanese stiltgrass, plumegrass, and bottlebrush.

Basics

WINGSPAN

1.75 to 2.60 inches

SEASONS

One brood, June to August in North; two broods in South, May to September

DISTRIBUTION

Across southern Canada, Saskatchewan to Nova Scotia; across the United States, Nebraska to the East Coast and then as far south as Alabama

(opposite page) You will most likely see a northern pearly-eye in the woods heading down a tree trunk.

(left and right) The bristly larvae are acid green with pink tails and salmon horns.

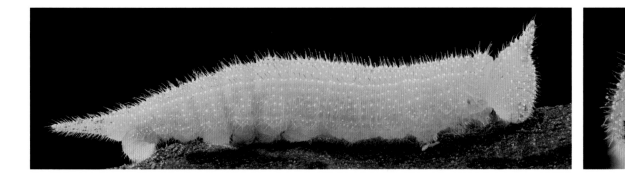

Common Wood-Nymph

Cercyonis pegala

Favorite plants

- purple coneflower
- lantana
- milkweed
- bee balm
- butterfly bush
- thistle
- alfalfa

Also known as the wood-nymph, grayling, blue-eyed grayling, and the goggle eye, the common wood-nymph is frequently found across southern Canada and the United States from coast to coast. Its range can be patchy, however, in parts of the South and Southwest, and it does not occur at all at the southern end of the Florida peninsula. These medium-sized butterflies prefer open, grassy areas like prairies, meadows, bogs, scrublands, coastal marshes, and old fields. They are often seen along woodland trails, and it has been reported that they roost overnight among the trees.

Common wood-nymphs are always a hazy brown, but beyond that they can vary greatly. They all have two large eyespots with yellow rings on the dorsal forewing, with the lower usually larger

Looking for Love

Most female butterflies choose their mates based on visual and olfactory data. Scent is especially important close up, which is why some males release sex pheromones, chemical communicators that attract females, as they approach potential mates. These can be produced by the scent spots on their wings or by the protruding, brushlike hair-pencils on their abdomens. Females are able to detect—and refuse—genetically weakened inbred males because they give off fewer pheromones.

than the upper. The ventral hind wing shows a variety of markings—it may have many, a few, or no eyespots. Butterflies of the southern or the coastal regions are generally larger and have a wide yellow or orange-yellow patch on both sides of the forewing in addition to the eyespots. Western butterflies are smaller and show a much smaller yellow area or no patch at all. Some northeastern subspecies lack the yellow patch entirely.

In breeding season, after mating, the female lays her eggs, one at a time, on or near the host plants, which can include a variety of grasses. The waxy eggs are pale yellow, later turning tan with pink or orange blotches. The larvae are yellowish

green, with darker green lateral stripes. They also have yellow spiracles covered with short hairs, and there are two pinkish projections at the end of the abdomen. The first-stage instar does not feed, but instead it climbs down the grass stem and burrows into the soil, where it will hibernate until spring. When the weather warms, it digs out and begins eating. The chrysalis it eventually forms is pale green, striped with pale yellow or white.

WOOING WOOD-NYMPHS

These butterflies have eclectic appetites, normally feeding on sap, aphid honeydew, dung, and carrion, but they also enjoy nectar-rich plants like purple coneflowers, bee balm, and lantana, and they may light on a platform feeder with ripe or even rotting fruit. They might also come to your yard to lay their eggs on host plants like purple topgrass or Kentucky bluegrass.

Basics

WINGSPAN
2 to 3 inches

SEASONS
One brood from late May to October; males emerge first.

DISTRIBUTION
Across most of the northern United States, a bit more spotty in the South and Southwest

(opposite page) Mating common wood-nymphs. Females are the active flight partners during mating season, although males do patrol with a dipping flight through the foliage.

(bottom) A common wood-nymph feeding on sap from a tree. Despite its name, this butterfly prefers meadows and roadsides, rather than dense woodland.

similar species: *common alpine*

This distinctive dark brown butterfly, the common alpine (*Erebia epipsodea*), with its vivid, orange-bordered eyespots is found throughout western North America, from Alaska south to the Rocky Mountain states. Common alpines prefer high altitudes; they are found in mountainous terrain, open meadows, and weedy scrub. Their dark color helps them absorb sunlight as they bask. Weak fliers, they often appear to bounce above grass and other vegetation as they forage for nectar. Males spend most of their days looking for females or congregating with other males at mud puddles. Females lay their eggs on both live and dead grasses.

Caramel-colored shading encloses the eyespots on the chocolate-hued wings of the common alpine.

Baltimore Checkerspot

Euphydryas phaeton

Favorite plants

- milkweed
- viburnum
- wild rose
- thistle
- dogbane
- wild blackberry
- white turtlehead

Checkerspots are small- to medium-sized butterflies that lay their eggs in layered clusters. The caterpillars are tiny, spiny, and feed in groups. They later form a hanging chrysalis that is white scattered with darker patches.

The Baltimore is an abundant, colorful checkerspot of the northeastern United States and the central South. It seeks out wet meadows and marshes where it lays eggs on its chief host, the white turtlehead (*Chelone glabra*) and may also be spotted in the uplands surrounding watercourses.

They are sluggish fliers and can sometimes be coaxed onto a human hand while nectaring. The dorsal wings are black with orange-red spots near the top of each forewing and rows of orange-red dots along the wing margins. Multiple rows of parallel pale yellow spots border the

Basics

WINGSPAN
1.75 to 2.75 inches

SEASONS
One brood—June to
August in the North,
May to June in the South

DISTRIBUTION
Northeastern United
States from the Great
Lakes south to Georgia

orange. The body is a dark brown and the antennae have pronounced knobs.

Males patrol for females close to the ground. Females lay 100 to 700 yellow, ribbed eggs in irregular, layered clusters on the undersides of host plant leaves. The eggs will eventually turn purplish. The caterpillars hatch together and then feed together in a web, which they use to envelop part of the host plant. The larva's head is black, and the orange body is marked with black rings. Most noticeable are the blue-black bristling spines along the back, which erupt out of papillae in bands of at least five on each segment. Fourth instar caterpillars hibernate inside the web, which forms a hard mass the size of a chicken's egg. Some leave the web and pass the winter wrapped inside leaves

on the ground. In spring, the larvae begin feeding again. The chrysalis is quite distinctive—bluish white with velvety black and pale orange markings over raised tubercles that mark the caterpillar's spines—though it may be well camouflaged among the trees. The larva pupates for 8 to 14 days before the adult emerges.

HOSTING BALTIMORES

Adult butterflies will come to your garden to feed on milkweed, viburnum, and wild rose and may appreciate marsh plants for hosting their larvae—white turtlehead, as well as hairy beardtongue, English plantain, and false foxglove. When the caterpillars emerge in spring, in addition to hosts, they may feed on arrowwood, Japanese honeysuckle, and white ash.

(opposite page) The black and orange checkers on its wings evoke the colors of the coat of arms of George Calvert, the first Lord Baltimore, from whom this butterfly takes its name. The Baltimore checkerspot has been the official insect of Maryland since 1973.

(left) Like the adults, the bristly caterpillars feature a distinctive black-and-orange patterning. These larvae are vulnerable to attacks by parasitic wasps and from falling off the plant.

(right) A tiny Baltimore checkerspot alights on a human finger. Up close, it is clear that these butterflies are much smaller than they appear when they are flying.

similar species: *chalcedon checkerspot*

Also known as the variable checkerspot, the chalcedon checkerspot (*Euphydryas chalcedona*), is a black-and-white butterfly with dark orange or blood red spots. It inhabits western North America from Alaska to the Baja and extends east past the Rockies. Males gather around host plants hoping to encounter females, and then put on a display prior to mating. Afterward, they deposit a mating plug that hinders females from copulating with other males. Larvae overwinter in a state of diapause inside a hollow stem or rock crevice. Adults live only about 15 days.

Its coloring provides defense for chalcedon checkerspots: intense red deters potential predators.

Silvery Checkerspot

Chlosyne nycteis

Favorite plants

- sunflower
- black-eyed Susan
- cosmos
- milkweed
- verbena
- purple coneflower
- daisy
- aster

With their complex patterning and silvery wing borders, these ornate checkerspots are among the most popular and attractive of the butterflies that visit suburban gardens. Silvery checkerspots are found in a variety of habitats across the northeastern and central states and as far south as Texas, frequenting open wetlands, streambanks, fields, meadows, roadsides, and nature trails—anywhere that their favored host plants grow

They are small- to medium-sized butterflies with yellow-orange dorsal wings that feature splashy black markings and black wing margins edged with white dashes. Their ventral wings are much lighter: tan veining on pale orange or yellow fields and a white crescent in the center of the darker hind-wing margin.

similar species: *Harris's checkerspot*

The Harris's checkerspot (*Chlosyne harrisi*) is a black-and-orange butterfly, similar to the silvery, but the underwing shows a checkered pattern in orange, white, and black and a red-orange stripe along the margin. Its range extends across southern Canada from Manitoba to the Maritimes and throughout the Northeast from the Great Lakes to New England and south to West Virginia. Larvae feed in a community web and hibernate at the base of the host, the flat-topped white aster; adults feed on nectar.

The Harris's checkerspot's preferred habitats are marshes, bog edges, and pastures.

Silvery checkerspots tend to fly lower to the ground than other butterflies—about waist high—and are fast on the wing, moving in straight lines from one sunny basking place to the next. Adults feed on cosmos, milkweed, and tall verbena and especially love sunflowers—as both a nectar source and a larval host.

The adults can be very active from spring to fall. Males pass the time puddling or spending their days patrolling for receptive females. The females will lay eggs in batches of 100 on the underside of the host plant's foliage. Their favored plants, besides sunflowers, include other Asteraceae: black-eyed Susans, asters, daisies, and goldenrod.

The caterpillars hatch in groups and quickly begin to skeletonize host leaves. Even large, mature sunflowers can be decimated by these hungry hordes, making them of concern to farmers when vulnerable young plants are developing. Fortunately, the caterpillars are not abundant enough to warrant the use of pesticides. These small larvae are black with orange stripes along the body, which is covered with purplish, bristling spines. When they are partially grown, they hibernate at the base of host flowers. Their suspended chrysalis is mushroom white with raised dark markings where the spines project from the caterpillar.

CHECKERSPOT CHECKLIST

If you want to attract these bright beauties to your garden, provide nectar-rich plants like cosmos, coneflowers, and milkweed, as well as host plants like black-eyed Susan and goldenrod. And don't forget to create a small mud puddle as a gathering spot for the males.

Basics

WINGSPAN
1.38 to 2 inches

SEASONS
One brood in the North, two in the South; three or more in the Deep South

DISTRIBUTION
Northeastern half of the United States, east from the Rockies; central states south to Texas

(opposite page) Perched on the flower head, a silvery checkerspot nectars on a variegated black-eyed Susan. These checkerspots are also called sunflower butterflies—not surprisingly, considering members of the sunflower family—the Asteraceae—are its favorite nectar and host plants.

(left) A silvery checkerspot basks on a rock.

(right) The undersides of the wings appear lighter than the dorsal sides. Silvery checkerspots tend to show more wear and tear on their wings than other butterflies, and as they age, their patterning loses contrast.

Pearl Crescent

Phyciodes tharos

Favorite plants

- New England aster
- tickseed sunflower
- daisy fleabane
- winter cress
- black-eyed Susan
- marigold
- swamp milkweed
- zinnia

The attractive orange-and-black crescent butterflies are closely allied to the slightly larger and similarly ornate checkerspots. A pale crescent on the margin of the under hind wing helps to identify these brush-foots. The larvae are social feeders, but they do not form webs like checkerspots. In general, summer broods result in paler butterflies than winter broods.

The pearl crescent is a common North American butterfly that ranges across southern Canada and throughout the United States—except for the Pacific coast—and down into Mexico. It flies from spring to fall in temperate regions but is active year-round in the South. It prefers open spaces like meadows, fields, airy pine woods, vacant lots, roadsides, and gardens, and it is likely to favor areas

where its host plant—members of the Asteraceae, or aster family—can be found.

Pearl crescents are easy to spot: they enjoy basking in the sunlight and tend to be low fliers. Their appearance can be variable, but the wings are generally a rich orange above, with dark brown or black markings and wing margins. The undersides of the wings are paler, and the hind wing has a dark marginal patch with a paler crescent. There is also less variegated coloring here than in the checkerspots or fritillaries. The antennae are black with orange-tipped knobs.

Like checkerspot males, these crescents also like to gather in groups at mud puddles and patrol actively for females. After mating, the females lay ribbed, glistening, pale green eggs in neat rows on the underside of smooth-leaved asters

such as *Aster pilosus, A. texanus,* and *A. laevis.* In 4 to 10 days, the larvae will hatch and begin feeding in groups on the host leaves, gradually moving down the plant. Larval coloring is dark brown or black with paler bands and rows of bristly spines. Third-stage caterpillars hibernate, possibly in crevices. Upon emerging in spring, they feed singly until ready to pupate. The suspended, "corrugated" chrysalis may range in hue from a pale mottled gray to deep brown. The adult emerges after 10 to 15 days.

CATERING TO CRESCENTS
These butterflies will be attracted to a yard containing flowers of the Asteraceae, such as sunflower, thistle, aster, gloriosa daisy (the wild variety), and other nectar-rich plants. They also seek out some of these same plants as hosts for their eggs and larva. Create a mud puddle or provide a basin of damp sand for moisture.

Basics

WINGSPAN
1.25 to 1.75 inches

SEASONS
Several broods in the North, April to November; continuous brooding in the South

DISTRIBUTION
Across southern Canada and the United States, except in the Northwest and extreme Southwest

(opposite page) A pearl crescent nectaring on daisy fleabane. Like most checkerspots and crescents, this butterfly is attracted to daisies and other members of the Asteraceae family.

(top) These butterflies take their name from the pale crescent shape near the center of the hind wing's submarginal markings.

(bottom) Mating pearl crescents. You are likely to spot these butterflies nectaring in groups, with males often actively wooing females. A male's courtship behavior might include a chase and wing fluttering displays.

similar species: *field crescent*

A small butterfly of the American West, the field crescent (*Phyciodes pulchella*) ranges from Alaska to Arizona but is quite prevalent in California. A brown-and-orange brush-foot, it has black margins, spots, and lines on the dorsal wings; the underside is pale yellow-brown with rusty markings. Adults frequent open areas such as meadows, fields, and streamsides from the flatlands to the mountains. The larvae feed on asters and may form a loose web before hibernating.

Their pattern is the same, but field crescents appear blacker than the orange pearl crescents.

Eastern Comma

Polygonia comma

Favorite plants

- butterfly bush
- milkweed
- Joe-pye weed
- sumac

Anglewing butterflies, genus *Polygonia*, are members of the brush-foot family that display distinctive angular notches on the outer edges of their wings and have a comma-shaped white spot on the hind underwing.

The eastern comma is a small- to medium-sized butterfly of deciduous woodlands, sunny fields, road edges, forest clearings, and marshes. There it feeds on tree sap, overripe fruit, and animal droppings. Its range extends across southeastern Canada, throughout the eastern half of the United States, and south into Texas and the Gulf Coast.

The upper wings are vivid orange with irregular deep brown blotches. The underwings are striped with a mix of muted browns with a white or silver comma-shaped mark on the hind wing.

Basics

WINGSPAN
1.75 to 2 inches

SEASONS
Overwintering adults brood until April; summer form broods May to September.

DISTRIBUTION
Southeastern Canada; eastern half of the United States, south to Texas and Gulf Coast

This dull coloration helps to camouflage butterflies hibernating among dead leaves. The hind wings also have short projections.

Courting males perch watchfully in the foliage, waiting for receptive females to fly past. These males are known to be aggressive and will actively defend their territories, pursuing any perceived threats—competing males or even birds. Females lay pale green, ribbed, barrel-shaped eggs in tidy columns on the underside of developing leaves. Host plants include several types of nettles, currents, elm trees, willows, and hop trees.

Eastern comma larval coloration is variable—the body and branching protective spines may range in hue from white to green to black. These larvae are solitary and generally feed at night. Some older caterpillars make daytime tents by sealing a leaf around their bodies with silk. The spiny chrysalis is light brown adorned with pale green streaks; pupation takes from 7 to 11 days. Second-brood adults that emerge in the fall will spend the winter hibernating under tree bark or in leaf litter, sometimes after first migrating farther south.

COURTING THE COMMA

These butterflies feed mainly on tree sap, fermenting fruit, and dung, but they will occasionally take nectar from butterfly bushes, common milkweed, Joe-pye weed, and smooth sumac. Yards that furnish host plants like elm and willow trees, currant bushes, and nettles will also encourage them to linger.

(opposite page) An eastern comma nectaring on a butterfly bush. When it rests with its wings open, the distinctive notching of the wings is very noticeable.

(left) With its wings tightly closed, the eastern comma resembles a dead leaf or piece of bark, a trait that helps to disguise this small butterfly from predators.

(right) An eastern comma butterfly alights on a bunch of ripening grapes. Like other anglewings, eastern commas prefer fruit, sap, and dung over flower nectar.

similar species: *satyr comma*

A butterfly of valley bottoms, wooded prairies, and marsh edges, the satyr comma (*Polygonia satyrus*) is found in western Canada, throughout the American West, and south to the Baja. Less abundantly, it ranges across the Great Lakes to New England. The satyr comma greatly resembles the eastern comma in both appearance and life cycle. Its larval hosts are a variety of nettles, while adult butterflies feed on tree sap, rotting fruit, and nectar from blackberries and almond trees.

A satyr comma. Males will spend their afternoons perched on tree trunks to watch for females.

Question Mark

Polygonia interrogationis

Favorite plants

- milkweed
- aster
- butterfly bush
- heliotrope

This vibrant anglewing haunts open woodlands throughout the eastern United States and across southern Canada. It also seeks habitats with trees and open spaces like city parks, fencerows, and suburban yards, where it feeds on sap flows, rotting fruit, carrion, and dung piles. Question mark butterflies will occasionally nectar on the blossoms of wildflowers, as well.

With its notched wings colored a bright red-orange and its brown or black markings, the question mark butterfly resembles its relative the comma. In addition to being slightly larger, however, the question mark's upper forewing shows four spots beside the wing margin, while the comma shows only three.

After returning north or emerging from hibernation, males bask on tree trunks,

Basics

WINGSPAN
2.5 to 3.0 inches

SEASONS
Spring brood from late June to mid-August; late brood from late August to October

DISTRIBUTION
Across southern Canada; throughout the eastern United States, south to central Florida

flying out to inspect passing butterflies for eager females. The females will lay their pale green, barrel-shaped eggs singly or in small stacks on leaves or twigs—typically not on the host plant. The larvae can be black, brown, or rust, with yellow lateral stripes and rows of bristly spines on the body. After hatching, these caterpillars must locate host plants on their own—these include elm trees, nettle, false nettle, hackberry, and possibly basswood.

The distinctive chrysalis, which often resembles a dead leaf, can be a brown, greenish, or tan color with olive spots; it sports ridges on the body and two hornlike projections on the head. Metamorphosis takes 11 to 17 days. An early summer brood, called the umbrosa form, has darker hind wings and emerges between late June and mid August; a later flight, known as the fabricii form, emerges from late August to October. Some late adults may hibernate, but the majority migrate south and return in the spring.

WOOING WITH WILDFLOWERS

Even though these anglewings prefer to dine on sap, fruit, and droppings, question marks will also nectar at milkweed and members of the aster family. You might consider hackberry for a host plant, but be careful of this butterfly's nettle favorites, which have stinging leaves. Males enjoy mud puddling, so be sure to furnish them with a patch of damp soil.

(opposite page) The mottled brown color and ragged shape of the question mark when it closes its wings give it the look of a dead leaf, a camouflage that can help it avoid predation. The narrow silver crescent with a dot below it—which resembles an inverted question mark—on the ventral surface of the hind underwing gives this species its common name.

(top) A question mark butterfly pays a rare visit to flowers. In the winter form of this anglewing, the upper surface of the long hind wing is tipped with a delicate pale violet.

(bottom) The appearance of the caterpillar is highly variable, and its spines range in color from yellow and orange to black.

Mourning Cloak

Nymphalis antiopa

Favorite plants

- willow
- black willow
- American elm
- hackberry
- hawthorn
- wild rose
- poplar
- thyme

This large, darkly elegant butterfly is a member of the *Nymphalis*, or tortoiseshell, genus, which is quite similar to the anglewings except that the inner margin of the forewing is straight, not concave. Adults hibernate in winter and emerge very early in spring, sometimes while there is snow on the ground. Tortoiseshells are found around the world in the Northern Hemisphere.

The mourning cloak is a spectacular species, a striking color-blocked purple-black with buff wing borders lined with iridescent blue dots—a standout in a genus of mottled black-and-orange butterflies. The underwings are a dark gray-brown with paler edges.

This butterfly was once called the white petticoat, and in Britain it is known as the Camberwell beauty or the grand surprise—

possibly because stowaways on a ship from Sweden were the first sighted. Its American common name, mourning cloak, came with Scandinavian or German settlers and is a literal translation from the Swedish *sorgmantel* or German *Trauermantel*.

These butterflies are unfussy roamers that can be found across most of North America in open woods, parks, clearings, and suburban yards and along waterways. Emergent males enjoy basking in sunny spots but will actively court females in the air. The female lays 30 to 50 eggs in a mass surrounding a host plant twig. Hosts include several varieties of willow, aspen, American elm, cottonwood, paper birch, and hackberry trees.

The larvae, called spiny elm caterpillars, are dark and hairy with red spots and feed together in a communal web. The chrysalis is brown and leaflike and has thorny protrusions. Adults usually emerge in June or July. During summer heat spells, they estivate—enter a state of dormancy—and when cool fall weather arrives they become active and start eating like crazy in preparation for winter. Mourning cloaks may spend as many as ten months as adults, a long life for a butterfly.

HOSTING MOURNING CLOAKS

It's true that these butterflies are not great nectar feeders, but they do frequent suburbs, most likely to lay their eggs on common landscaping trees like willow, elm, aspen, and paper birch. They also enjoy lapping up sap from oak trees.

Basics

WINGSPAN
2.25 to 4.0 inches

SEASONS
One flight from
June to July

DISTRIBUTION
Most of North America
south of the tundra and
down to Mexico

(opposite page) A mourning cloak on a paper birch. These butterflies are often the first to emerge from hibernation. This allows them to take advantage of one of their main food sources: tree sap, which starts to rise in early spring.

(top) Even though they feed in groups, the larvae move apart to pupate; all their collective waste can attract hungry birds.

(left) The gray pupa can look like old leaves with two rows of red-tipped points.

(right) A mourning cloak in spring, just after emerging from hibernation. Clothing has inspired two of this butterfly's common names: mourning cloak comes from its somber coloration, and white petticoat from the snowy edges on its wings, which resemble a frilly crinoline peeking from beneath a skirt.

Painted Lady

Vanessa cardui

Favorite plants

- thistle
- aster
- cosmos
- Joe-pye weed
- red clover
- privet
- milkweed
- heliotrope

The thistle butterflies are named for their primary larval host—members of the thistle, or aster, family. Adults of some species, like the painted lady, migrate, while others hibernate over the winter. Thistle butterflies occur in many temperate and some tropical regions.

The graceful and elegant painted lady is the most widely distributed butterfly in the world; it is sometimes called the cosmopolitan because it occurs on every continent except Antarctica. It is part of the *Cynthia* group—a subgenus of the *Vanessas*—that includes the American lady *(V. virginiensis)*, the Australian painted lady *(V. kershawi)*, and the West Coast lady *(V. annabella)*. Although this specific butterfly, *V. cardui*, does not reside in the United States, it frequently

migrates from Mexico to colonize northern regions well into Canada, sometimes in great numbers, especially after rainy spells in the desert.

A lover of open spaces like prairies and fields, these butterflies can be found in almost any disturbed area—vacant lots, parks, garden, even oil fields. They feed on nectar from tall composite plants, as well as privet, red clover, and milkweed.

The overall visual effect of this butterfly is one of delicacy and contrast. The wings are gently scalloped and edged in white. The dorsal surfaces are deep orange with black veining, and the apex of the forewing is black with a white bar. The ventral forewing shows contrasting patches of red-orange and black; the hind wing is a patterned tan, gray, and white with four small submarginal eyespots.

Western males scout for females from hilltop shrubs; eastern males perch on bare patches of ground. The pale green, ridged eggs are the size of a pinhead and are laid on the leaves of the host plants— including thistle, mallow, sunflower, hollyhock, and some legumes—and hatch in three to five days. The caterpillars are dark purple or black with yellow-green stripes and pale spines on each segment. After hatching they feed for five to ten

days inside a silk-webbed nest and then form a pearly while chrysalis with golden flecks. The adult butterfly will emerge in seven to ten days. In the South or during milder winters, adults may hibernate. Sadly, the lifespan of this lovely butterfly is often only two to four weeks.

LURING PAINTED LADIES

Bring these attractive butterflies to your yard with plantings of tall composites such as asters, cosmos, ironweed, and Joe-pye weed. They will also feed from and lay eggs on thistles.

Basics

WINGSPAN
2.0 to 3.5 inches

SEASONS
Three flights in the East from May to October; three to four in southern Texas from October to April

DISTRIBUTION
Migrates north from Mexico and colonizes much of the United States and Canada

(opposite page) A painted lady. With the monarch, this lovely species was chosen to become the first butterflies in orbit aboard the International Space Station in 2009.

(left) A painted lady caterpillar. After each successive molt, the instars become increasingly bristly.

(middle) The pearl-colored chrysalis will darken to brown just before the adult butterfly emerges.

(right) Two painted ladies show their best angles while perched on thistle, their preferred host plant. The underside of the wings are very different from the top.

(bottom) A painted lady nectaring on a sunflower. The origin of the genus name, *Vanessa*, is unclear. Many experts believe it was simply taken from the familiar girl's name.

Red Admiral

Vanessa atalanta

Favorite plants

- butterfly bush
- milkweed
- marigold
- aster
- cosmos
- mistflower
- privet
- lantana

These colorful, medium-to-large butterflies are found worldwide in northern temperate zones. In North America, they range from southern Canada, across the United States and south to the Mexican highlands and Guatemala. They favor rich, moist bottomland, sunlit forest edges, and well-watered gardens. And even though they prefer to feed on tree sap, rotting fruit, and animal droppings, they are not averse to taking nectar from composite plants such as asters and milkweed, and verbenas like lantana. Although the red admiral is often considered a thistle butterfly along with its *Vanessa* cousins, its primary larval plant hosts are members of the nettle, or Urticaceae, family.

The red admiral's distinctive coloration makes it hard to mistake—the upper

surfaces of the wings are black with white spots scattered near the apex, with a red-orange band across the forewing and a red-orange band at the hind-wing margin. The underwings are a mottled brown with red, blue, and yellow splashes on the forewing. Their markings do not vary geographically, but they do alter based on season: the summer form of the red admiral is larger and brighter; the winter form is smaller and drabber.

Males are very territorial, chasing off any competitors with swift, erratic flight patterns, and then perching on ridgetops as they wait for females. After mating, females lay barrel-shaped, pale green eggs singly on the top of leaves in the nettle family. The larvae, which hatch in about a week, are dark gray with deep red spots and rows of bristling spines. Young caterpillars feed inside a shelter of folded leaves; some older larvae make a nest of leaves bound together with silk to pupate, and others form a brown chrysalis that resembles a leaf with protruding spines. Adults sometimes migrate south from the extreme northern parts of their range; others hibernate, typically under tree bark, but sometimes inside sheds, garages, or the cooler parts of houses.

ATTRACTING RED ADMIRALS

Red admirals will feed on nectar-producing flowers and shrubs, including butterfly bush, milkweed, aster, lantana, and red clover. Some of their nettle host plants cause painful stings, so it is not advisable to include them in home gardens.

Eclectic Appetites

In spite of their delicacy and grace, many species of butterflies are drawn to what humans would consider disgusting food sources—rotting fruit, dung, and even animal carcasses. Scientists believe that this nondiscriminating diet is an adaptation that helped sustain the butterflies that emerged from hibernation in late winter or early spring when nectar was not yet available.

Basics

WINGSPAN
1.8 to 3.0 inches

SEASONS
Two broods, March through October

DISTRIBUTION
Central Canada; throughout the United States, south to Mexico and Guatemala

(opposite page) A red admiral feeding at a sap flow. Its red bands are similar to the chevrons on naval uniforms, hence the common name.

(left) A red admiral soaks up some sunshine atop a ripening pear.

(middle) Like many other butterfly species, red admirals will bask on wet rocks on the ground, often taking in water and minerals from the earth.

(right) From the side, its richly marbled underwings are visible. This butterfly prefers other food sources, but will take nutrition from nectar-rich flowers like butterfly bush.

Common Buckeye

Junonia coenia

Favorite plants

- aster
- chicory
- coreopsis
- white clover
- knapweed
- peppermint
- globe amaranth
- cosmos

The genus *Junonia* features beautifully marked butterflies known as buckeyes, pansies, peacocks, or commodores. There are about 35 species of these medium-to-large butterflies, and the genus is represented on every fertile continent.

Most notable of the *Junonia* butterflies' markings is a large, bold eyespot or series of eyespots in orange, pink, or blue on the dorsal wings. A number of these species occur in different color forms.

The common buckeye ranges across eastern Canada, throughout the United States, except in the Pacific Northwest, and south to Central America and Colombia. It is particularly prevalent in the South and Southern California. It seeks open land with low vegetation and patches of bare earth and can be found in agricultural areas, disturbed ground, dry ravines, canals, and desert water courses.

The upper wings are a muted brown with two bright orange cell bars and two eyespots on the forewing and a white band below the apex that merges with the lower, larger eyespot. The dorsal hind wing has two eyespots; the top is the larger and contains a magenta crescent. The ventral forewing is a slightly muted version of the upper wing. The ventral hind wing is yellow-brown in the wet season (summer) form, the linea morph, but is a rose-red in the dry season (fall) form, the rosa. It is believed that the large, startling eyespots are used to deter predators.

Male buckeyes laze around on low plants waiting for females to fly by, but they might bestir themselves to chase intruders or male competitors from their territory. Females lay single pale green, ribbed eggs on or below host plant leaves. These include snapdragon, toadflax, plantains, and members of the acanthus family. The spiny gray, black, or reddish larvae are solitary and feast on the foliage,

flowers, and fruit of their host plants. They complete five instars before pupating into a pale brown, ridged chrysalis. Both adults and late-brooded caterpillars overwinter in the South.

BRINGING IN BUCKEYES

These wide-ranging butterflies will visit yards with nectar-rich plants like asters, white clover, and coreopsis, and herbs like peppermint. They also enjoy taking moisture from a basin of damp sand.

(opposite page) The common buckeye. These butterflies prefer to take nectar from flowers with short throats—their small proboscis isn't long enough to reach the bottom of deep, tubular-shaped flowers.

(top) In 2006, the U.S. Postal Service featured the common buckeye on the 24-cent stamp.

(left)The common name buckeye is used to describe plants and insects that have a feature that resembles the eye of a deer, like the fruit of the Ohio buckeye tree and the wing spots on the *Junonia* butterflies.

(right) The late-stage caterpillar of the common buckeye is black with numerous blue-black branched spines.

Great Spangled Fritillary

Speyeria cybele

Favorite plants

- butterfly weed
- boneset
- red clover
- marigold
- verbena
- bee balm
- thistle
- purple coneflower

The fritillaries are brightly patterned butterflies, members of the Heliconiinae, a subfamily of the brush-foots; they are also called longwings due to their noticeably elongated forewings. There are 14 species of greater fritillaries (genus *Speyeria*) and 16 species of lesser (genus *Boloria*). Their coloring ranges from reddish and black to complex patterns of orange, yellow, and deep brown. The name fritillary comes from the Latin word *fritillus,* which means "chessboard," reflecting the typical checkered pattern on their wings.

The great spangled fritillary is widespread and abundant, found across southern Canada and throughout the United States, except in some southern regions. It is the most common fritillary in the East. These butterflies generally seek out moist open

The lovely Aphrodite fritillary *(Speyeria aphrodite)* is a smaller copy of the great spangled but has a narrower submarginal band on the ventral hind wing. The two species are often seen nectaring together. The Aphrodite prefers high elevations and ranges from Connecticut to Georgia in the East and as far west as the Rockies. The Atlantis *(S. atlantis),* is another similar fritillary, but it has a dark margin on the forewing and a purplish or chocolate hind underwing.

Like the great spangled, the Aphrodite fritillary uses members of the *Viola* genus as its host plants.

spaces like fields, valleys, meadows, marshy woodlands, and prairies. The wings are scalloped on both sexes. The male's coloration is tan or orange with black scales on the veins of the forewings; females are similar but darker than males. The underside of the hind wing shows a wide, pale submarginal band and pronounced multiple silver spots.

These fritillaries mate in the summer. Males patrol for females, and females, meanwhile, give off enticing pheromones. After mating, the females enter a state of dormancy called diapause. They rouse in late summer and lay their pale brown eggs near their host plants—members of the *Viola,* or violet family. Even if the upper plant has wilted by then, females can likely

smell the roots and know where to deposit their eggs. The larvae hatch in the fall and enter hibernation in the leaf litter without eating. They time their emergence in the spring with the growth of the violets, which they feed on by night, hiding in the leaf litter by day. Mature larvae are black with orange tubercles and black spines. They typically pupate in June, forming a chrysalis that is dark brown and misshapen.

FEEDING FRITILLARIES
Draw these bright beauties to your garden or lawn by encouraging the growth of nectar-rich wildflowers like milkweed, Joe-pye weed, and ironweed, as well as by planting verbena, butterfly bush, bee balm, and purple coneflower. You can also provide a small patch of violets for their larvae to feed on.

Basics

WINGSPAN
2. 5 to 4 inches

SEASONS
One brood, mid-June to early October; possibly two in the South

DISTRIBUTION
Southern Canada; the United States, except some southern and southwestern states

(opposite page) A great spangled fritillary on a purple thistle flower. This butterfly's specific name is *cybele,* which means "mountain mother" or "earth mother."

(top) Great spangled fritillaries will descend en masse to dine in a field of their favorite flowers.

(bottom) Fritillaries are also known as silverspots because of the silvery blotches on the underwings; these markings possibly help camouflage them when they are resting wings-up in dappled sunlight.

Silver-bordered Fritillary

Boloria selene

Favorite plants

- goldenrod
- black-eyed Susan
- thistle
- butterfly weed
- blackberry bush
- ajuga
- alfalfa

An eye-catching example of a lesser fritillary, the silver-bordered fritillary (genus *Boloria*) is also known as the small pearl-bordered fritillary. (The pearl-bordered fritillary, *B. euphrosyne*, resides in Europe and northern Asia.) These butterflies are widespread across northern Europe and Asia, as far east as Korea, as well as across the north and central reaches of North America. Here, they range from Alaska, along the Rocky Mountains, to northern New Mexico, and east to Illinois, Maryland, and New Jersey. Habitat preferences include marshes, wet meadows, bogs, and the edges of watercourses. Silver-bordered fritillaries feed on nectar-rich wildflowers like thistles and members of the composite, or aster, family such as black-eyed Susan and goldenrod.

Visually, these butterflies don't have a bad angle—both their upper and lower wing surfaces are beautiful. The dorsal surfaces are a rich orange with black veins and markings—two distinguishing features being the dark wing margins and rows of orange chevrons on the wings, each displaying a large central black dot. The ventral wings have random patterns of pale orange, rust, and white, with rows of silver spots.

Males typically scout for females in wet areas. Eggs are laid singly on the host plants—a variety of violets—or nearby. When they hatch, these larvae move to the host plant to feed. They are dark gray with numerous black spots and orange or yellow spines with black tips. Third-stage caterpillars hibernate over the winter in cooler climates and emerge in spring to feed and pupate. The chrysalis is a deep tan and adorned with silver spots and thorny spines.

Populations of this butterfly are fairly stable, but there is concern that they are suffering loss of habitat in some regions across the country as wetlands are filled in. Commercial insecticides intended for use against gypsy moths are also reducing their numbers. The Peggy Notebaert Nature Museum in Chicago is working to bolster a number

of endangered butterfly populations, including the silver-bordered fritillary, with their Butterfly Restoration Project.

FOOD AND WATER
Draw these attractive butterflies to your yard by offering favored foraging plants like purple coneflower, milkweed, and red clover. Or provide a water garden, pond, or bog that replicates their moist habitats.

(opposite page) A delicate silver-bordered fritillary flits among tiny forget-me-nots. The pale edging on its wings gives it its common name.

(top) The stained-glass effect of its patterning is particularly noticeable on its underwings, which are a rich mix of earth tones enlivened by patches of pearlescent silver.

similar species: *meadow fritillary*

The meadow fritillary *(Boloria bellona)* is similar to the silver-bordered fritillary, but the forewing is squared off below the tip, and it lacks the black wing margins. These adaptable butterflies are typically found across southern Canada and throughout the northern and central United States as far south as northeast Tennessee—but they are currently expanding their range deeper into the South. Adults feed on flowers of the aster family, and the larvae use violets as host plants.

Despite its common name, the meadow fritillary prefers cool, moist forests and forest edges.

Variegated Fritillary

Euptoieta claudia

Favorite plants

- butterfly weed
- sunflower
- milkweed
- coreopsis
- red clover
- dogbane
- hibiscus

At first glance, these striking butterflies might look like their close cousins, the *Speyeria* genus fritillaries, but there are a number of differences between the variegated fritillaries (*Euptoieta claudia)* and the *Speyeria.* Variegateds produce three broods per year as compared to the one, or possibly two, generated by the *Speyeria.* They are also nomadic as opposed to sedentary, and their larvae feed on a number of host plants beside violets. And because they eat poisonous passionflowers, these butterflies are linked to the Heliconians of the tropics, which have similar appetites. Variegateds are swift fliers that remain vigilant when nectaring. They are so difficult to approach that their genus name comes from the Greek *euptoietos,* meaning "easily scared."

Basics

WINGSPAN
1.75 to 3.15 inches

SEASONS
Three broods, April to October in the North; four in the South, from February or March to November

DISTRIBUTION
Throughout the United States, except the Northwest; south to Argentina

Although they reside in the American South, these butterflies will migrate throughout the United States—except the Northwest region—and south to Mexico, Cuba, and Jamaica, all the way to the highlands of Argentina. Their preferred habitat is open, sunny fields, prairies, landfills, road edges, and gardens. Their scalloped wings display typical fritillary patterning—the dorsal surfaces are checkered with orange and black and the forewings and hind wings show submarginal black spots and black median lines. The ventral forewing is pale orange with a black-rimmed spot. The hind wing is a mottled, leaflike tan and brown with no silver spots.

Males patrol short distances, seeking receptive females. Eggs are laid singly on the leaves or stems of host plants, which include violets, pansies, passionflowers, stone crop, moonseeds, and may apples. When they hatch, the larvae consume both the flowers and leaves of the host.

WILDFLOWERS ON THE MENU
Variegated fritillaries prefer wildflowers such as butterfly weed, milkweed, red clover, and dogbane. You can also try planting coreopsis, sunflowers, and peppermint to lure them onto your property. And don't forget to offer host plants like violets, pansies, stonecrop, passionflowers, and purslane.

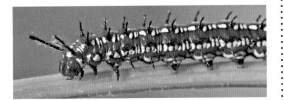

(opposite page) The variegated fritillary is a graceful butterfly, with elegant scalloped wings.

(left) With its underside visible, the variegated fritillary is a mix of muted browns. Unlike any of the other North American fritillaries, this species has a pale, very wide band near the middle of the hind wing.

(right) The pupae of the fritillary butterflies are downright spectacular— a lustrous pearly white, often with black or reddish splashes and golden spikes.

(bottom) These caterpillars can be surprisingly pretty, with a vivid red-orange body and white stripes set off by shiny black spines.

similar species: *Diana fritillary*

A large, lovely fritillary, the Diana (*Speyeria diana*) is notable for the disparate coloration displayed by males and females—the male's upper wing surfaces are brown-black with bright, relatively unbroken orange margins. The female's wings are black with even white markings on the forewing and blue patches on the hind wing. They range across the southern Appalachians to the Ozarks, and south to northern Georgia.

With such extreme dimorphism, a male Diana fritillary (left) and a female (right) look like two species.

FOCUS ON
Exotic Heliconians
GLAMOROUS LONGWINGS FROM THE TROPICS

While nectaring on lantana, a Julia heliconian shows off its slim, graceful wings. The large, lovely Julia measures 3.25 to 3.6 inches across. It is a popular species at butterfly houses and learning centers because it is pretty, long-lived, and stays active all day.

The Heliconian subfamily includes a host of exquisite butterflies. Most of them are found in the tropics of South America, where the larvae of some species feed on poisonous passionflower vines, making them—and the adults—distasteful to predators. Over time, these butterflies also evolved aposematic, or "warning," coloration, which signals to predator birds and animals that it would be best to avoid them. Three species of these tropical beauties can be found in Florida and Texas—and sometimes even farther north.

ZEBRA LONGWING

The zebra longwing (*Heliconius charithonia*) is a striking black butterfly with narrow white and yellow stripes, a pattern that accounts for its name. The species inhabits South and Central America but is also found in Texas and peninsular Florida. In warm weather, migrations to other states are common. Zebras prefer moist forests and open fields, and forage on a set path called a trap line. Each night, they roost in the same trees in groups of 60 or more for protection and to retain warmth. The larvae are white with black spots and long black body spikes. Adults are unusual in that, in addition to nectar, they feed on pollen, which may help synthesize the toxins from passionflowers that make them unsavory to predators. Pollen nutrients might also account for their longevity—they live up to three months in the wild.

JULIA HELICONIAN

Also known as the flame, flambeau, or the Julia butterfly, the Julia heliconian (*Dryas iulia*) is a vivid orange with darker markings on its exaggerated forewings. Its ventral wings are a soft ocher. Julias range from Brazil to Central America, the West Indies, southern Texas, and Florida. Migrants may stray as far north as Nebraska. They prefer semitropical hammocks, fields, and forest edges, and they forage for nectar along trap lines. The caterpillars, which feed on passionflower vines, are black with orange legs and long, ominous black spikes.

GULF FRITILLARY

In spite of its name, this butterfly (*Agraulis vanillea*) is not closely related to the other fritillaries. Its dorsal surfaces are bright orange with darker, patterned markings, while the underside is buff with a series of

Feeding on Tears

While basking in the sun, turtles and alligators often shed tears, possibly to clear irritants from their eyes. Some butterflies, like Heliconians, will lap up these tears—not in commiseration, but to take in sodium and other nutrients necessary for egg production and metabolism. This phenomenon is called lachryphagy or "tear feeding." Meanwhile, their reptile hosts don't seem to mind all those butterfly kisses.

silver spots. These butterflies are found from Argentina through Central America, Mexico, and the Caribbean, and range into the southern states, often as far north as San Francisco. They seek out open country, but will also visit parks and gardens. The larvae, which feed on passionflowers, have orange bodies and rows of long black spines that warn predators away.

Three species of these tropical beauties can be found in Florida and Texas.

(left) Zebra longwings feeding in a group. This large heliconian, which measures an impressive 2.75 to 4 inches across, was declared the official butterfly of Florida in 1996.

(middle top) A gulf fritillary. This butterfly, which has a 2.4-to-3.7-inch wingspan, got its name from its migration route over the Gulf of Mexico.

(middle bottom) Caterpillars of the Julia heliconian (left) and zebra longwing (right) butterflies. The larvae of both species feature long, fearsome spikes.

(right) A side view of the gulf fritillary shows its silver-spotted underwings.

Viceroy

Limenitis archippus

Favorite plants

- milkweed
- thistle
- New England aster
- goldenrod
- coneflower
- red clover
- zinnia
- cosmos

The viceroy and the monarch are well-known look-alikes, yet these two black-and orange butterflies are not closely related. The monarch is a milkweed butterfly, while the viceroy is an admiral, of the brush-foot subfamily Limenitidinae. Admirals lay eggs on trees, and their larvae are not as spiny as other brush-foots. To pinpoint a viceroy, look for a black line across the vertical veins of the hind wing parallel to the margin. The viceroy's flight is swift and erratic compared to the monarch's "flap and glide" technique. Viceroys are the smaller of the two, and they do not migrate, but overwinter as caterpillars.

These butterflies range from the Northwest Territories in Canada south to the Sierra Nevadas and Mexico and east across most of the United States. They

Basics

WINGSPAN
2.50 to 3.40 inches

SEASONS
Two to three flights from May to September in most of its range; year-round in Florida

DISTRIBUTION
From the Northwest Territories in Canada south to Mexico; east across the United States to the Atlantic coast

prefer moist, open spaces, shrubby terrain, lake edges, willow thickets, roadsides, and gardens. Early spring

butterflies feed on aphid honeydew, dung, and rotting fungi. As more flowers become available, they will nectar at members of the Asteraceae family, such as asters, milkweed, and Joe-pye weed.

Males patrol for females near host trees of the willow family—willow, poplar, and cottonwood. Females lay two or three eggs on the tips of leaves. The larvae's bodies are able to sequester salicylic acid from their willow leaf diet, which sickens any predators that consume them. (Although it was once believed that the viceroy mimicked the distasteful monarch, researchers now know that the viceroy's diet makes it just as unpalatable.) The caterpillar and chrysalis are further protected by camouflage—both resemble bird droppings. Third-stage larvae overwinter rolled up in a leaf.

VICEROY INVITATIONS
These energetic butterflies will feed at wildflowers like goldenrod, thistle, and milkweed, as well as at cultivated asters and similar perennials.

Warning Colors

The larvae of some butterflies, such as the viceroy, consume plants that make them and, possibly, the adults distasteful or harmful to predators. Often, they display aposematic coloring, which warns animals of this possibility. When harmless species evolve to copy the appearance of these harmful species, it is known as Batesian mimicry, after British naturalist Henry Walter Bates. If two species are distasteful and evolve to resemble each other to reinforce this threat—as with viceroys (left) and monarchs (right)—it is called Müllerian mimicry, after German naturalist Fritz Müller.

(opposite page) A viceroy lights on a zinnia. The viceroy was named the official state butterfly of Kentucky in 1990.

(left) A viceroy larva resting on a twig with its abdomen lifted in a classic viceroy caterpillar pose. At this stage, the caterpillar looks like mottled olive green bird droppings with bristly tufts behind the head.

(middle) An adult prepares to emerge from its chrysalis. A viceroy chrysalis is brownish with silvery or creamy markings that make it, too, look like droppings. When the butterfly emerges, a fluid called hemolymph will circulate through its body, inflating the wings.

(right) A viceroy in profile. The black lines running parallel to the margins of the hind wings can help distinguish this butterfly from the monarch. The underside of its wings are also more brightly pigmented than the monarch's, which are paler on the ventral surfaces.

White Admiral

Limenitis arthemis

Favorite plants

- spirea
- privet
- viburnum
- daisy fleabane
- butterfly bush
- boneset

Also known as the red-spotted purple, this unusual butterfly exhibits two completely different color forms, which for many years were considered separate species. The white admiral (*Limenitis arthemis arthemis*) is a black butterfly with broad white median bands across both wings and small blue spots along the hind wing. The ventral surface is a reddish brown with similar white bands. The upper side of the red-spotted purple (*L. a. astyanax*) is blue to bluish green with iridescent patches on the outer hind wing. The underside is dark brown; the forewing shows two red-orange bars, while the hind wing has three red-orange spots near the base and a row of submarginal reddish spots.

The white admiral ranges from Alaska across Canada to the Maritimes, and

aphid honeydew, rotting fruit, carrion, dung, and occasionally nectar.

Males rarely patrol, preferring to perch in bushes or trees awaiting females. The gray-green eggs are laid singly on the tips of host leaves, including those of wild cherry, aspen, poplar, cottonwood, oak, hawthorn, birch, and willow. The larvae are misshapen, brown or green, with a white midsection meant to mimic bird droppings. Spring broods pupate in a brown-and-white chrysalis and as adults may produce same-season offspring. These late-summer larvae often overwinter rolled inside a leaf—or hibernaculum.

MESS CALL FOR ADMIRALS

Regardless of the color morph, these impressive butterflies occasionally feed on the nectar of small white flowers, including spirea, privet, and viburnum. They also enjoy dining on overripe fruit.

south into New England, New York, and Pennsylvania. The red-spotted purple occurs south of this region, from the Plains states and Texas to the East Coast down to Florida. Where their ranges overlap, hybridization between the color morphs is common, creating intermediate species. These butterflies inhabit open woodlands and deciduous or mixed evergreen forests. Adults feed on tree sap,

(opposite page) A white admiral. This striking butterfly is the unofficial insect emblem of the province of Quebec.

(top) Ripe oranges and other fruit can tempt red-spotted purples—and white admirals—to your yard.

(bottom) A red-spotted in profile This harmless species is a mimic of the poisonous pipevine swallowtail (*Battus philenor*).

(right) The white admiral, meanwhile, benefits from disruptive coloration via the white wing bands that break up its silhouette.

similar species: *Lorquin's admiral*

The Lorquin's admiral (*Limenitis lorquini*) is a medium-sized West Coast butterfly, occurring from British Columbia to the Baja. Its black wings have a sweeping row of white spots, with orange tips on the forewings. Lorquin's admirals feed on nectar and dung; the larval hosts include wild cherries, willows, poplars, and orchard trees. This species is named for Pierre Joseph Michel Lorquin, a French naturalist who came to California for the gold rush and stayed to study its natural history.

The ventral side of the Lorquin's admiral is richly patterned in chocolate, chestnut, and white.

Gray Hairstreak

Strymon melinus

Favorite plants

- milkweed
- garlic chives
- white clover
- dogbane
- coneflower
- yarrow
- liatris
- tickseed sunflower

A member of the gossamer wing family, the Lycaenidae, and part of the hairstreak subfamily, the Theclinae, gossamer wings are small- to medium-sized butterflies, typically gray, copper, or blue. Hairstreaks get their name from thin hairlike projections on their lower wings, which are believed to deter predators. There are roughly 70 hairstreak species north of Mexico.

The gray, or common, hairstreak, is one of the most widely distributed butterflies in North America—and the most widespread hairstreak. It ranges across the United States, south to Central America and northern South America and is found in open terrain, disturbed or weedy areas, and suburban gardens.

The adult coloration is attractive but subtle—the upper surface of the wings is

similar species: *atala butterfly*

The atala butterfly *(Eumaeus atala)*, a small, colorful gossamer wing, was a longtime favorite in Florida, Cuba, and the Bahamas. Its larval diet of cycads—ancient palmlike plants—gives it an unpleasant taste, and the adult coloration, blue-speckled black wings and bright orange abdomen, warns predators away. In 1965, the Florida subspecies was thought to be extinct due to the overharvesting of its host plant, a ferny cycad called coontie, and the loss of pine flatlands. The atala was reintroduced and rebounded, in part by feeding on ornamental cycads used in landscaping.

Two new atala butterflies emerge from their chrysalises on a coontie plant.

blue-gray bordered in white with a large orange spot on each hind wing near the small tail. Males can be territorial, but they typically spend their afternoons on bushes awaiting receptive females. Eggs are laid singly on a variety of hosts, especially members of the pea (Fabaceae) and mallow (Malvaceae) families. The larvae are green, grayish white, or pink, as well as fat and hairy. They first consume flowers and fruit and then may switch to leaves. While they feed, lycaenid larvae are often tended by groups of ants. In this symbiotic relationship, the ants are sustained by a sweet substance the caterpillar secretes and in return they protect the larvae. The chrysalis is brown with fine hairs and shaped like a jelly bean. Adults emerge in seven to ten days—although most pupae hibernate until spring.

HAPPY HAIRSTREAKS

These butterflies are among the least fussy feeders and will take nectar from a wide range of plants. Wildflower favorites include goldenrod, clover, and milkweed. Cultivated perennials like aster, lantana, and coneflower all draw them in. They also readily feed on herbs like oregano, mint, and garlic chives.

Basics

WINGSPAN

1 to 1.35 inches

SEASONS

Two flights from May to September in the North; three or four in the South, February to November

DISTRIBUTION

Throughout the continent, south to Central America

(opposite page) A gray hairstreak alights on a lantana bloom. In the spring and fall forms of this butterfly, the ventral wings are a steely gray.

(left) In the summer form, the ventral wings of the gray hairstreak are a pale tan-gray.

(right) A tiny gray hairstreak basking atop a dandelion is smaller than this diminutive flower. This butterfly will bask with its wings open, a behavior not characteristic of the hairstreak group.

American Copper

Lycaena phlaeas

Favorite plants

- white clover
- zinnia
- aster
- yarrow
- ox-eye daisy
- milkweed
- dandelion

The coppers, a subfamily of the gossamer wings, are represented throughout North America, Europe, Asia, and North Africa. As the names suggests, they are a rich reddish brown in color. In the Western Hemisphere, there are roughly 16 species that range across Canada and the United States.

The American copper, also known as the small copper and the common copper, occurs in pockets in Alaska and the Canadian arctic and in greater concentrations from Nova Scotia south to Georgia, and across the Plains states to the Dakotas. There is evidence that the eastern populations of this butterfly were unintentional imports from Scandinavia of the Eurasian small copper, subspecies *Lycaena phlaeas phlaeas,* during the 18th century. These butterflies prefer open or disturbed habitats such as old fields, vacant lots, road edges, rocky, alpine terrain, and landfills.

The American copper's coloration makes it hard to miss: a shiny, vivid red-orange on the dorsal forewing, contrasting with deep brown borders, and eight or nine black spots, and a gray-brown hind wing with a red-orange border. The ventral surfaces are a paler version of the upper wings. They are rapid fliers and often show iridescence on their wings. Female coppers sometimes display blue dots on the dorsal hind wings above the orange border, a form that is known as caeruleopunctata.

When males are not challenging intruders to their territory, they perch on grassy stems or weeds to watch for passing females. After mating, females lay pale green, turban-shaped eggs singly on the upper surfaces of host plants—chiefly herbs in the buckwheat family (Polygonaceae) like common sorrel, mountain sorrel, and curled dock. The

rosy red or grass green larvae feed from beneath the leaves, but do not pierce the upper epidermis, creating opaque "windows." Some American coppers overwinter as pupae in an ovoid chrysalis that is medium brown with darker spots, while others hibernate as larvae and pupate in spring.

CATERING TO COPPERS

These butterflies will take nectar from many types of flowers, including white clover, zinnia, buttercup, butterfly weed, ox-eye daisy, yarrow, and a number of flowers in the aster family.

Basics

WINGSPAN
0.875 to 1.40 inches

SEASONS
One flight for alpine or arctic populations; two broods in the North between June and September; three in the South, April to September

DISTRIBUTION
Alaska to the Arctic; northeastern Canada to the Deep South; west to the Dakotas

(opposite page) A tiny and strikingly beautiful butterfly, the American copper feeds on the nectar of a minuscule wildflower in a western Wisconsin wetland.

(top) Its coppery color makes this butterfly seem to glow as it lights on a daisy. The specific name *phlaeas* may come from the Greek *phlego*, meaning "to burn up," or the Latin *floreo*, which means "to flourish."

similar species: *ruddy copper* ⌒

An attractive copper of the American West, the ruddy copper (*Lycaena rubidus*) is found throughout the Rocky Mountain states. It is slightly larger than the American copper, with bright orange wings with white borders, and it has fewer spots on the grayish ventral hind wings. Female coloration is more subdued, usually orangey brown to dark brown. These butterflies inhabit dry sandy terrain and can be found in scrublands, arid streamsides, and sagebrush. When watching for females, male ruddy coppers will perch in open areas and along streams or gulches.

A male ruddy copper. This butterfly has more uniformly orange wings than the American copper.

Eastern Tailed-Blue

Cupido comyntas

Favorite plants

- milkweed
- aster
- coreopsis
- zinnia
- clover
- oregano
- dogbane
- boneset

As their name suggests, members of the blue subfamily of gossamer wings are generally blue or gray in color. The larvae secrete a sweet substance and are attended by ant guardians that feed off this "honeydew."

The eastern tailed-blue is a beautiful, diminutive butterfly of southeastern Canada and the eastern half of the United States. There are also isolated pockets of this butterfly along the Pacific Coast, possibly transported there by humans. (The Plains states form a boundary between this species and the far-less-common western tailed-blue.) These butterflies prefer open, sunny terrain like fields, pastures, vacant lots, parks, and gardens. Because they fly close to the ground and have a short proboscis, they feed on low-growing flowers with short

Basics

WINGSPAN
0.85 to 1.14 inches

SEASONS
Three broods in the North, April to November; many in the South, February to November

DISTRIBUTION
Southeast Canada; eastern half of the United States

tubes. These include white clover, wild strawberry, cinquefoil, shepherd's needle, oregano, and aster.

The male's dorsal coloring is a rich iridescent blue; summer females are brown or slate gray, and spring females, which tend to be small, are pale blue with a darker shade at the base. The wings of both males and females have a white fringe. There are also purple and pink variations found in both sexes. The speckled ventral wings range in color from pale whitish gray-blue to tan or white and sport two or three orange-and-black chevrons at the edge of the hind wing near the narrow tail.

Males scout for females during the day, usually near host plants. The eggs are laid on the flower buds of legumes—yellow sweet clover, alfalfa, vetch, wild pea, and bush clover. The larvae are green or tan, hairy, and sluglike and will eat the buds, flowers, and leaves of host plants. Caterpillars hibernate and emerge in spring to pupate. The chrysalis, which transforms from yellow-green to deep gray, is covered with fine hairs.

BECKONING BLUES
To attract these dainty, colorful butterflies to your garden, try planting asters, zinnia, coreopsis, wild strawberries, oregano, and coneflowers. You might also supply host plants such as clover, vetch, wild peas, and other members of the legume family.

(opposite page) A male eastern tailed-blue is iridescent cobalt, with black-edged dorsal wings fringed in white. It gets its name from the tiny white tail trailing from the fringe on the hind wings.

(left) A dorsal view shows the pale spotted gray underside of this butterfly.

(right) A female eastern-tailed blue is uniformly brown or charcoal with splashes of bright orange. Unlike most Lycaenids, which perch with wings closed, this butterfly is known to bask with its wings at a 45-degree angle.

similar species: *western pygmy-blue*

The western pygmy-blue (*Brephidium exilis*) is one of the tiniest butterflies in the world and the smallest in North America—with only a half-inch wingspan. It is a ruddy copper color with drab blue at the base. The ventral hind wing is copper and white with black spots at the base and near the margin and has a white fringe. This butterfly roams alkaline deserts and wastelands in the American West from central California to Texas and has even reached Hawaii.

It would be easy to miss this gossamer wing, but its copper and silver markings are worth a viewing.

Spring Azure

Celastrina ladon

Favorite plants

- black-eyed Susan
- milkweed
- coltsfoot
- mint
- clover
- heliotrope
- oregano
- dogbane

Surely one of the loveliest of all North American butterflies, this member of the blue subfamily is found in Alaska and Canada and throughout the United States, except for peninsular Florida and the coast of Texas. It prefers moist woodland terrain including marshes, wetlands, swamps, and old fields.

Celastrina ladon may be a single species or, more likely, multiple species flying under one name. What is problematic to scientists is that there are a number of seasonal color forms, many populations feed on different host plants, and even though the northern butterflies brood only once, in the South they brood all year. Some potential species in the spring azure complex include the 'Summer', 'Northern' or 'Blueberry', 'Cherry Gall', 'Atlantic Holly', and 'Pine Barren' azure. Ongoing research

Basics

WINGSPAN
0.85 to 1.40 inches

SEASONS
One in North, May to August; will brood from January to October in warm regions

DISTRIBUTION
Alaska and Canada south of the tundra; the United States, except Florida peninsula and Texas coast

will eventually supply some answers about this intriguing little gossamer wing.

The male's coloration ranges from a light blue to a bright cerulean on the upper wing surface, while darker females may show some black on the outer forewing. Both sexes have a white wing fringe, and late spring and summer forms may display white above. The undersides of the wings are pale gray or bluish gray with speckles and margins of varying intensity.

These butterflies feed on milkweed, blackberry, dogbane, privet, American holly, and other nectar-producing plants. Scouting males typically become active in the afternoon. Eggs are laid singly on the buds of host plants—woody shrubs and herbs that include flowering dogwood, blueberry, viburnum, New Jersey tea, and

meadowsweet; sometimes whatever plant is in flower. The chunky, pink-and-green caterpillar feeds on both host flowers and fruit and is attended by ants that take nourishment from the honeydew it secretes. Caterpillars pupate in a glossy yellowish brown chrysalis and overwinter in that form. The adult spring azure is one of the earliest butterflies to emerge, thus ushering in the warmer weather.

SPRING AZURE APPETITES

These delicate blue beauties enjoy a wide range of nectar-rich plants: wildflowers such as milkweed and dogbane; herbs and vegetables like mint, oregano, and radish; legumes like white and red clover; and perennials like black-eyed Susan, butterfly bush, and sedum.

(opposite page) A 'Summer' form of the spring azure butterfly tends to be a nearly white pale gray.

(top left) The dorsal color of the spring azure makes it clear how this gossamer wing got its name.

(top middle and right) Coloration varies greatly in the spring azure, and the undersides can appear a pale blue or a light gray.

(bottom left) A female 'Summer' azure shows the black edging typical of the *Celastrina* butterflies.

(bottom right) A 'Cherry Gall' morph of the spring azure. This delicately pretty form is often listed as a distinct species, *C. serotina*.

Silver-spotted Skipper

Epargyreus clarus

Favorite plants

- perennial pea
- blueberry
- zinnia
- lavender
- aster
- Brazilian verbena
- coneflower
- red clover

Skippers, which appear to be a combination of a butterfly and a moth, are members of the Hesperiideae superfamily. There are more than 3,500 species worldwide, most of them a bit drab and difficult to identify. The common name comes from their quick, darting flight. Unlike true butterflies, skippers' antennae are spaced far apart and end in curled knobs. Their bulky bodies are also similar to those of moths. The larvae have a distinct head that narrows before the first segment.

The silver-spotted skipper, of the subfamily Eudamimae, might be the most recognized skipper in North America, perhaps because it is marked by splashes of both gold and silver. The dorsal wings are a deep brown to brownish black, with transparent gold spots on the forewing.

The undersides are brown, and the lobed hind wing has a wide silver band. This skipper is found in southern Canada and throughout most of the continental United States, except western Texas and the Great Basin. Open woodlands, disturbed terrain, streamsides, old fields, prairies, and suburban gardens are among its favorite haunts. Adults will feed on nectar from perennial and herb flowers of many colors—red, pink, blue, purple, and white—but rarely from yellow or orange blossoms.

When it is hot or cloudy, or during the night, adult skippers cling to the underside of leaves. Males either perch on tree branches or patrol to find receptive females. The pink-and-green eggs are laid singly near, but not on, host plants in the legume (pea) family, including black locust, honey locust, and false indigo. The emerging larvae—which are greenish yellow with a distinct brown head and orange "eyes"—must locate the proper host in order to feed. Young caterpillars live inside a folded leaf; older ones stitch together a leaf tent with silk. The larvae pupate over the winter inside a smooth brown chrysalis.

SKIPPER FARE

These intriguing butterflies will flock to a perennial border with blossoms in their favorite colors—blue, pink, purple, white, and sometimes cream. Try planting coneflower, aster, liatris, bee balm, lavender, salvia, thistle, milkweed, mint, zinnia, and red and white clover. Also consider false indigo as a host plant; it thrives in sunny locations and puts out long spikes with lovely purple flowers.

Basics

WINGSPAN
1.75 to 2.65

SEASONS
Two flights in East, May to September; one brood in the North and West; three to four broods from February to December in the Deep South

DISTRIBUTION
Southern Canada; the continental United States, except West Texas and the Great Basin

(opposite page) A silver-spotted skipper sipping from red clover, one of its favorite sources of nectar.

(top) With its plump, fuzzy body, the silver-spotted skipper might be mistaken for a moth. The wings of the skippers, the fastest flying butterflies, can beat up to 20 times per second.

(bottom) The silver-spotted skipper larva is surely a memorable sight, with its thick lemon-lime colored body topped by a knobby chestnut head sporting bright orange "eyes."

(right) A bright pink zinnia is the landing pad for a skipper. These butterflies show a distinct preference for pink, purple, blue, red, or white flowers, and they generally avoid orange or yellow blossoms.

Luna Moth

Actias luna

Favorite plants

- black walnut
- white birch
- American beech
- sumac
- white oak
- hickory

The Saturniidae family of moths includes some of the largest species, not only of moths, but of all insects. There are an estimated 1,500 saturniid species found throughout the world, the majority in tropical or subtropical regions. North America is home to 68 of them, including giant silkmoths, royal, and emperor moths. In addition to their imposing wingspans, adult saturniids have heavy bodies with hairlike scales, lobed wings, small heads, and reduced mouthparts. Though they lack the frenulum that interlocks the forewings and hind wings in flight, their wings overlap, creating a single-winged effect. Many species are beautifully colored and display notable eyespots.

Perhaps the most lovely of the saturniids, the ethereal luna moth flutters

out of the night like something from a dream—its wings a pale jade green with yellow or pink margins, transparent eyespots, and a graceful drooping tail. The luna is a type of giant silkmoth, so-named for the fine silk the larvae produce to create their cocoons. Luna moths range across southern Canada from Saskatchewan to Nova Scotia and are found throughout the eastern half of the United States. They prefer deciduous hardwood forests that are home to host trees and shrubs.

Adult luna moths emerge from winter hibernation in late spring or early summer, usually by midmorning, giving them all day to inflate and dry their wings. By evening, they are primed for their chief purpose: reproduction. These moths do not eat or drink; they have no working mouthparts and rarely live beyond one week. Females

perch and wait for males, luring them with powerful pheromones that the males detect with their antennae. Mating takes place after midnight. Females lay four to seven eggs at a time—more if the climate is favorable—on or under the leaves of native trees and shrubs such as black walnut, white birch, American beech, red maple, willow, sweetgum, sumac, white oak, and hickory. The fleshy larvae are lime green with yellow or magenta dots along their sides. Fifth-instar caterpillars spin a single-layer silk cocoon and pupate for about two weeks, unless the insect is entering diapause for winter hibernation.

LOOKING FOR LUNAS

These nocturnal moths live only a short time, but they are common in their ranges. Lunas are highly attracted to light, so try luring them with a spotlight on a June night. If a newly emerged female should land nearby, she will likely attract multiple males, providing a great opportunity for study and photography.

Basics

WINGSPAN
4.5 to 5.0 inches

SEASONS
One brood in the North; possibly two in the mid-Atlantic region; three or more in the South

DISTRIBUTION
Central and southeastern Canada; across the eastern half of the United States

(opposite page) The luna moth's common and specific name comes from the moonlike whitish spots on its hind wings. The family name, Saturniidae, derives from the eyespots many of these moths display, which contain concentric circles similar to the rings around the planet Saturn.

(top) A newly emerged luna moth. Before pupating, this caterpillar performs a "gut dump," expelling any excess food, water, waste, or fluids. If disturbed inside the cocoon, the pupa visibly wiggles and makes noise.

(bottom) A closeup of a luna shows its tan, feathery antennae, as well as the downy white hair and maroon legs that set off its jade green wings. Lunas are strong fliers, and males may travel relatively long distances to follow the pheromone trail of females.

Silken Secrets

FROM MOTH COCOON TO LUXURY FABRIC

The silkworm, *Bombyx mori*, is cultivated mainly for the production of its cocoons, which produce filaments that are woven into luxurious silk fabric.

Silk production, also known as sericulture, has a long and intriguing history, not the least of which is how the Chinese, the first culture to use moth silk to weave fabric 4,000 years ago, kept the secret for at least two millennia.

Moths that spin silken cocoons occur in many regions in the world, but China could boast a moth that produced a silk strand that was finer, smoother, and rounder than any others—*Bombyx mori,* a wild moth that lived exclusively off the white mulberry tree. After centuries of cultivation and refinement, *Bombyx* evolved into a blind, flightless, domestic moth that simply mated, produced eggs, and died.

Today, careful temperature control and feeding programs ensure healthy *Bombyx* larvae that pupate inside puffy white cocoons. After nine days, the cocoons are steamed (to prevent adults emerging and ruining the filaments) and then soaked in water to release the strands. One silk filament may be more than 2,000 feet long; five to eight filaments are twisted together to form a thread.

A Tangled Trade

Naturally, America wanted to establish its own silk trade, and from colonial times onward, farmers were encouraged to grow mulberry trees to support a budding silkworm industry . . . with little success. Then, in 1844 a fatal blight affected almost all domestic mulberries. The invasive gypsy moth was imported in the 1860s as a possible silk producer (result: no silk, escaped moths, lots of destroyed trees), and attempts with giant silkmoths—the imposing polyphemus and the double-brooding promethea—were deemed commercially impractical. Eventually, one city, Paterson, New Jersey, became home to dozens of silk manufacturers, and as the center of the industry in the United States, earned the title Silk City.

Silk honors the moths that perish to produce it—the fabric is lightweight, strong, cool in summer, warm in cool weather, and takes color beautifully. Initially worn by royalty, and then court members, over time it became available to anyone who could afford the precious commodity. The demand for this fabric led to increased caravan traffic between the Mediterranean and Asia—and the trade routes they established became known as the Silk Roads.

Silk honors the moths that perish to produce it . . .

(top) The large promethea (*Caliosamia promethea*) of the eastern United States is dimorphic: males are a velvety black, females a rusty brown. This moth was once considered a possible source of cocoons for an American silk industry.

(left) A woman in a kimono and elaborate obi sash. One of the most exquisite examples of silk coloration and styling is the Japanese kimono, a belted robe with long, open sleeves that is worn for formal or ceremonial occasions.

(right) A silkmoth among cocoons. In the United States, small-scale silk producers are now making efforts to allow the moths to mature and emerge.

Cecropia Moth

Hyalophora cecropia

Favorite plants

- elm
- ash
- maple
- birch
- box elder
- dogwood
- willow

This burly and beautiful behemoth is North America's largest native moth, with an imposing wingspan of up to seven inches. A member of the Saturniinae, or giant silkmoth subfamily, it is found across southern Canada, and east of the Rocky Mountains in the United States, from Maine to Florida. It has adapted to many habitats, including rural, urban, and suburban settings.

These moths are hard to mistake, not only because of their great size, but also due to their rich coloration. The robust body is a warm vermilion with white abdominal bands, the legs are also red-orange, and the wings are dark brown, with red crescent spots and an overlay of white scales that give the brown areas a frosted appearance. Their dorsal forewings are red-orange at the base and

similar species: *polyphemus moth*

This richly appointed giant silkmoth, the polyphemus (*Antheraea polyphemus*), occurs throughout the United States, except for Nevada and Utah, and reaches four to six inches in width. The wings are tan with ruddy borders and a single large, purplish eyespot on each hind wing. Larval coloring is lime green with silvery yellow side stripes. Host plants include many backyard deciduous trees, including oak, maple, birch, elm, basswood, sassafras, ash, willow, beech, butternut, walnut, and sycamore.

This moth gets its name from Polyphemus, the one-eyed Cyclops in the *Odyssey*.

display a black eyespot at the apex, and the hind wings show a wide red band. The underside has similar but muted markings.

Males will seek out females from more than a mile away. Females lay from two to six eggs in a row on both sides of host leaves, which include elm, ash, maple, willow, wild cherry, box elder, dogwood, and birch. The tiny larvae are born covered with black hairs and mature to a dull waxy green, with rows of orange, yellow, or blue tubercles along the back and sides. They may reach four inches in length and an inch in width. New larvae feed in groups, then turn solitary. Caterpillars overwinter in a spindle-shaped cocoon that is well camouflaged—spun with brown silk and attached lengthwise to a branch or twig in a dark, protected part of a tree. The adults will emerge in early summer and live for only two weeks.

SEEKING CECROPIAS

These butterflies occur in many urban and suburban settings and may sometimes be seen fluttering under street or gas station lights or near porch lights. Their great size makes them difficult to miss.

Basics

WINGSPAN
5 to 7 inches

SEASONS
One flight, March to July, in most areas; two possible in the Midwest, May to early June, then two weeks later

DISTRIBUTION
Southern Canada; the central and eastern United States east from the Rockies, from Maine to Florida

(opposite page) A mating pair of cecropia moths. Males have larger, bushier antennae than females. Females, meanwhile, have rounder abdomens.

(left) A pair of fat cecropia larvae. These caterpillars occur in such low numbers that they cause little harm to the ornamental landscape trees that they feed on.

(top) A silken cocoon of the cecropia lies hidden in willow tree branches.

(bottom) One of the largest moths in the world, the cecropia spans the length of a man's hand.

Imperial Moth

Eacles imperialis

Favorite plants

- pine
- oak
- box elder
- maple
- sweet gum
- sassafras

Royal moths, of the saturniid subfamily Cetatocampinae—also known as regal moths—are lepidopteran royalty, encompassing some of the most beautiful and sizable night fliers. The imperial moth—and its many regional morphs and subspecies—make up the imperial complex, which scientists continue to sort and classify. Human confusion notwithstanding, the imperial adult, with its yellow and purple-brown coloring, is simply spectacular.

These moths may vary greatly in appearance, but the typical upper side of the wings is a sunny yellow with irregular patches of pinkish brown to purple-brown. The stout body echoes these colors, and the underwings can be distinctly lavender. The purplish wing patches may be less prevalent in females or in northern

populations, but both light and dark forms occur in the northern and southern states.

These nocturnal, light-seeking moths can be found across the eastern United States, from New England to Florida, and west to Nebraska and Texas, with denser numbers occurring in the South. The subspecies *E. I. pini,* which is mostly yellow, inhabits the Great Lakes region. Imperials frequent both conifer and deciduous forests, and some suburban habitats.

In spring and summer, adult moths emerge from underground before sunrise and mate after midnight the following day. Females lay two to five pale elliptical eggs on both sides of host leaves, including those of many conifers and deciduous trees. Newly hatched larvae are bizarre looking, even by caterpillar standards—school bus yellow with three long branching black spines, or scoli. Fifth instar larvae are black-and-orange or lime green with pale spiracle spots on their sides. When ready to pupate, they crawl along the forest floor seeking a suitable site for burrowing and then hibernate in a glossy brown cocoon.

STALKING THE IMPERIAL

This impressive moth of the eastern woodlands is definitely worth seeking out on a balmy summer night. With a flashlight in hand, look for misshapen emergents that have crawled up from their holes and now cling to tree bark waiting for their wings to inflate.

similar species: *royal walnut moth*

The royal walnut moth *(Citheronia regalis)* is a robust saturniid with orange-and-brown striped wings. Also known as the regal, it is the largest moth, by mass, north of Mexico. Adults can reach six inches across and the substantial caterpillar spans a human palm. This bright green larva, with its projecting horns and spikes, is known as the hickory horned devil and, not surprisingly, feeds on hickory trees, as well as black walnut, sumac, and cottonwood.

The hickory horned devil, like the moth it will turn into, is one the largest of its kind in North America: about the size of a large hot dog. It may look fierce, but it is quite harmless.

Black Witch

Ascalapha odorata

Favorite plants

- banana
- mango

The black witch, an enormous moth of the semitropics, is a member of the superfamily Noctuoidea, the owlets, so-called because the moths' eyes glow when struck by light. This is the largest superfamily of Lepidoptera, with more than 70,000 species. Its family, Erebidae, comprises owlets, underwings, and tiger moths, among others, which are found on every fertile continent. The black witch occurs in Central America, Mexico, Texas, and Florida, and it ranges south to Brazil and, during spring and summer, will migrate north well into the United States. Specimens have been found as far north as Newfoundland and Minnesota.

Adult moths have a pointed forewing and a dark gray dorsal surface with hints of iridescent pink or purple and zig-zagging lines. Females show a wavy white

Very Superstitious

There are few insects with as much superstition surrounding them as these massive gray moths. In Mexican and Caribbean cultures, a black witch is believed to be a harbinger of death. In Mexico, it is called *mariposa de la muerte,* the "butterfly of death," and in the Nuhuatl (Aztec) language as *miquipapalotl,* the "black death moth." Still, there is a less tragic side to the belief: death only occurs if the black witch flies to all four corners of a house. In Jamaica, it is called the duppy bat, after a malevolent spirit who returns from the dead to harm the living, and the moth is thought to be the embodiment of that soul. As in Jamaica, in Hawaii, the black witch is also thought to be the embodiment of a human soul—but in this case, it is a benevolent presence that is returning to say farewell to loved ones. Other happier superstitions surrounding the black witch include its reputation on Cat Island in the Bahamas, where it is called the money moth. A legend goes that if one lands on you, riches are coming your way.

Black witches fly at night; during the day they may be seen resting under house eaves or in carports. Their flight patterns are erratic, like those of bats, and they are often mistaken for those winged mammals. Tympanic organs in their ears help them detect echolocating bats and avoid them in flight. Adults feed on overripe fruit, like bananas, and tree sap.

The caterpillars, which can reach three inches in length, are brown with three pale splotches on their backs and two dark parallel stripes. They feed at night on legumes like acacia and mesquite. The cocoon is smooth and black with visible abdominal rings. Adult moths are thought to live from three to four weeks, although some details of the black witch life cycle remain sketchy.

WATCH FOR BLACK WITCHES

These monumental moths may be night fliers, but black witches are easily attracted to lights, ripe fruit, stale beer, and puddles. You can also look for them by day—they often rest in secluded spots like porch eaves or garage overhangs.

median band across the wings, and are a lighter gray than males, which display eyespots on each forewing.

Basics

WINGSPAN
4.35 to 7 inches

SEASONS
Breeds year-round

DISTRIBUTION
Mexico and Central America; range extends south to Brazil, north to the southern United States and beyond

(opposite page) A black witch, with its gigantic wingspan and gracefully pointed wings, is an impressive sight. Because of its size and nocturnal habits, this moth is often mistaken for a bat.

(left) The black witch's body is fuzzy and rust colored, and the rarely seen underside of the wings a mix of grays and violets.

(right) Caught on camera in a suburban backyard, a black witch displays the violet-indigo iridescence of its wing markings. This harmless moth has gained a reputation as foreboding and mysterious and bears many unearned nicknames, such as *sorciére noire* (or "dark sorcerer"), which is used in the French-speaking Caribbean islands.

White Underwing

Catocala relicta

Favorite plants

- hickory
- oak
- walnut
- poplar
- willow
- quaking aspen

Underwing moths at rest possess a secret: drab forewings obscure brightly marked hind wings . . . until they fly off and reveal their hidden glory. Underwing moths are medium-to-large members of the Noctuoidea superfamily. Roughly 100 of the 250 recognized underwing species are found in North America; the balance are native to Eurasia. Their genus name *Catocala*

means "beautiful hind wing," taken from the ancient Greek *kato*, the "hind one," or "lower one," and *kalos*, "beautiful."

The contrasting concentric markings on the hind wings are meant to startle predators: when they flash in flight, they resemble the eyes of a cat or owl. With their many color variations, it is no surprise that these moths have become popular with butterfly collectors.

The white underwing moth, also called the relict, is the only North American species with arching black-and-white bands on the hind wings. The forewing coloring—gray or mottled black and white—effectively camouflages this moth on birch trunks. The ventral wings show arched bands of black and white. The body is visibly furry, black above and white below, with striped legs.

These moths occur across southern Canada to Newfoundland, south to Pennsylvania, and west to Missouri, with strays reported in Mississippi and Kentucky. They haunt the deciduous forests that are home to their larval hosts. They lay their eggs in the fall, which overwinter before hatching into pale gray larvae with spots on each segment and dark heads.

The larvae then feed on the leaves of hickory, oak, walnut, poplar, quaking aspen, beech, birch, and willow trees. The mature larva spins a dun-colored pupa deep in the leaf litter. Adults emerge relatively late—from August to September—and they fly from just after dusk until daybreak. As do some other noctuids, white underwings have special organs in their ears that help them avoid bats while in flight.

ATTRACTING UNDERWINGS
A small fluorescent lamp left burning overnight near a white sheet draped on a clothesline will likely bring in a number of moths that are attracted to light, possibly even white underwings. Specimens that light on the sheet are likely to remain there, especially after daylight arrives.

(opposite page) Paper birch bark forms the perfect background for a white underwing moth, which can hide undetected as it rests against the tree trunk. Research has shown that underwings are predisposed to light on the exact trees upon which their camouflage (called cryptic coloration) will be most effective.

(left) The white underwing is also known as the relict. Unlike most underwings, it lacks the bright coloration on the hind wings.

(right) The white underwing's close cousin the semirelict underwing *(Catocala semirelicta),* with its bright crimson hind wings circled in black, is more typical of this genus.

similar species: *locust underwing*

The locust underwing *(Euparthenos nubilis)* of the Erebidae family resembles its *Catocala* cousins in color and pattern and shares their habit of resting on tree trunks. The gray forewing is paired with a vibrant black-and-orange hind wing, with jagged concentric circles. These underwing moths range from Maine to Florida and as far west as Arizona; they produce two broods a year. Larvae feed on locust trees, while adult moths sip on fermenting fruit.

A locust underwing lights on a tree. Even though they are nocturnal, many underwing species have a period of activity for a few hours around noon.

Garden Tiger Moth

Arctia caja

Favorite plants

- raspberry
- blackberry
- honeysuckle
- common nettle
- burdock

Tiger moths are colorful, small-to-medium moths with conspicuous stripes or spots. They are noctuiids, part of the Erebidae family, and the Arctiinae subfamily. Roughly 200 tiger moth species occur north of Mexico, most with limited mouthparts. Tiger larvae are known for their dense, bristly hair—accounting for the subfamily name derived from the Greek word for "bear."

A richly patterned example is the garden tiger moth, also called the great tiger. This is a medium-sized moth that ranges from Central America north into the United States and Canada and is also found in Great Britain, Eurasia, and Africa. The garden tiger seeks a variety of open, often damp, habitats—marshes, river valleys, sparse woodlands, sand dunes, meadows, scrub areas, parks, and gardens.

This striking moth displays a distinctive brown-and-cream pattern on the forewings. Hidden beneath this cryptic, or camouflaging, forewing, the hind wing shows blue-black spots on an orange ground, which the resting moth may flash at lurking predators. Its sharply contrasting colors also serve as a warning to predators that the moth's body is poisonous, containing neurotoxic choline esters, the chemistry of which is not yet fully known. Garden tigers can show many variations—hundreds of color and pattern aberrations have been reported.

Clutches of bluish white eggs are laid under host plant leaves starting in July. The dark, hairy caterpillars feed on raspberry, blackberry, honeysuckle, common nettle, burdock, and many garden plants. The garden tiger larva finds a protected niche in which to overwinter and in spring pupates inside a thin, fuzzy cocoon. Adult moths emerge from June to July.

TIGER BAIT

Garden tiger moths are attracted to light, so try luring them with either fluorescent or incandescent sources. Once temperatures rise above 50 degrees, you can entice a variety of night fliers by "baiting" tree trunks at dusk—painting on a mixture of brown sugar, beer, ripe fruit, and molasses that has fermented for a day or two. It is always exciting to see which species have been drawn to the sweet scent.

Basics

WINGSPAN

1.8 to 2.6 inches

SEASONS

One brood, from June to July

DISTRIBUTION

New England and the Great Lakes region; the Rocky Mountains and the Great Basin; the Pacific Northwest

(opposite page) A garden tiger moth. These handsome moths are widespread, occurring around the world. In the United Kingdom, they are protected because their numbers have declined by 92 percent over the past 40 years, possibly due to climate change.

(top) This moth's common name may at first seem confusing—the patterning of the forewings is more reminiscent of a giraffe than a tiger. It is actually, however, the striped body that inspired the name.

(bottom) A garden tiger at rest on a narrow leaf. In order to deter predators, it can make a rasping noise by rubbing its wings together.

Creating a Moon Garden
THE PROPER SETTING WILL ENCOURAGE MOTHS TO VISIT—AND POLLINATE

An elephant hawk-moth (*Deilephila elpenor*) on honeysuckle. This eye-catching moth, with its delicate pink-and-olive coloration, typically occurs overseas, but it has recently been discovered in the Lower Fraser Valley of British Columbia. It may only be a matter of time before it crosses unmarked borders and enters the United States—as a most-welcome visitor.

Imagine lounging on your deck or veranda after dark and watching as stately, beautiful moths sail into the soft beams of patio lights before fluttering down to feed on ghostly, scented blossoms. It's not as dreamlike as it sounds. Many white or pale night-blooming plants, called vespertines, can lure moths to your backyard. A number of them also give off scents that nocturnal fliers find intoxicating and that intensify after dark. The creation of such a "moon" garden takes only a small investment of time and money—and a little imagination.

Naturally, you will want to place your night garden in a spot where you can observe it while comfortably seated. A patio or deck just beyond the garden edges or a bench or swing within the garden itself work well. Many species of moths are attracted to light, so it helps to have a source of gentle illumination—a few hanging mason jar lights, perhaps, or glittering white fairy lights. On the other hand, you won't want your outdoor speakers turned up or noisy guests chatting and moving around the deck.

Many white or pale night-blooming plants, called vespertines, can lure moths to your backyard.

Appropriate plants with pale flowers include evening primrose, moonflower (a favorite of hummingbird sphinx moths), angel's trumpet, and night phlox. For heady scents, consider honeysuckle, nicotiana (especially Indian peace pipe), columbine, pinks, and mock orange, or night-blooming jasmine in warmer regions.

PROVIDING CONTRAST

Foliage is important for creating visual contrast in these shadowed spaces. Plants with silver, gray, blue-green, or variegated leaves are perfect for night gardens. Some foliage options include silver artemisia, dusty miller, lamb's ear, sage, thyme, variegated hosta, and any coleus with large amounts of lime green on dark red leaves, such as 'Rose Wizard' or 'Kong'. Miniature white pumpkins or variegated eggplants also provide contrast.

Bear in mind that many of the above plants can also be grown in containers and arranged in groups at the edge of your patio or deck, a movable feast for moths and nectar-feeding bats.

(*top left*) With its curving demi-lune border, this uncomplicated moon garden features pale flowers, variegated foliage, soft lighting, and even some dense trees for moths to hide in by day.

(*top*) Planting angel's trumpets (*Datura* spp.) is sure to encourage moths that like tubular blossoms. These night-bloomers are also known as moonflowers, a name given to a number of other plants, including some species of cacti, which might also bring moths to a Southwestern moon garden.

(*bottom*) Evening primrose (*Oenothera biennis*) is a biennial wildflower with a soft lemony scent and buttery yellow blooms. It blossoms at night and closes again by noon.

(*bottom right*) A white-lined sphinx moth (*Hyles lineata*) feeds on a petunia. This brown-and-pinkish moth, also known as the hummingbird moth, ranges from South America to Canada and is often seen feeding from columbines, clovers, thistles, and lilacs in suburban gardens.

Moths as Pollinators

Some moth larvae are considered major agricultural pests, yet adult moths have a critical place in nature's food chain. Not only are they a key food source for birds and other animals, their hairy bodies also make them effective pollinators. Still, for years scientists were unsure of how much pollen these night feeders actually transferred from plant to plant. Recent research has shown that they do indeed effectively pollinate, either while sipping nectar from flowers or laying eggs on them.

Hummingbird Clearwing

Hemaris thysbe

Favorite plants

- angel's trumpet
- bee balm
- viper's bugloss
- petunia
- thistle
- nicotiana
- butterfly bush
- verbena

Sphinx moths are often mistaken for hummingbirds, which they closely resemble, down to the throbbing hum. These members of the Sphingidae family, which includes 1,450 mostly tropical species, are also known as hawkmoths and hornworms. Not only are they capable of reaching speeds of 12 miles per hour, some species also hover in midair to feed and can even hover from side to side in a predator evasion tactic called side slipping. They have plump bodies, narrow wings, and the tips of their tails open into a fan. Diurnal sphinxes feed by day; the night fliers prefer flowers with long corolla tubes and sweet scents.

The hummingbird clearwing is so named not only for its thrumming flight, but because sections of its wings have no scales, creating a clear "window." This

sphinx flies by day, feeding on bee balm, red clover, lilac, and thistle. It is abundant throughout the eastern United States from Maine to Florida and ranges inland from Texas and the Great Plains, and then northwest into Oregon, British Columbia, and Alaska. Preferred habitats include open woodlands, second-growth forests, and suburban gardens.

The furry spindle-shaped body is golden-olive on the thorax and burgundy on the abdomen with light olive or dark gold patches. The ventral body is yellow or white at the thorax with a burgundy or black abdomen. Later broods or southern broods tend to be darker. When the adult emerges, its wings are a solid dark red or black, but it sheds many scales in flight, leaving a clear wing with reddish brown veins and borders.

The female lays translucent greenish eggs singly on host leaves of honeysuckle, snowberry, hawthorn, cherry, plum, and European cranberry bush. The caterpillars are plump, yellow-green with bands of dark green and reddish brown and a horn at the posterior end. Larvae burrow into the soil to pupate over the winter in brown, hard-shelled cocoons; the adults emerge in the late spring.

HOSTING SPHINX MOTHS

The hummingbird clearwing will eagerly lap nectar in your perennial or wildflower border by day, enjoying nectar-rich species like phlox, dogbane, and verbena. Later, many of its fellow sphinx moths will be busy feeding in your moon garden—with their long curling tongues, they are well equipped to feed from tubular flowers like angel's trumpets and petunias.

Basics

WINGSPAN
1.6 to 2.2 inches

SEASONS
One brood in the North, April to August; two broods in the South, March to June and August to October

DISTRIBUTION
From Alaska south to Oregon; east across southern Canada and the Great Plains to the eastern seaboard

(opposite page) While hovering at a thistle bloom, a hummingbird clearwing bears a striking resemblance to its namesake. It also favors similar flowers.

(top) A hummingbird clearwing nectaring on wild bee balm. These moths prefer flowers with long corolla tubes and sweet scents, a pollination form known as sphingophily.

(bottom) The larvae are yellow-green through most of their stages, and then turn pinkish in the final instar before pupating.

similar species: *Carolina sphinx*

This brown moth, the Carolina sphinx (*Manduca sexta*) of the eastern and far western United States, is less well known than its larva—the tobacco, or goliath, hornworm. A strapping lime green caterpillar with diagonal white stripes, it eats nightshades and can reach nearly three inches in length. Children—and moth lovers—often keep these hornworms as short-term pets, allowing them to observe metamorphosis firsthand. Some pet stores even offer them for sale.

The larva of the Carolina sphinx moth. The sphinx moth's family name comes from the caterpillar's posture of raised forelegs and tucked-down head, resembling the Egyptian Sphinx.

APPENDIX

Index & Additional Information

....

(opposite page) A colorful border of coneflowers, marigolds, petunias, sage, and black-eyed Susans will lure many birds, bees, and butterflies.

Growing Guide

SELECTED GARDEN PLANTS THAT ATTRACT BIRDS, BEES, & BUTTERFLIES

AJUGA
(Ajuga spp.)
Also known as bugleweed, this popular evergreen to semi-evergreen ground cover may have purplish, rose, or white flowers. It blooms in early spring and lasts until mid-July and accepts most types of soil and levels of sun exposure. It spreads in runners, creating a carpet of foliage and controlling erosion with its extensive root system. The flowers attract hummingbirds, bees, and butterflies like the painted lady.

ALFALFA
(Medicago sativa)
Alfalfa can be grown in a greenhouse, on the balcony, or in the garden. It requires light soil, mild sun exposure, and plenty of water. Spring seeds can be sown directly in the ground or in pots. They will germinate within six days. Sprouts can be grown in special plastic sprouter boxes. Alfalfa is a major source of bee nectar, and it is also popular with butterflies, like the orange sulphur, as well as some birds.

ANGELICA
(Angelica spp.)
Known for its bright green foliage, aromatic angelica is part of the celery family. It will grow from seeds in late autumn or early spring. Tamp seeds gently into the ground and cover with a light layer of soil. Variations of temperature, but not actual freezing, help seeds to sprout. Plant seedlings in partial shade, near water, spaced at least a foot apart. The tiny lime green flowers attract many pollinators, including honeybees.

ASTER
(Aster spp.)
These daisylike perennials brighten fall gardens and borders with their blue, white, or pink flowers. They range from 8 inches to 6 feet in height. Plant nursery stock in spring—loosen enriched soil to 15 inches—in a cool, moist spot with full sun to light shade. Asters attract bees and swallowtail, sulphur, gray hairstreak, fritillary, pearl crescent, monarch, painted lady, and silver-spotted skipper butterflies.

BASIL
(Ocimum basilicum)
Also known as sweet basil, this king of culinary herbs prefers rich, moist soil and six hours of sun a day, yet it will adapt to partial shade. It is easy to raise in the garden, but should be started indoors in flats, with seeds arranged 3 to 4 inches apart. Transplant seedlings outdoors, 12 to 16 inches apart, once the risk of frost is past. Fertilize for more robust plants. Basil flowers will bring bees and smaller butterflies to the yard.

BEE BALM
(Monarda spp.)
Tall, colorful bee balm enjoys moist, light soil, and a location with only morning sun to prevent it from getting leggy. Propagate plants by their creeping roots or by slips or cuttings. If using cuttings, place in a shady spot in May, and plants will root just like other mints. Its tufted, nectar-rich red, pink, or purple flowers attract honeybees, hummingbirds, and black swallowtail and silver-spotted skipper butterflies, among others.

BLACK CHOKEBERRY
(Aronia melanocarpa)
This attractive, low-maintenance shrub reaches up to 5 feet in height and 9 feet across. It does best in sun or partial shade in moist, well-drained soil. The plant spreads easily from root sprouts. Black chokeberry develops clusters of small white flowers that draw honeybees in spring and summer. The bluish black fruit, which can be used to make jams, syrups, and teas, is a favorite of songbirds during the fall and winter.

BLACK-EYED SUSAN
(Rudbeckia spp.)
The hardy, long-blooming black-eyed Susan typically has a dark center and bright yellow petals, but new color combos appear each year. Place seeds in moist, well-drained soil in a sunny spot and loosely cover with soil. They will grow from 1 to 3 feet tall. Divide every three or four years. Bees and butterflies feed on the nectar, while house finches, chickadees, and American goldfinches flock to the seeds.

BLUEBERRY
(Vaccinium spp.)
These hardy berry bushes, which once grew wild, are now popular in backyard gardens. They prefer slightly acidic soil high in organic matter. Plant nursery stock in early spring and space plants 5 feet apart. Fertilize one month after planting, and mulch to keep roots moist. Prune after four years to stimulate new growth. The blooms are magnets for honeybees, bumblebees, and silver-spotted skippers: birds love the plump berries.

BONESET
(Eupatorium spp.)
These showy perennial wildflowers bloom from late summer to fall with clouds of tiny blossoms in white, purple, or pink. Boneset prefers moist soil, but will tolerate some drought. A reliable butterfly lure, its nectar draws orange sulphurs, swallowtails, eastern tailed-blues, spring azures, gray hairstreaks, great spangled fritillaries, pearl crescents, monarchs, red-spotted admirals, painted ladies, and silver-spotted skippers.

BORAGE
(Borago officinalis)
The herb borage thrives in ordinary soil, in sun or shade with moderate watering. Grow from seeds in fall or early spring, or sow indoors in late winter or early spring. Plant seeds ½ inch deep and 4 inches apart. As seedlings mature, thin them to 15 inches apart. If allowed to self-seed, it may re-bloom in the fall. Its deep blue flowers, which boast a high level of nectar production, are honeybee favorites.

BRAZILIAN VERBENA
(Verbena bonariensis)
This hardy garden plant, with its tiny purplish blossoms and "see through" profile, thrives in poor, well-drained soil but likes full sun. Purchase seedlings; reseed annually in cooler climates. This verbena is a pollinator favorite, enticing swallowtails, cabbage whites, gray hairstreaks, sulphurs, fritillaries, red-spotted admirals, painted ladies, silver-spotted skippers, and sphinx moths, as well as honeybees and hummingbirds.

BURDOCK
(Arctium spp.)
A bristling wildflower, burdock accepts partial shade to full sun and prefers light, sandy soil. Sow seeds in fall or start indoors four weeks before final frost, cover lightly with soil, and keep moist. Transplant to pots when leaves first show and then to ground after final frost. Mature burdock self-seeds. This is a favorite of bumblebees, honeybees, and butterflies, including fritillaries. Finches love the seeds. May be considered noxious.

BUTTERFLY BUSH
(Buddleia spp.)
This large, arching shrub produces masses of nectar-rich flowers in red, yellow, violet, pink, and white from midsummer to fall. Plant nursery stock in well-drained soil in a sunny location; till soil to 16 inches, and mix in compost. Prune back old growth each spring. This bush attracts swallowtail, cabbage white, orange sulphur, fritillary, monarch, painted lady, red admiral, and silver-spotted skipper butterflies.

CALENDULA
(Calendula officinalis)
Cheerful flowering calendulas (pot marigolds) grow best in full sun, in rich, well-drained soil. Sow seeds in April; keep seedlings weeded and thin out to 9 or 10 inches apart. Plants will begin to flower in June and continue until frost kills them. Seeds ripen in August and September; plant will self-seed and spread. Calendulas attract bees and butterflies, including swallowtails, checkerspots, buck-eyes, and painted ladies.

CATMINT
(Nepeta spp.)
Like most mints, catmint is easy to cultivate in full sun and well-drained soil. Depending on the variety, plants can be a foot tall or reach 4 feet in height. Its blue-gray foliage makes it attractive all year long. Place nursery specimens in light, sandy soil, and water well. Pinch top growth as the herb matures to encourage bushiness. Catmint blooms heavily in early summer, and the purple, pink, or white blossoms lure bees and butterflies.

CHERRY
(Prunus avium)
This graceful tree bears pale pink blossoms and small, smooth round red fruit. (It shares its genus with plum, peach, nectarine, apricot, and almond). Cherries grow in most temperate latitudes and bloom in May in North America. Seeds require exposure to cold to germinate, so plant them in fall for spring seedlings. Cherries rely on bees for pollination, and birds take shelter in their foliage and enjoy the summer fruit.

CHIVES
(Allium schoenoprasum)
These hardy, pungent herbs thrive in rich, moist soil. As cold-tolerant perennials, they can be planted in early spring in a sunny location or start indoors eight to ten weeks before the last frost. If the flowers ripen and the seeds disperse, chives can pop up randomly in moist spots. The spiky purple blooms attract bees, moths, and butterflies, including swallowtails.

CLOVER
(Trifolium spp.)
Clover, a member of the pea family, grows wild in many lawns, but it can also be cultivated. It will survive in most soils and with varied levels of sun, although lime will bring the soil up to the proper pH 6.0 or 7.0. Bumblebees and fritillary butterflies like red clover; cabbage white, orange sulphur, eastern tailed-blue, spring and summer azure, gray hairstreak, pearl crescent, and American lady butterflies prefer white clover.

COLUMBINE
(Aquilegia spp.)
The ethereal, multihued blooms of columbine resemble small orchids, yet the plant is surprisingly hardy. Grow it from seeds or from nursery specimens. It prefers partial shade and well-drained soil, but it can handle sun and drier soil. Avoid too much fertilizer, which can result in fewer blooms. Hummingbirds and butterflies flock to this plant in spring. Removing spent blossoms will encourage a greater number of flowers to form into early summer.

COMFREY
(Symphytum spp.)
Prepare a bed for this healing herb by weeding thoroughly, loosening the soil with a garden fork, and dressing it with manure. Locate the bed in full sun or partial shade. Plant seeds or cuttings in permanent spots, because the roots go deep, and the plants are long-lived. Make sure to water regularly. The nectar-rich, bell-shaped, pale purple flowers are popular with bumblebees, honeybees, and solitary bees.

CONEFLOWER
(Echinacea spp.)
Grow this reliable perennial from seeds in fall or from bare-root stock or nursery containers in spring. Coneflowers thrive when temperatures fluctuate, so get them into the ground before summer arrives. Choose a location with rich soil and at least five hours of sun daily. Water regularly; fertilize lightly. The large, showy blooms will attract butterflies and bees, and the seed heads will nourish birds in winter.

CORAL BELLS
(Heuchera spp.)
Perennial coral bells are valued in shade or rock gardens for their colorful foliage that comes in varied patterns. Long-lasting clouds of small coral flowers form atop wiry stems in late spring. They enjoy rich, fertile soil and partial shade. Place container plants in soil tilled to 15 inches in depth and space them 1 or 2 feet apart. Hummingbirds will feast here in spring and early summer.

COREOPSIS
(Coreopsis spp.)
Also known as tickseed, this hardy perennial's daisylike flowers range in color from yellows and oranges to pinks and reds. The stems reach 2 to 4 feet in height. Plant seeds or nursery stock in full sun and well-drained, enriched soil; thin seedlings to 3 feet apart. The nectar-rich blooms last through summer into fall, drawing butterflies and hummingbirds, while the seeds nourish finches, sparrows, chickadees, and other songbirds.

CORNFLOWER
(Centaurea cyanus)
Also known as bachelor's buttons (the round sapphire blue flowers look like buttons), cornflowers bloom from late spring through summer. For spring blooms, sow seeds in the ground in fall or early spring. They do best in average, well-drained soil and full sunlight. The seeds, nectar, pollen, sap, and foliage of these plants nourish birds, especially finches, buntings, and sparrows, as well as bees and butterflies.

COSMOS
(Cosmos spp.)
These cheerful annuals with fernlike leaves and yellow centers are easy to grow. Plant seeds after the last frost in full sun or partial shade in well-drained soil, and deadhead them throughout the summer to keep them blooming from June until late autumn. Their bright, open flowers draw in honeybees and bumblebees. They come in a wide variety of colors and some have rich scents. Cabbage white, painted lady, silvery checkerspot and other butterflies also enjoy the sweet nectar.

CRABAPPLE
(Malus spp.)
These decorative deciduous flowering trees produce magenta buds and white blossoms in spring and tiny apples—that linger into winter—in late summer. Place nursery stock in full sun, in rich, slightly acidic, well-drained soil, and water regularly. Plant bare-root trees in spring; balled roots go in any time except winter. Honeybees love the blooms; the fruit attracts cedar waxwings, robins, orioles, cardinals, and other songbirds.

CROCUS
(Crocus spp.)
From snow crocuses that signal the end of winter to giant Dutch crocuses, these goblet-shaped blooms come in colors from yellow to purple, and many offer enticing perfumes that lure bees and hawkmoths that require nectar in early spring. Plant the corms, 6 inches apart and 3 inches deep in rich, well-drained soil. For an autumn bloom, try the exotic saffron crocus (*C. sativus*). Plants will bloom in the fall.

DAISY FLEABANE
(Erigeron speciosus)
This charming wildflower, with its frilly white blooms with yellow centers, adapts well to perennial borders and rugged rock gardens—in fact, it thrives on neglect. Simply supply a sunny location and well-drained soil, and most of the available hybrids, which come in short and tall versions, will do fine. After three years, divide the clumps. It will attract pearl crescent, eastern tiger swallowtail, and cabbage white butterflies.

DAME'S ROCKET
(Hesperis matronalis)
This showy member of the mustard family, with its spring-blooming lavender or white flowers, has many names, including dame's violet, dame's gilliflower, and mother-of-the-evening—possibly because the scent grows stronger at night. Sow seeds in full sun in soil with good drainage; plant produces low rosettes the first year, flowers the second. It is a favorite of eastern tiger swallowtail, cabbage white, and orange sulphur butterflies.

DANDELION
(Taraxacum spp.)
Dandelions play an important part in bee culture, providing nectar for bees emerging in early spring before fruit trees and other flowers blossom. You can simply let these lawn invaders be or sow seeds in early spring, directly in a garden. They are a major food resource for honeybees and also draw cabbage white, clouded and orange sulphur, pearl crescent, and silver-spotted skipper butterflies.

DILL
(Anethum graveolens)
This delicate culinary herb thrives in loamy soil and full sun. It does not like being transplanted from starter trays, so sow seeds directly in the ground in early summer. Set seeds ¼-inch deep and 18 inches apart, and then gently rake them into the soil. Plants will appear in 10 to 14 days. In two weeks, thin seedlings 12 to 18 inches apart. Dill flowers attract bees, and the plant serves as a host for black swallowtail larvae.

DOGBANE
(Apocynum cannabinum)
Known as Indian hemp, this wildflower oozes sticky white sap when broken. Mature plants can reach 5 feet in height and have white or greenish clusters of small flowers. It grows in most types of soil in varied light. Dogbane draws many butterflies including the swallowtail, eastern tailed-blue, spring and summer azure, gray hairstreak, fritillary, red admiral, eastern comma, and silver-spotted skipper butterflies.

DOGWOOD
(Cornus spp.)
This small landscape tree offers creamy white or pale peach blossoms (the flower's bracts) in early spring and rich foliage and red berries in the fall. Dogwoods do best in full sun to partial shade with moist soil. Plant nursery stock in a hole three times wider than the root ball, and water regularly. Dogwoods are larval hosts to giant silk moths and some butterflies, and the berries sustain robins, bluebirds, and cardinals in winter.

ELDER
(Sambucus spp.)
A hardy shrub that tolerates most soil types, elder thrives best in loamy, moist soil in a sunny spot. Purchase it as a bare-root or potted plant; place in a bushel basket–sized hole with compost. Plant two or more cultivars about 5 feet apart to ensure cross-pollination. Flat white clusters of flowers are followed by purple berries, which are more plentiful the second year. Gray catbirds, robins, bluebirds, and other songbirds love the fruit.

EVENING PRIMROSE
(Oenothera biennis)
Hardy biennial evening primrose, a columnar wildflower that lends a buttery glow to gardens and borders, grows easily on dry stony ground or in well-drained sandy soil. Sow seeds in late spring and keep watered until established. The vibrant yellow flowers bloom overnight from late afternoon and close during the heat of the day. The small seeds are brown-black. The plant reseeds readily and appeals to both hawkmoths and honeybees.

FENNEL
(Foeniculum vulgare)
Fennel is an anise-flavored perennial culinary herb that will grow—and continue to produce—in almost any sunny spot. Sow seeds in early April in ordinary soil, in drills 15 inches apart, lightly covered with soil. Separate the seedlings to the same distance apart. If sowed in April, the plant will be in full flower by July. Fennel blossoms attract honeybees and butterflies; the plant hosts the larvae of the black swallowtail.

FOUNTAIN GRASS
(Pennisetum alopecuroides)
This tufted ornamental grass can be used as a backdrop in a border, as an accent plant, or as a transitional plant between formal and natural areas. It flowers with pale plumes from July to fall, when it turns a golden brown. Some cultivars can reach 5 feet in height. Grow container stock in sun to light shade locations in fertile well-drained soil. At the end of its growing season, this grass becomes an appreciated source of birdseed.

FOUR O'CLOCK
(Mirabilis jalapa)
The blooms of this heirloom flower open in the midafternoon and fade before sunrise. Plant the seeds directly in the ground in spring or early summer in sun or partial shade. Cover lightly with soil, and press down. The trumpet-shaped flowers—in red, white, yellow, pink, or peach—will bloom from midsummer to the first frost. Their sweet scent makes them a favorite with bees, hummingbirds, butterflies, and moths.

FOXGLOVE
(Digitalis spp.)
A short-lived perennial or biennial, the tall-growing foxglove has tubular, bell-shaped blooms that come in purple, lavender, apricot, pink, coppery rose, and more. Plant container stock in a sunny spot with moist, well-drained soil, at least 1 or 2 feet apart. The flower's configuration provides an inviting lip so that bumblebees can lap nectar from the deep interior. Hummingbirds also favor these speckled beauties.

GARLIC CHIVES
(Allium tuberosum)
This pungent, perennial member of the onion family features strap-shaped leaves and tall, thin, white-flowering stalks. It expands in clumps or can be grown from seeds and is often used as an ornamental. The flowers, which bloom in late summer or autumn, feed honeybees, eastern tiger swallowtails, eastern tailed-blues, gray hairstreaks, great spangled fritillaries, red-spotted admirals, eastern commas, and silver-spotted skippers.

GLOBE AMARANTH
(Gomphrena globosa)
This tender annual broadcasts its presence with rounded magenta blooms and blue-green foliage. Sow seeds in average, well-draining soil after the last frost in full sun (soaking them overnight will aid germination). This plant is an extremely popular nectar source for eastern tiger swallowtail, orange sulphur, gray hairstreak, variegated fritillary, pearl crescent, common buck-eye, and silver-spotted skipper butterflies.

GRAPE
(Vitis spp.)

Twining grape vines give an Old World charm to the patio and provide food and shelter for wildlife. The woody, deciduous vines grow up to 30 feet in length, thrive in full sun, and produce late-summer and autumn fruit. Plant dormant, bare-root plants in early spring at the base of a trellis or support. The high-sugar fruit provides energy for birds, and bees may be drawn to the nectar. Butterflies like red admirals also drink from the rotting fruit.

HELIOTROPE
(Heliotropium arborescens)

With pretty clusters of purple, lavender, or white flowers, drought-resistant heliotrope makes a great rock garden plant. Sow seeds in spring or start indoors 12 weeks before final frost. Plants require full to part sun and well-drained, fertile soil. The flowers emit a faint cherry pie aroma and supply nectar for bees and swallowtail, spring and summer azure, painted lady, and question mark butterflies. Heliotrope can be toxic to dogs.

HOLLY
(Ilex spp.)

Spiky evergreen holly makes a strong statement in the yard or garden. Species range from small bushes to 60-foot trees. Plant container specimens in the spring, in full sun, and bed them in soil that is well drained, loamy, and slightly acidic. Holly trees and bushes nurture visiting winter birds— the dense foliage protects them from the cold, and the red berries are nourishing. To ensure berries, plant both female and male varieties.

HOLLYHOCK
(Alcea spp.)

Back your garden or border with these towering perennials that display large, papery flowers in many shades of pink, purple, and red. Sow seeds just below the surface a few weeks before the last frost in a bed of rich, moist soil that gets full sun. Thin to 24 to 36 inches apart. Bare-root hollyhocks are also available at most nurseries. The imposing flowers attract hummingbirds and butterflies; songbirds enjoy the seeds.

HONEYSUCKLE
(Lonicera spp.)

Sweet-smelling perennial honeysuckle occurs in two types: climbers prefer humus-rich, moist soil and full sun; shrubby plants like well-drained soil and sun or partial shade. Plant in spring or fall, 5 to 15 feet apart. They bloom from spring to midsummer, producing tubular yellow, orange, red, or white blossoms. Hummingbirds and butterflies feed on the nectar, Baltimore orioles eat the flowers, and thrushes eat the fruit.

HYSSOP
(Hyssopus officinalis)

Perennial hyssop features tall spikes of scented flowers and deep green, edible leaves. It enjoys full sun to partial shade and light, dry soil enriched with organic matter. Sow seeds indoors eight weeks before last frost close to the soil surface. Transplant after final frost, 12 to 24 inches apart, in a well-worked bed. Hummingbirds, butterflies, and bees all feed on the purple, red, pink, or white flowers.

JOE-PYE WEED
(Eupatorium purpureum)

This tall, native, perennial wildflower creates an impressive mass of nectar-rich pink or purple blossoms when it matures in late summer. Grow container specimens in average-to-moist soil in full sun or partial shade, allowing several feet on either side of the plant for spread. Older plants can be divided. The vanilla-scented blooms attract many bees and butterflies; songbirds feast on the seeds and use the fluff in their nests.

LANTANA
(Lantana spp.)

Lantana is an easy-to-grow garden favorite with extended blooms in shades of yellow, orange, red, pink, and white. It prefers a sunny location and slightly acidic soil, achieved by mulching with pine needles. Grow from seeds sown in pots and kept in plastic bags, cuttings in starter mix, or six-pack seedlings. The clustered flowers attract swallowtails, admirals, fritillaries, and buckeyes, as well as honeybees and bumblebees.

LAVENDER
(Lavandula spp.)

A versatile herb, lavender prefers dry, sandy soil and full sun. Start seeds indoors, eight to ten weeks before final frost. The small seeds need light to germinate, so cover thinly with soil. Place seedlings in pots, and then transplant them in your garden, 12 inches apart, after threat of frost is over. Keep roots barely covered with soil. It attracts butterflies, silver-spotted skippers, honeybees and bumblebees, and hummingbirds

LIATRIS
(Liatris spicata)

Also known as gayfeather or blazing star, this spiky perennial with pale purple, white, or rose flowers blooms from late spring through summer. The foliage turns bronze in fall. Plant corms or nursery specimens in any sunny spot—the plants are not fussy about soil type and will even grow in rocky terrain. The flowers attract hummingbirds, while tufted titmice, American goldfinches, and other seedeaters savor the seed heads.

LILAC
(Syringa spp.)

With its clustering spring blooms in pale purple, violet, or white, this shrub adds color and sweet scent to your landscape. Plant nursery stock in humus-rich, well-drained soil with an alkaline to neutral pH. Full sun is also critical. Plant in spring or fall, with the latter preferred. Prune dead wood to ensure lush blooms that draw butterflies, hummingbirds, moths, and bees.

MARIGOLD
(Tagetes spp.)

These hardy garden annuals offer brilliant and lasting colors, blooming through the fall. They grow from 6 inches to 3 feet tall, depending on variety. Start from seeds indoors, six weeks before the final frost, or from nursery seedlings. Place in a sunny location with moderately fertile soil; they also make excellent container plants. They attract monarch, blue, and tortoiseshell butterflies, among others, as well as bees.

MARJORAM
(Origanum majorana)

This popular, aromatic culinary herb can be started indoors on a windowsill and transferred to the garden in a sunny location. Handle the dustlike seeds carefully: sprinkle over soil and water gently. Thin seedlings in the ground to 10 inches apart. Stem cuttings can be taken in summer and propagated in a starter mix to overwinter. Its blossoms are favored by many types of bees, including honeybees and bumblebees.

MILKWEED
(Asclepias spp.)

This native wildflower of North America serves as a monarch butterfly host. The vibrant flowers of its many species, such as *A. tuberosa* (known as butterfly weed) or *A. incarnata* (called swamp milkweed), give way to large seedpods. Sow seeds in full sun; plants from early sowings bloom will that year. Not only butterflies will flock to its blooms—hummingbirds, too, love its nectar, and goldfinches and orioles, among other birds, use the silky seed down as nesting material.

MINT
(Mentha spp.)

Mints are hardy herbs that require minimal care. Plant seeds in fall before the first frost or after the final frost of spring in fertile, moist soil. Space seedlings 18 to 24 inches apart. Most mints prefer full sun or partial shade. Some, like peppermint, can send out runners, so keep them in containers. Mints attract cabbage white, spring azure, silver-spotted skipper, and gray hairstreak butterflies, as well as bees and hummingbirds.

MISTFLOWER
(Conoclinium coelestinum)

This perennial member of the sunflower family grows wild in many regions of eastern and central North America, but it can also be cultivated in the garden. The clustering bluish purple flowers are fall favorites of cabbage white, clouded sulphur, eastern tailed-blue, variegated fritillary, pearl crescent, monarch, queen, red admiral, common buck-eye, and silver-spotted skipper butterflies.

MULLEIN
(Verbascum thapsus)

Mullein is a tall, columnar wildflower with small yellow blossoms that appear in July and August. It does best in sandy, well-drained soil with full or partial sun exposure. Seeds should be started indoors in flats after 30 days in the refrigerator in moist medium. Once seedlings have leaves, transplant outdoors at 16 inches apart. Flowers appear the second year. These blooms attract bees and butterflies. Songbirds love the seeds.

NASTURTIUM
(Tropaeolem spp.)

Nasturtiums are hardy, attractive trailing plants with funnel-shaped orange, copper, or yellow flowers. Nasturtiums like full sun, but grow well in part shade and cool, well-drained soil. Sow the large seeds outdoors, 10 to 12 inches apart, a week before the last frost. Seedlings can also be started indoors using peat pots that go straight into the garden. Hummingbirds and butterflies visit the blooms, which are also edible for humans.

NICOTIANA
(Nicotiana alata)

Also known as flowering tobacco, this annual plant's star-shaped flowers of pink, red, lavender, yellow, or white give off a seductive odor. Heights can range from a few inches to 5 feet. Nursery seedlings or seeds need a sunny or semi-shaded location with well-drained soil. They can be grown in patio boxes so homeowners can enjoy the scented flowers that attract bees, butterflies, several types of moths, and hummingbirds.

OREGANO
(Origanum vulgare)

This widely popular Mediterranean herb prefers loamy soil and full sun. Start from seeds or cuttings from established plants. Plant seedlings 10 inches apart. Pinch tops for fuller growth, and keep them a bit dry. Thin older plants after three years; self-seeding oregano will fill in the gaps. Popular with swallowtail, orange sulphur, eastern tailed-blue, spring and summer azure, silver-spotted skipper butterflies, and bees.

PARSLEY
(Petroselinum spp.)

This versatile garden herb prefers loamy soil and full or partial sun. Plant seeds indoors (after soaking overnight) in small pots 10 or 12 weeks before final frost, or plant in ground 3 weeks before final frost. Space seedlings 6 to 8 inches apart. Keep well watered. Harvest when leaf stems have three segments, trim outer leaves first. Will grow indoors in cold weather. Parsley draws butterflies, including black swallowtails, and honeybees.

PENSTEMON
(Penstemon spp.)

These tall flowering plants require full or partial sun and well-draining soil; damp or rich soil can make them rot. Plant seeds directly in the garden after danger of frost is over, or purchase rhizomes, which need to be divided every three to five years. Penstemon blooms for most of the summer. Hummingbirds love the tubular red, purple, blue, pink and white flowers. Bees and butterflies also flock to them.

PETUNIA
(Petunia spp.)

This hardy, nectar-rich garden staple offers 35 species with bell-shaped flowers in a host of colors. These annuals require at least five hours of sun daily and humid, moist soil. Grow from seeds indoors (10 to 12 weeks before you intend to transplant seedlings) or nursery six-packs, and space 1 foot apart. Arrange mature plants in hanging baskets so that honeybees, swallowtails, sphinx moths, and hummingbirds can feed.

PHLOX
(Phlox spp.)

These old-fashioned perennials can be grown in full sun or partial shade from seeds or cuttings/transplants, 1 to 2 feet apart in moist soil. Loosen earth to a depth of 12 to 15 inches, and then mix in a 4-inch layer of compost. The scented flowers bloom in spring or summer and come in many colors and sizes with staggered bloom times. These clustering blossoms attract hummingbirds, swallowtails, and silver-spotted skippers.

PRIVET
(Ligustrum spp.)

These shrubs and small trees are often trimmed for ornamental hedging. Many have scented white flowers followed by clusters of black berries. Privet can be evergreen or deciduous and prefers slightly moist soil. Plant in full or partial sun, and prune often. It is favored by butterflies like the spicebush swallowtail, black swallowtail, clouded sulphur, spring and summer azure, red admiral, eastern comma, and silver-spotted skipper.

RASPBERRY
(Rubus spp.)

These perennial berries produce tangy red or black fruit. Plant canes in late winter or early spring; cut them back to 10 inches after planting. These shrubs prefer enriched soil in a sheltered location and will produce fruit by their second season. They can be invasive, spreading by basal shoots. The blooms are a major source of honeybee nectar, and the berries attract catbirds, mockingbirds, and thrushes.

RHODODENDRON
(Rhododendron spp.)

These sturdy shrubs, along with their azalea cousins, produce large, knockout blooms in vibrant colors in late spring. Situate nursery stock in a lightly shaded area with protection from winter sun and winds, and plant in moist, acidic, well-draining soil. These perennials offer shelter and nectar to hummingbirds; the tubular flowers also entice honeybees, bumblebees, and butterflies, including the swallowtails.

ROSE
(Rosa spp.)

Growing roses can be a challenge, but many new varieties resist insects and disease. Plant bare-root roses in early spring; plant potted roses from early spring to early fall. Ensure at least five hours of sunlight and loamy soil, and feed often during the blooming period. Bees and butterflies feed at the blooms, and rose hips (the fruits) attract many songbirds. Two good hip-producing cultivars are the wild roses *R. canina* and *R. rugosa*.

ROSEMARY
(Rosmarinus officinalis)

Rosemary is an unfussy culinary herb that is easy to grow. Situate a nursery plant in a sunny garden spot with good drainage and air circulation. Fertilize in spring with fish-kelp emulsion. In colder climates, plants can winter indoors in a sunny window or under artificial light. Harvest cooking sprigs above the woody growth. This aromatic herb is a favorite of bees and many butterflies.

SAFFLOWER
(Carthamus tinctorius)

Safflowers grow best when rainfall is less than 15 inches per year. Sow seeds 1 to 1½ inches deep, 6 to 10 inches apart in April or May after last frost. Mature plants have prickly spines, so do not attempt to transplant. To harvest seeds, allow heads to mature for one month after flowering ends. Use gloves to collect flower heads, and crush to remove seeds. Safflowers furnish seeds for songbirds like cardinals and chickadees.

SAGE
(*Salvia* spp.)

Sage's silvery-hued foliage makes it a favorite with gardeners. It grows best in a warm, dry border, but the hardy perennial will root in almost any slightly alkaline soil in semi-shade. Use cuttings to propagate rather than seeds. It makes an excellent potherb; harvest leaves any time before the plant flowers. It attracts hummingbirds, honeybees, and butterflies like the cabbage white, gray hairstreak, and silver-spotted skipper.

SEDUM
(*Sedum* spp.)

During fall, when most of the garden is declining, 'Autumn Joy' sedum—or stonecrop—brightens the landscape with its deep pink, star-shaped blooms. Start with nursery stock and divide every three or four years. Sedums are hardy except in extremely cold regions. The flowers attract bees and cabbage white, spring azure, gray hairstreak, and pearl crescent butterflies. Late-autumn seed heads attract finches and chickadees.

STAGHORN SUMAC
(*Rhus typhina*)

Staghorn sumac, so named because its elongated velvety fruit looks like deer antlers, is a durable, attractive shrub that reaches 15 feet in height. Plant container specimens or suckers from an existing plant next to pavement or a solid surface that will block it from becoming a thicket. Dig a hole nearly twice the width of the root ball. In summer, the flowers provide nectar for bees. In winter, the red fruit provides nutrition for birds.

SUNFLOWER
(*Helianthus annuus*)

These large-faced yellow flowers simply shout summer. Various cultivars range from 2 to 15 feet tall and include some red or brown varieties. Grow from seeds in full sun and in a well-dug, compost-rich bed with dryish soil; stagger planting times. Thin seedlings to a minimum of 2 feet apart. Sunflowers attract bees and swallowtail butterflies, and in fall they are magnets for seed-eating songbirds like finches, chickadees, and nuthatches.

SWEET PEA
(*Lathyrus odoratus*)

These traditional garden beauties offer scented flowers in many hues. They prefer cooler weather, so it is important to start them early in the growing season: indoors before the last frost or outdoors in early spring. Harden indoor seedlings for a week before transplanting to a moderately sunny spot. The flowers are popular with solitary bees and honeybees, as well as swallowtails.

THISTLE
(*Carduus, Cirsium,* and *Onpordum* spp.)

This large tribe of prickly plants, with their signature spiky purple flower heads, belongs to the Asteraceae family. They prefer sunny or partially shady spots. Sow seeds after last chance of frost, three to five seeds per hole at a depth of 1 inch, 12 to15 inches apart. Thin out weaker seedlings. Thistles are important food sources for bees, butterflies, finches, and hummingbirds, and birds often use the soft seed floss to line nests.

THYME
(*Thymus vulgaris*)

This earthy Mediterranean garden herb prefers full sun. Start seeds indoors, and set out seedlings after the last frost in well-drained, slightly alkaline soil. Add lime if needed. Use slow-release fertilizer when planting and then again each spring. Prune lightly after the first year. Thyme attracts honeybees and many butterflies, including swallowtails, cabbage whites, blues, coppers, and tortoiseshells.

TICKSEED SUNFLOWER
(*Bidens polylepis*)

This easy-to-grow wildflower, also known as midwestern tickseed-sunflower, bur marigold, and bearded beggartick, flowers from August to October. Plant in full sun in moist-to-wet soil that is rich in organic matter. Its nectar draws swallowtail, cabbage white, gray hairstreak, and pearl crescent butterflies and bumblebees, and the seeds attract sparrows and purple finches. Considered invasive in some regions.

TRUMPET VINE
(*Campsis radicans*)

Trumpet vine, with its showy, shaded, trumpet-shaped flowers, can grow up to 40 feet in length, making it an ideal cover for a messy wall or fence. Plant nursery stock in full sun or partial shade in almost any soil, but be sure to supply a trellis or support. The orange-to-red blossoms are tubular, making them a favorite of many moths and hummers—the plant is even known as hummingbird vine. Birds eat and spread the seeds, so it may become invasive.

VIOLET
(*Viola* spp.)

These small, clumping plants with their delicate purple, white, or yellow flowers are generally hardy but do best in partial shade and with moist soil. Sow indoors in March, outdoors in fall or April. Replant seedlings about 6 inches apart. Fritillaries use violets as host plants, and long-tongued butterflies feed on the flowers. Pollinators are drawn to the bright colors, not the scent.

VIPER'S BUGLOSS
(*Echium vulgare*)

This hardy, long-blooming wildflower, with its upright, brushlike blooms, can be cultivated in a border or edging as an annual. It does well in full sun to partial shade and well-drained soil. Sow under cover or directly in May through July. The blue-violet flowers that will occur the following year are popular with butterflies and moths; they also produce nectar and pollen into September, critical to bees that are stocking up for winter.

VIRGINIA CREEPER
(*Parthenocissus quinquefolia*)

Purchase this hardy, fast-growing vine, also known as woodbine, as nursery stock, and plant from early spring to fall. Space 5 to 10 feet apart. Virginia creeper will thrive in any well-drained soil in shady or sunny locations—or a mix of the two. The blooms are insignificant, but the crimson fall foliage is spectacular, and the blue fruit provides an important winter resource for thrushes, catbirds, cardinal, chickadees, and starlings.

WOOD GERANIUM
(*Geranium maculatum*)

Also called wild geranium or spotted cranesbill, this perennial wildflower displays pink or purple blooms and adapts well to garden life. Start seeds indoors or plant nursery stock in semi-shade in enriched soil. Flowers bloom from late spring to midsummer and attract honeybees, bumblebees, and butterflies like swallowtails and eastern tailed-blues. Hummingbirds prefer garden geraniums, genus *Pelargonium*.

YARROW
(*Achillea millefolium*)

Tall, easy-to-grow yarrow is a rock garden staple and is perfect for drying. It is hardy in most regions and prefers full sun. Plant seeds in spring in well-drained, average soil with a fine layer of compost. Thin seedlings to 2 feet apart. Divide plants every three to five years in early spring or fall. The flattened clustering flowers attract butterflies and hummingbirds in midsummer, and in fall, the seeds appeal to songbirds.

ZINNIA
(*Zinnia* spp.)

These bright, easy-going garden favorites are known for long-lasting blooms. Sow seeds in the ground (or indoors in peat pots) in a sunny spot, six weeks before the last frost. Thin to roughly a foot apart. The flowers attract bees and butterflies, including swallowtails, cabbage whites, orange sulphurs, fritillaries, pearl crescents, monarchs, painted ladies, and silver-spotted skippers. Red-hued blooms draw hummingbirds.

Glossary

androconia: Pheromone-emitting glands located on the dorsal hind wings of some butterflies, such as the queen.

anting: The practice of some birds, including grackles, of rubbing ants onto their feathers. The reasons for this behavior are unclear; the formic acid secreted by ants may kill parasites, or the birds may possibly use the insects as preening oil.

aposematic coloring: Warning colors or patterns evolved by prey animals to indicate to predators that they are poisonous or distasteful.

archaeopteryx: From the Greek for "ancient feather," a more refined flying dinosaur than the pterodactyl that appeared in the late Jurassic.

arthropod: An invertebrate animal having an exoskeleton, a segmented body, and jointed appendages. Insects, such as bees, butterflies, and moths are arthropods.

bib: Color marking below the chin of a bird.

biological control: A living organism used to control agricultural pests employing predation, parasitism, or other natural mechanisms.

brood: A group of young birds hatched at the same time.

brood parasite: A bird species, such as the brown-headed cowbird, that lay its eggs in the nests of other species: the offspring are often larger than the host bird's actual chicks and get more food and attention, ensuring that they will thrive.

brooding: Incubating—warming, covering, and protecting—eggs in a nest.

cache: A hidden storage space, such as under tree bark or behind house shingles, in which birds wedge seeds and nuts.

cap: Color marking at the back of a bird's head.

chaparral: An area of dry land, especially in Southern California, that offers a dense cover of short trees, evergreen shrubs, and thorny bushes.

chitin: A tough, semitransparent substance that is the main component of the exoskeleton of arthropods.

chrysalis: A hardened covering formed during the third stage of butterfly and moth metamorphosis, when the larva pupates and sheds its outer skin, and the skin beneath forms into this resilient casing.

clutch: The number of eggs laid at a single time by a bird, reptile, or amphibian. Removal of eggs by a predator—or by conservationists trying to increase breeding—can result in double-clutching, the laying of a second brood.

cocoon: A silken or protective covering used by a moth larva in order to pupate and become an adult moth.

colony collapse disorder syndrome: The name (usually shortened to CCD) given to a phenomenon in which bees leave the hive to collect nectar and then the majority of them never return, leaving behind the queen, larvae, and nursemaid worker bees; CCD is especially prevalent in large-scale, commercial apiaries.

color morph: This occurs when members of the same species develop different coloration or patterning. Those with two color morphs, such as the Diana fritillary butterfly, are dimorphic. Those that display multiple color variations or different markings, such as rock pigeons, are polymorphic. Also called color phase.

conspecific: Organisms that belong to the same species.

convergent evolution: This occurs when animals with different ancestry develop similar traits; for instance, different bird species developing the same type of forest camouflage.

cremaster: A hook or series of hooks used to attach the hind end of a butterfly or moth pupa to a twig or other structure; often attaches to a silken pad created by the insect.

crop: An expanded, muscular pouch near the gullet or throat of a bird used to temporarily store food.

crop milk: Regurgitated fluid from the lining of a bird's crop that is used to feed the young: found in pigeons, flamingos, and penguins. Also known as pigeon milk.

cryopreservation: Keeping the bodily fluids of a hibernating insect, such as a mourning cloak butterfly, from freezing, partly by creating "antifreeze" in the blood.

cryptic coloration: A form of camouflage in which an animal's coloring, patterning, or texture allow it to blend in with its surroundings; found in both predator and prey animals.

cuticle: The exoskeleton of a butterfly or moth larva that is shed as the insect grows

diapause: A state of animal dormancy in which the body conserves resources and does not continue development; can be triggered by adverse environmental conditions.

dimorphic: Animals showing two forms, such as differences in colors, markings, or size. In sexual dimorphism, males and females show different coloration from each other or differ greatly in size.

disruptive coloration: Markings that break up the distinctive silhouette of an insect, making it blend in with its background.

diurnal: Active primarily during daylight hours.

echolocation: A means of navigating that involves the emitting of ultrasound calls that reflect off objects, indicating their identity and location. This form of navigation is used by bats and some birds so that they can forage in the dark.

eclosion: The emergence of an adult Lepidoptera from its pupa.

egg tooth: A small projection on a baby bird's bill used to chip away the shell so that the bird can hatch from the egg.

evolution: Change in the heritable traits of biological populations over successive generations.

extinction: The disappearance of a species from the earth; according to the fossil record, 99.9 percent of species that ever existed are now extinct.

flight feathers: The long, stiff, asymmetrically shaped, yet symmetrically paired feathers on the wings or tail of a bird that are necessary for flight.

frenulum: A small ridge of bristles on the hind wing that keeps it in contact with corresponding barbs on the forewing; found on many moths and at least one skipper butterfly.

gaping: A feeding method in which a bird stabs its closed bill into fruit and then opens it to lap at the juice inside. It also refers to inserting its partially opened bill into bark or foliage to seek out insects.

gleaning: A feeding method that involves birds plucking invertebrate prey from foliage or the ground, from rock crevices or under bark or shingles, or even from living animals.

gorget: A patch on the throat of a bird or other animal, distinguished by its color, texture, or other attribute.

hair-pencil: A pheromone-signaling structure that is normally inside a male butterfly's abdomen; it is levered outside the body during courtship.

head: A bird marking description that indicates a solid color from the neck up.

hemolymph: The fluid that circulates through an arthropod's body, analogous to blood; in butterflies and moths, it fills and inflates the wings after the adult emerges from pupation.

hibernaculum: A space—such as under tree bark or roof shingles, in leaf litter, or in rock crevices—for butterflies that do not migrate during cold weather to overwinter.

holometabolous: Insects that must go through complete metamorphosis—egg, larva, pupa—before becoming an adult.

imago: The last stage an insect attains during metamorphosis; an adult, sexually mature butterfly or moth.

indicator species: Any sensitive species that allows scientists to monitor environmental conditions.

instar: The stages of growth between molts for butterfly and moth caterpillars; also an individual in a specified instar.

Johnston's organ: A collection of sensory cells found at the base of insect antenna that is believed to aid in balance and orientation during flight.

labial palpi: Bristling hairs found on the "faces" of Lepidoptera that contain olfactory sensors; may also filter dust from the eyes.

malar stripe: A distinctive stripe located along the cheek of a bird adjacent to the throat.

melanin: A group of natural black, dark brown, reddish brown, or yellow pigments found in most organisms.

metamorphosis: The process by which an insect matures from egg to adult. In complex metamorphosis, there are four stages: egg, larva, pupa, and adult.

migration: Movement of animals, birds, or insects from one location to another based on increasing or diminishing resources.

mimicry: The similarity of one species to another—in appearance, behavior, scent, or sound—that protects one or both from predation.

mobbing: Noisy, overt behavior of birds surrounding and harassing a predator that has strayed into their territory; displayed by mockingbirds, crows, chickadees, and jays, among other avian species.

murmuration: A flock of starlings; also used to describe the complex and coordinated swooping movements as the flock soars upward and outward and then turns back on itself.

nape: Color marking at the back of a bird's neck.

nares: Nostril openings on a bird's bill.

nectar: A sugar-rich liquid protein produced by a plant that enables it to attract pollinators.

neonicotinoid pesticide: A synthetic nicotine used to disrupt the nervous systems of insect pests in order to kill them; this kind of pesticide may also affect honeybees and is a suspected cause of colony collapse disorder.

nocturnal: Active primarily at night.

nyjer: The small, dark, nutritious seed of the African yellow daisy (*Guizotia abbysinica*). Nyjer is especially popular with finches and sparrows at bird feeders. Also known as niger, nyger, and blackseed.

osmeterium: A defensive organ found on the forehead of swallowtail butterfly caterpillars, which everts as fleshy "horns" that secrete volatile organic acids when the larva is threatened.

pappus: The soft floss of seed heads that many birds use to line their nests.

pishing: A human imitation of the scolding or alarm call of birds such as tits and chickadees used to bring the birds closer to an area of study.

pollen: A fine-to-coarse powder produced by the anthers of plants that contains male gametes. It is carried to the female stigma by pollinating animals in order to effect fertilization.

polygynous: A pattern of mating in which a male animal has more than one female mate.

proboscis: In insects, an elongated, sucking mouthpart that is tubular and flexible.

proleg: A small, fleshy, footlike stub found on the ventral surface of the abdomen of most larval forms of Lepidoptera.

propolis: A sticky, resinous red or brown substance collected by honeybees from tree buds and sap and used to fill in crevices in the hive and to varnish and seal honeycombs.

royal jelly: A nutritious substance secreted by worker bees to feed new larvae and larval and adult queens.

sallying: A feeding method that involves birds darting from the cover of foliage to hunt for food and then hurrying back to safety with their captured prize.

scoli: Bristle-bearing spinal structures in caterpillars.

setae: Long hair resembling fuzzy pile, typically found on the bodies of insects and their larvae.

sonation: A sound produced by a bird using a mechanism or structure other than the syrinx, such as the bill, tail, feet, or body feathers, or by the use of tools. The popping sound made by the tail feathers of the Anna's hummingbird is an example.

sphingophily: A pollination syndrome in which certain moths seek out plants with long corolla tubes and sweet scents.

spiracle: An opening on the surface of some organisms, such as caterpillars, that lead to the respiratory system.

swarming: The process by which a significant portion of an established—often crowded—honeybee colony flies off in search of a new home. The bees are often docile at this time because they do not yet have a hive to protect.

syrinx: From the Greek for "Pan pipes," a bird's voice box.

tubercle: A wartlike, round or knobbed protuberance found on the dorsal surfaces of caterpillars; it may contain hairlike bristles called setae.

vagrant: A bird that has strayed out of its normal migration, feeding, or breeding territory; North American birds, such as the red-eyed vireo, are sometimes blown off course and end up in Ireland or Great Britain.

vespertine: A night-blooming plant; many vespertines attract moths and bats.

xeriscaping: A landscaping plan designed to conserve water, especially by using native plants and eliminating large areas of thirsty grass lawn.

Image Credits

Garden illustrations on pages 19, 161, and 193 by Lizzie Harper (www.lizzieharper.co.uk)

Cover
Front: *tl*, Markus Keller/imageBROKER/age fotostock; *tmt*, Darrell Gulin/Corbis; *tmb*, constantgardener/Getty Images; *tr*, Tim Zurowski/Getty Images; *bl*, Danita Delimont/Getty Images; *brt*, James Laurie/Shutterstock; *bm*, Frank Cezus/Getty Images; *br*, setsuna/Getty Images. Back: *l*, Lorraine Hudgins/Shutterstock; *m*, rtbilder/Shutterstock; *r*, AC Rider/Shutterstock.

Half title page
1*l* Cynthia Kidwell/SS; 1*m* MMCez/SS; 1*r* John E Heintz Jr/SS

Title page
2*bl* Tessa Palmer/SS; 2*br* Zsolt Biczo/SS; 2*t* Mahony/SS; 3*bl* Philip Lange/SS; 3*br* Maxine Livingston/SS; 3*tl* Tyler Keim/SS; 3*tr* Paul Reeves Photography/SS

Introduction: Welcoming Wildlife 4 Michael G. Mill/SS; 5*l* Josef Iber/SS; 5*r* Doug Lemke/SS; 6*l* mubus7/SS; 6*r* feathercollector/SS; 7 Ratikova/SS; 8 Paul Sparks/SS

PART 1: BIRDS OF THE YARD & GARDEN
Chapter 1: Creating a Habitat for Birds
10*t* Natalia Paklina/SS; 10*bl* Bildagentur Zoonar GmbH/SS; 10*br* Bonnie Taylor Barry/SS; 11*tl* Darren Baker/SS; 11*tr* Steve Byland/SS; 11*blt* Boris Bort/SS; 11*blb* Birdiegal/SS; 11*br* Elaine Davis/SS; 12 asharkyu/SS; 14 KellyNelson/SS; 15*l* kukuruxa/SS; 15*m* FloridaStock/SS; 15*r* AlekseyKarpenko/SS; 17*tl* Maria Bell/SS; 17*tm* Maria Bell/SS; 17*tr* Martha Marks/SS; 17*bl* Grey Cat/SS; 17*br* John E Heintz Jr/SS; 20*l* Nadia Borisevich/SS; 20*r* Sutichak Yachiangkham/SS; 21 Ravennka/

SS; 23*tl* Rigucci/SS; 23*tr* Igor Sokolov (breeze)/SS; 23*bl* pics721/SS; 23*br* Elena Elisseeva/SS; 24*l* Warren Price Photography/SS; 24*m* Elena Elisseeva/SS; 24*r* Steve Robinson/SS; 25*l* Anatoliy Lukich/SS; 25*m* Sari ONeal/SS; 25*r* Robert A. Mansker/SS; 26 KellyNelson/SS; 27*tl* Beth Van Trees/SS; 27*bl* Lee Prince/SS; 27*r* Steve Byland/SS; 27*s* TTphoto/SS; 28 Yatra/SS; 29*tl* Steve Biegler/SS; 29*tr* Antonina Potapenko/SS; 29*b* White78/SS; 30*t* Mark R Layman/SS; 30*b* Tom Middleton/SS; 31*tl* Abeselom Zerit/SS; 31*bl* Eiji Ueda/SS; 31*r* Jill Lang/SS; 32*tl* geertweggen/SS; 32*tr* Paul Orr/SS; 32*bl* Johnwoodkim/SS; 32*br* David Kay/SS; 33*tl* LianeM/SS; 33*tr* B Brown/SS; 33*ml* Kwanjitr/SS; 33*mr* Vahan Abrahamyan/SS; 33*bl* Adam J/SS; 33*br* Howard Sandler/SS; 34*tl* Doug Lemke/SS; 34*tr* David Byron Keener/SS; 34*bl* Birdiegal/SS; 34*br* Teri Virbickis/SS; 35*tl* Dale Wagler/SS; 35*tr* Kenneth Rush/SS; 35*ml* ConstanzeK/SS; 35*mr* Studio Barcelona/SS; 35*bl* Matt Cuda/SS; 35*br* kamnuan/SS

Chapter 2: Backyard Birds
36 Bruce MacQueen/SS; 38*l* Sari ONeal/SS; 38*m* Stubblefield Photography/SS; 38*r* KOO/SS; 39*l* Gerald Marella/SS; 39*r* Annette Shaff/SS; 39*b* Stubblefield Photography/SS; 40 Stubblefield Photography/SS; 41*t* Dave Courey/SS; 41*s* dirkr/SS; 42 kojihirano/SS; 43*l* Martin Good/SS; 43*m* David Spates/SS; 43*r* Anatoliy Lukich/SS; 44 teekaygee/SS; 45*t* Pacific Northwest Photo/SS; 45*b* Charles Brutlag/SS; 46 Feng Yu/SS; 47*t* Mark Scott/SS; 47*b* Ron Rowan Photography/SS; 48 LorraineHudgins/SS; 49*l* Nancy Bauer/SS; 49*r* MVPhoto/SS; 50 Matt Cuda/SS; 51*s* Paul Reeves Photography/SS; 51*b* Pacific Northwest Photo/SS; 52 Menno Schaefer/SS; 53 Ginger Livingston Sanders/SS; 54 Stubblefield Photography/SS; 54*t* Robert L Kothenbeutel/SS; 54*s* MVPhoto/SS; 56 Phil Lowe/SS; 57*l* Steve Byland/SS; 57*t* Steven Russell Smith Photos/SS; 57*b* Ivan Kuzmin/SS; 58 Will Howe/SS; 58*l*

PART 2: BEES & OTHER BENEFICIAL WILDLIFE

Chapter 3: Creating a Habitat for Bees

Chapter 4: Bees & Other Pollinators

Contributors

Author **NANCY J. HAJESKI** writes adult and young adult nonfiction under her own name. Recent titles include *Life-size Birds, National Geographic Complete Guide to Herbs and Spices, Ali: The Official Portrait of the Greatest of All Time,* and *The Beatles: Here, There and Everywhere.* Writing as Nancy Butler, she has produced 12 Signet Regencies, two of which won the RITA award from the Romance Writers of America. She has adapted the work of Jane Austen into graphic novels for Marvel Entertainment. Her *Pride and Prejudice* remained on the *New York Times* bestseller list for 13 weeks. An avid gardener who focuses on natural landscaping, Hajeski lives in the Catskill Mountains of New York.

Consultant **Kelley Edkins** is the owner of Gardens by Kelley, a sustainable, organic landscape design company. The facilitator and operator of the first DEC compost facility site in Sullivan County, New York—a static-pile vermi-compost called The Bee Green Community Garden—Edkins has been cultivating medicinal herbs, native plants, and endangered species for 20 years. Her organic farm, Honeybee Herbs, focuses on plants that provide food for honeybees, and she sells herbal and honeybee products at farmer's markets and festivals. Edkins is a Master Gardener, holistic beekeeper, and compost expert who shares her knowledge with school students, politicians, and clients.

Index

Since 1888, the National Geographic Society has funded more than 12,000 research, exploration, and preservation projects around the world. National Geographic Partners distributes a portion of the funds it receives from your purchase to National Geographic Society to support programs including the conservation of animals and their habitats.

National Geographic Partners, LLC
1145 17th Street NW
Washington, DC 20036-4688 USA

Become a member of National Geographic and activate your benefits today at natgeo.com/jointoday.

For information about special discounts for bulk purchases, please contact National Geographic Books Special Sales: ngspecsales@ngs.org

For rights or permissions inquiries, please contact National Geographic Books Subsidiary Rights: ngbookrights@ngs.org

ISBN: 978-1-4262-1741-8
ISBN: 978-1-4262-1759-3 (deluxe)

Printed in the United States of America

16/QGT-QGLM/1

Acknowledgments

Thanks to Susan Tyler Hitchcock, Barbara Payne, Elisa Gibson, Susan Blair, R. Gary Colbert, Jennifer Hoff, Lisa Walker, and Judith Klein of National Geographic Books, and to Lisa Purcell and Sean Moore of Moseley Road. Also, thank you to Saturniidae expert Bill Oehlke for his input on giant silkmoths.

Outdoor Enthusiasts Rejoice

with more great books from National Geographic

NATIONAL GEOGRAPHIC
ILLUSTRATED GUIDE TO
Nature
FROM YOUR BACK DOOR
TO THE GREAT OUTDOORS
Wildflowers | Trees & Shrubs | Rocks & Minerals
Weather | Night Sky

NATIONAL GEOGRAPHIC
The
NATIONAL PARKS
An Illustrated History
100 YEARS OF AMERICAN SPLENDOR
KIM HEACOX

NATIONAL GEOGRAPHIC
ILLUSTRATED GUIDE TO
Wildlife
FROM YOUR BACK DOOR
TO THE GREAT OUTDOORS
Birds | Mammals | Reptiles & Amphibians
Insects & Spiders | Aquatic Life

NATIONAL GEOGRAPHIC
SECOND EDITION
COMPLETE BIRDS
OF NORTH AMERICA
Now covering more than 1,000 species with the most-detailed
information found in a single volume
COMPANION TO
*National Geographic's
Field Guide to the Birds
of North America*
Edited by
Jonathan Alderfer

NATIONAL GEOGRAPHIC
Backyard
GUIDE TO THE
Birds of North America
JONATHAN ALDERFER
AND PAUL HESS

Kids' Companion to the Best-selling Field Guide to the Birds of North America
NATIONAL GEOGRAPHIC KIDS
BIRD GUIDE
OF NORTH AMERICA
Identify Birds
THE BEST BIRDING BOOK FOR KIDS FROM
NATIONAL GEOGRAPHIC'S BIRD EXPERTS!
For Kids!
Get Inside a Bird's Habitat
Birding Activities & Crafts
JONATHAN ALDERFER

NATIONAL GEOGRAPHIC KIDS
CENTENNIAL EDITION
NATIONAL PARKS GUIDE U.S.A.
THE MOST AMAZING SIGHTS, SCENES, & COOL ACTIVITIES FROM COAST TO COAST!
Kids' Companion to the popular National Geographic Guide to the National Parks of the U.S.

NATIONAL GEOGRAPHIC POCKET GUIDE
Birds
OF NORTH AMERICA
• For beginners
  & beyond
• 160 species
• Coast-to-coast
  coverage
• Full-color
  index
LAURA ERICKSON best-selling author and radio host
JONATHAN ALDERFER best-selling birding author

NATIONAL GEOGRAPHIC POCKET GUIDE
Insects
OF NORTH AMERICA
• 160 species,
  coast to coast
• Includes 35 spiders
  and other species
• Photos and art to
  show significant
  features
FROM YOUR FAVORITE FIELD GUIDE EXPERTS

NATIONAL GEOGRAPHIC POCKET GUIDE
Wildflowers
OF NORTH AMERICA
• Photo & illustration
  of each flower
• 160 species,
  coast to coast
• Organized by
  color
FROM YOUR FAVORITE FIELD GUIDE EXPERTS

NATIONAL GEOGRAPHIC POCKET GUIDE
Mammals
OF NORTH AMERICA
• 160 species, coast to coast
• Large and small, rare and
  common
• Photos and tracks of
  every species
FROM YOUR FAVORITE FIELD GUIDE EXPERTS

NATIONAL GEOGRAPHIC POCKET GUIDE
Trees & Shrubs
OF NORTH AMERICA
• 160 species,
  coast to coast
• Photograph &
  illustration of
  each tree or shrub
• Handy
  identification tips
FROM YOUR FAVORITE FIELD GUIDE EXPERTS